India-Vietnam
Agenda for Strengthening Partnership

India-Vietnam

Agenda for Strengthening Partnership

Edited by

Rajiv K. Bhatia

Vijay Sakhuja

Vikash Ranjan

SHIPRA

INDIAN COUNCIL OF WORLD AFFAIRS

Some of the contents in this volume have been translated from Vietnamese language. Some chapters have also been drawn from power point presentations made at 'India-Vietnam Strategic Partnership: Future Directions' seminar held at Hanoi on 17 July 2012. The text has therefore been edited and suitably modified for the readers. The views expressed in this volume are of individual contributor and do not represent the viewpoint of the editors or the council.

Rs. 750; US$ 37.50

ISBN: 978-81-7541-703-8

First Published in India in 2013

India-Vietnam: Agenda for Strengthening Partnership

Published by:
SHIPRA PUBLICATIONS
H.O.: LG 18-19, Pankaj Central Market, Patparganj,
Delhi-110092, Tel: 91-11-2223 5152, 2223 6152
Br.Off.: 4617/18, Ansari Road, Darya Ganj,
New Delhi-110002, Tel: 9650028065, 9810522367
E-mail: info@shiprapublications.com
www.shiprapublications.com

Foreword

India and Vietnam are two friendly countries which have been cooperating closely for a long time. For India, the Strategic Partnership with Vietnam is undoubtedly one of the most important external relationships and figures prominently in India's Look East Policy. Also, the Indian people have great admiration for the people of Vietnam for their strong sense of discipline, capability to sacrifice, and a deep commitment to the cause of nation. Vietnam thus enjoys a very positive image in India.

The collective memory and history of rich connections and exchanges through trade, culture, religious influences and ideas provide a solid foundation for India-Vietnam Partnership. India and Vietnam have shared experiences of colonialism, and have fought hard for independence. The bonding between the two countries has been revitalised by the endeavours of several generations' of leaders from both countries and the positive trends continue today.

Jawaharlal Nehru was among the first foreign leaders who visited Vietnam after its historic victory against France in Dien Bien Phu in 1954. Subsequently, President Ho Chi Minh visited India in 1958 and President Rajendra Prasad visited Vietnam in 1959. This tradition has continued, culminating in the last two major visits, one by Prime Minister Manmohan Singh who attended the 8th ASEAN-India Summit and 5th East Asian Summit in Hanoi in October 2010; and the other by President Truong Tan Sang who visited India in October 2011.

Regular dialogues at the highest political levels and the existing institutional arrangements have been useful and effective in sustaining multiple engagements at different levels between the two countries. The Joint Commission has ensured consultations on political, diplomatic, trade, economic, cultural, scientific and technological cooperation. Different mechanisms at the level of Minister of Defence and Minister of Home Affairs have contributed immensely to the bilateral relationship.

Three pillars of bilateral relationship have attracted considerable public attention. The first relates to trade, economic and energy cooperation. Bilateral trade has seen a steady growth and a target of US$ 7 billion has been set for 2015. Other areas of economic relationship are investment, capacity-building, technological cooperation and various lines of credit extended by India for infrastructure development. The potential for energy cooperation, both in conventional and non-conventional spheres is enormous.

The second pillar relates to security and defence cooperation. Being maritime nations, India and Vietnam face common security challenges. India is committed to an atmosphere of peace, tranquillity and stability in the Asia-Pacific region and considers it essential for continuation of the region's economic progress. India is particularly concerned about rising tensions in East Sea/South China Sea. It attaches great importance to international law and the security and freedom of navigation. India favours resolution of all disputes and differences through peaceful means and negotiations. Defence and security relations between India and Vietnam have made significant progress, as evident from regular high-level visits, strategic dialogues, military training, and joint exercises. India and Vietnam also need to address non-traditional threats and challenges such as climate change, environmental degradation, natural disasters, energy security and communicable diseases.

The third pillar of the bilateral relationship is India's support for multilateral institutions led by ASEAN. As part of its Look East Policy, India recognises Vietnam's significant position in ASEAN. India is committed to the ASEAN principles of friendship and cooperation, supports the ASEAN Regional Forum (ARF) and ASEAN Defence

Ministers' plus (ADMM+) Eight Dialogue Partners Meeting, and acknowledges the vital role of the East Asia Summit (EAS).

When the history of India-Vietnam relations is written, historians will no doubt recall the exceptional importance of the year 2012 when 40 years of the establishment of full diplomatic relations, 5th anniversary of commencement of Strategic Partnership, India-Vietnam Friendship Year and Year of India in Vietnam were celebrated. The year 2012 is also historic for India-ASEAN relations, as both sides celebrated two decades of India's Dialogue Partnership with ASEAN, culminating in the commemorative India-ASEAN Summit, which was hosted by India for the first time.

India and Vietnam remain committed to strengthening bilateral relationship and also cooperate at the regional and international fora with the aim to promote peace, stability, development and prosperity in East Asia.

This book emerges from the bilateral dialogue held between the Indian Council of World Affairs (ICWA), New Delhi and the Diplomatic Academy of Vietnam (DAV), Hanoi, and it serves a two-fold purpose. Firstly, it evaluates the relationship as it stands today and secondly, it offers a constructive perspective as experts reflect on and chart future directions for bilateral relations. This book should make a valuable contribution to the expanding relationship between Vietnam and India.

Rajiv K. Bhatia
Director General,
Indian Council of World Affairs

Message

It gives me great pleasure to participate in this important Seminar on India–Vietnam Strategic Partnership. The seminar provides an important opportunity for our scholars, strategic thinkers and diplomats to analyse the development of India–Vietnam cooperation and outline a road map for the future.

The foundations of the contemporary India–Vietnam relationship were laid by our great leaders-Prime Minister Pandit Jawaharlal Nehru and President Ho Chi Minh. Forged in the crucible of our respective struggles for freedom and liberation, India and Vietnam have stood by each other during difficult times.

Changes in the global geo-political and economic scenario have impacted positively on India-Vietnam partnership. The economic reform programmes of both countries and the global integration of our economies have opened myriad opportunities for mutually beneficial cooperation. The series of high level visits and exchanges over the years have taken our cooperation to higher levels. Today, we have upgraded our cooperation to a Strategic Partnership, based on a commonality of interests and shared perceptions on global and regional developments. Our wide ranging Partnership encompasses cooperation in Defence and Security, Trade and Investment, IT, Science and Technology, Culture and Academic Exchanges and Capacity Building. We have achieved concrete progress in some areas and need to work harder in others.

After a sustained focus for over two decades, India's Look East

Policy has matured. India sees itself as an integral part of the dynamic Indo-Pacific region. India's strong ties with ASEAN are being celebrated in the first ever India-ASEAN Commemorative Summit to be organised in New Delhi on 20-21 December 2012. A series of events are being organised to mark 20 years of the ASEAN-India dialogue partnership and 10th anniversary of ASEAN-India Summit meetings. The, India-ASEAN car rally and a Sail Training Ship expedition will demonstrate the physical connectivity between India and ASEAN. A number of business seminars and cultural programmes to be organised in Hanoi, Danang and Ho Chi Minh City will bring our peoples closer together and strengthen bilateral friendship.

The regional and global context within which India and Vietnam are enhancing their relationship is in a state of fluidity. New security and economic paradigms are evolving in this region and the world. Both India and Vietnam share a common vision of an open, inclusive and democratic regional and global architecture where every country can play its rightful role. This will contribute to peace, security and stability in the region, and facilitate mutually beneficial cooperation.

I take this opportunity to express my sincere gratitude and appreciation to the Diplomatic Academy of Vietnam and to Ambassador Dang Dinh Quy, President of DAV for co-hosting the seminar. Equally I wish to thank the Indian Council for World Affairs for sponsoring this important event. The fact that Ambassador Rajiv Bhatia, Director General ICWA has chosen Vietnam as his first destination after assuming charge of the ICWA, testifies to the importance that our strategic community places on India–Vietnam partnership.

I am confident that the deliberations in the seminar would provide concrete recommendations on the ways and means to further develop and enhance India-Vietnam Strategic Partnership in the future.

Ranjit Rae

Ambassador of India to Vietnam

Message

Vietnam-India relationship is a long traditional friendship nurtured by President Ho Chi Minh and Prime Minister Jawaharlal Nehru. During the past 40 years, despite historical ups and downs, Vietnam and India have always been faithful friends, reliable partners with shared interest and vision.

For the past 40 years, a long progress has been made in the Vietnam-India relationship. Apart from being traditional friends, Vietnam and India have become strategic partners. The relationship has developed in all areas, which has brought practical benefits to the people of the two countries and has contributed to the peace, stability and prosperity of the region.

There remain untapped potentials in the relationship between the two countries. Many projects and cooperation programmes agreed between the two countries has not been implemented efficiently, even in critical areas like economics, commerce, science and technology, and security and defence sectors.

Rapid changes have taken place in the regional and international spheres, and both countries have faced new opportunities and challenges. To further strengthen the relationship, India and Vietnam need to do objective assessment of their past relations, and put forward new initiatives and ideas for future cooperation.

The seminar is an effort in that direction, which will do an objective assessment of the existing relations and suggest ways to further strengthen the relationship in near future.

Dang Dinh Quy

President, Diplomatic Academy of Vietnam

Contents

Section IV
Development of a Knowledge Economy: Cooperation in IT, Science and Technology and Related Fields

Section V
Tracing Civilisational Links and Potential for Tourism

The Contributors

Dr. Shantanu Chakrabarti, Associate Professor, Department of History, University of Calcutta, Kolkata, India.

Mr. Tran Viet Phuong, Department of South East Asia, South Asia and South Pacific, Ministry of Foreign Affairs, Vietnam.

Mr. Shantanu Srivastava, Managing Director, Ishan International Private Limited; Chairman, Ishan Foundation; founder Chairman Indian Business Chamber in Vietnam; and Chairman, India–ASEAN Business Promotion Council, ASSOCHAM, India.

Dr. Vikash Ranjan, Research Fellow, Indian Council of World Affairs, New Delhi, India.

Mr. Ly Quoc Hung, Head, Africa, Western and South Asia Markets Units, Ministry of Industry and Trade, Hanoi, Vietnam.

Dr. Nguyen Van Lich, Associate Professor and Dean, Economic Faculty, Diplomatic Academy of Vietnam, Hanoi, Vietnam.

Ms. Lydia Powell, Senior Fellow, Observer Research Foundation, New Delhi, India.

Mr. Jesudas Bell, President and CEO, Futurelinks, Singapore.

Dr. Hoang Anh Tuan, Director General, Institute for Foreign Policy and Strategic Studies, Diplomatic Academy of Vietnam, Hanoi, Vietnam.

Professor Tridib Chakraborti, Professor, Department of International Relations, Jadavpur University, Kolkata, India.

Mr. Nguyen Nam Duong, Director, Centre for Political and Security studies, Institute of Foreign Policy and Strategic Studies, Diplomatic Academy of Vietnam, Hanoi, Vietnam.

Dr. Vijay Sakhuja, Director (Research), Indian Council of World Affairs, New Delhi, India.

Colonel Nguyen Hong Quan, Deputy Director General, Institute for Defence Strategy, Ministry of National Defence, Hanoi, Vietnam.

Professor K. Raja Reddy, former Director, Centre for Southeast Asian and Pacific Studies, Sri Venkateswara University, Tirupati, India.

Mr. Pham Hoang Ha, Senior Expert, in-charge of Vietnam-India cooperation, International Cooperation Department, Ministry of Science and Technology, Hanoi, Vietnam.

Dr. Tran Quy Nam, Department of IT, Ministry of Information and Communications, Hanoi, Vietnam.

Dr. Do Thu Ha, Associate Professor, Department of Social Sciences and Humanities, Vietnam National University, Hanoi, Vietnam.

Mr. Tran Phong Binh, Chief of Division, Tourism Marketing Department, Vietnam National Administration of Tourism, Hanoi, Vietnam.

Abbreviations

ADMM+	ASEAN Defence Ministers' Meeting plus
ADMM+8	ASEAN Defence Ministers' Meeting plus Eight
AIF	ASEAN Infrastructure Fund
AITIG	ASEAN-India Trade in Goods
ANZUS	Australia, New Zealand, United States Security Treaty
APEC	Asia-Pacific Economic Cooperation
APSC	ASEAN Political-Security Community
ARC-ICT	Advanced Resource Centre in Information and Communication Technology
ARF	ASEAN Regional Forum
ASEAN	Association of South East Asian Nations
ASEM	Asia-Europe Meeting
BARC	Bhabha Atomic Research Centre
bcm	billion cubic metres
BIMSTEC	Bay of Bengal Initiative for Multi-Sectoral Technical and Economic Cooperation
BP	British Petroleum
bpd	barrels per day
BPO	Business Process Outsourcing
BRIT	Board of Radiation and Isotope Technology
C-DAC	Centre for Development of Advanced Computing
CE	Christian era
CENTO	Central Treaty Organization
CEPEA	Comprehensive Economic Partnership for East Asia
CEPT	Common Effective Preferential Treatment

CLV	Cambodia, Lao Peoples' Democratic Republic and Vietnam
CMMI	Capability Maturity Model Integration
DAE	Department of Atomic Energy
DRDO	Defence Research and Development Organisation
DRVN	Democratic Republic of Vietnam
DST	Department of Science and Technology
EAS	East Asia Summit
EEZ	Exclusive Economic Zone
EIA	Energy Information Administration
EVN	Vietnam Electricity
FDI	Foreign Direct Investment
FS	Feasibility Studies
FTA	Free Trade Area
GMC	Ganga-Mekong Cooperation
GOI	Government of India
HADR	Humanitarian and Disaster relief
HMC	Hoan My Medical Corporation
HPC	High Performance Computing
IAEA	International Atomic Energy Agency
IBF	India Business Forum
ICC	International Commission of Control and Supervision for Vietnam
ICP	International Consumer Product
IMF	International Monetary Fund
IT	Information Technology
ITO	Information Technology Outsourcing
JAPC	Japan Atomic Power Company
JBC	Joint Business Council
JCM	Joint Commission Meeting
JVs	Joint Ventures
LoC	Line of Credit
LWR	Light Water reactor
MGC	Mekong-Ganga Cooperation
MIC	Ministry of Information and Communication
MOST	Ministry of Science and Technology

MoU	Memorandum of Understanding
MPAC	Master Plan on ASEAN Connectivity
MPI	Ministry of Planning and Investment
MSME	Micro, Small and Medium enterprises
mtoe	million tonne oil equivalent
NATO	North Atlantic Treaty Organisation
NEP	New Economic Policy
NGLs	Natural Gas Liquids
NHPC	National Hydropower Corporation
NOC	National Oil Company
NRI	Nuclear Research Institute
NTPC	National Thermal Power Corporation
ODA	Official Development Assistance
OECD	Organisation for Economic Co-operation and Development
OGJ	Oil & Gas Journal
ONGC	Oil and Natural Gas Commission
OSCE	Organisation for Security and Cooperation in Europe
OVL	ONGC Videsh Limited
PIDC	Petro-Vietnam Investment and Development Company
POF	Pakistan Ordnance Factories
PSC	Production Sharing Contract
PSI	Proliferation Security Initiative
PVEP	PetroVietnam Exploration and Production
PVN	PetroVietnam
RCA	Regional Cooperation Agreement
RE	Renewable Energy
SAARC	South Asian Association for Regional Cooperation
SCO	Shanghai Cooperation Organisation
SEATO	Southeast Asia Treaty Organisation
SLOCs	Sea Lines of Communication
SMEs	Small and Medium Enterprises
SOEs	State-Owned Enterprises
SPV	Solar Photovoltaic
TAC	Treaty of Amity and Cooperation

TC	Technical Cooperation
TPP	Trans Pacific Partnership
TSD	Trilateral Strategic Dialogue
UNCLOS	United Nations Convention on the Law of the Sea
UNEP	United Nations Environment Programme
UNPKO	United Nations Peacekeeping Operations
UNSC	United Nations Security Council
VAEC	Vietnam Atomic Energy Commission
VAIP	Vietnam Association for Information Processing
VARANS	Vietnam Agency for Radiation and Nuclear Safety
VARANSAC	Vietnam Agency for Radiation and Nuclear Safety and Control
VAST	Vietnam Academy of Science and Technology
VCP	Vietnam's Communist Party
VEIA	Vietnam Electronic Industries Association
VINASA	Vietnam Software Association
VINSC	Vietnam-India Nuclear Science Centre
VND	Vietnamese Dollar
VNISA	Vietnam Information Security Association
WB	World Bank
WMD	Weapon of Mass Destruction
WTO	World Trade Organisation

Introduction

India's sustained friendly and cooperative relations with Vietnam are rooted in antiquity and are based on similarities in history, geography, culture and economy. Both countries endured colonial rule, and won their independence through intense nationalistic movements. The ties between the two countries are marked by mutual trust and a near identical outlook on bilateral, regional and international issues. In a span of 35 years, the relationship graduated from diplomatic to strategic and in 2007, India and Vietnam signed the Strategic Partnership that envisages bilateral political and economic engagements, security and defence cooperation, scientific and technological capacity building and enhanced cultural contacts.

India-Vietnam bilateral relationship is marked by high level political exchanges and both sides have supported each other on a number of issues. Vietnam has played a constructive role in forging closer linkages between India and ASEAN, which has provided content and depth to India's 'Look East' Policy. India is committed to ASEAN's principle of friendship and cooperation, endorsed Treaty of Amity and Cooperation (TAC) and supports ASEAN Regional Forum (ARF). It acknowledges the viability of the East Asian Summit (EAS) and participates in other ASEAN initiatives such as the ADMM plus Eight Dialogue Partners Meeting.

There is considerable potential for the two countries to enhance India-Vietnam cooperation through comprehensive engagements, based on key pillars of political, economic, defence and security, culture and human resource cooperation.

India-Vietnam economic relations have expanded gradually since the establishment of diplomatic relations between the two countries in 1972. Since the signing of the India-Vietnam Strategic Partnership in 2007 and coming into force of India-ASEAN Free Trade Area (FTA) in goods in 2010, the two-way trade has increased and has become much more balanced. India-Vietnam bilateral trade reached US$ 2.7 billion in 2010, and increased to US$ 5.4 billion in 2012. Both countries have set the target of US$ 7 billion to be achieved by 2015. Both countries have also agreed to work for the early finalisation of the India-ASEAN FTA in Services and Investments.

In the energy sector, Petro Vietnam and ONGC Videsh Limited (OVL) have agreed to develop a long-term cooperation in oil and gas sector based on the principle of equality and mutual benefit. Economic interactions in several other sectors through cooperation between Chambers of Commerce and Industry, Joint Business Council and other initiatives for economic development have increased between the two countries. However, the overall level of trade and investment between the two countries is not commensurate with the political understanding between the two partners. Hopefully, with the expansion of India-ASEAN FTA in Goods, and the Free Trade in Services and Investments in the future, the situation is likely to change.

Vietnam is the sixth largest economy in ASEAN with a dynamic and youthful population. India is cooperating closely with Vietnam in skill enhancement and human resource development efforts. There has also been progress in sharing knowledge in the field of biotechnology, health and agriculture. A good example of Vietnam-India cooperation in high technology is the Vietnam-India Advanced Technology Resource Centre, which was constructed with the help of Centre for Development of Advanced Computing (C-DAC) of India, at a cost of US$ 2 million.

India is a stakeholder in the evolving security architecture in East Asia. In geostrategic terms, India and Vietnam are highly dependent on sea for their economic vitality. Their geographical location bestows on them the responsibility to safeguard international shipping routes in the Indian Ocean and through the South China

Sea. The ongoing developments in the East Sea South China Sea involving China, and some ASEAN claimant countries, are of concern to India. India and Vietnam have instituted a mechanism of biennial dialogue on security issues between Ministry of Home Affairs of India and Ministry of Public Security of Vietnam. India and Vietnam also signed a Memorandum of Understanding on defence cooperation, which has led to significant defence cooperation between the two countries including high level visits, military training and joint exercises. Both countries have also signed an Extradition Treaty.

The year 2012 marks the establishment of 40 years of diplomatic relations and 5th anniversary of the Strategic Partnership between India and Vietnam. The year was also celebrated as 20th year of India's Dialogue Partnership with ASEAN and commemorated as 10th year of ASEAN-India Summit Level Partnership.

In this backdrop, India and Vietnam need to evaluate the current relationship and explore opportunities to further strengthen the partnership. This edited volume provides a unique opportunity to understand India-Vietnam relations in its totality and offers a firsthand insight into the thinking of the stakeholders, from a practitioner, corporate and an academic perspective. It will be useful to mention that some of the papers included in this volume were contributed in Vietnamese language; the text has been suitably translated, edited and modified for the general readers. Ms. Ly Vu Nhat Tu, a Vietnamese student at the Delhi University has done a commendable work in the translation of Vietnamese papers into English.

Vijay Sakhuja
Vikash Ranjan

Section I

Evolving India-Vietnam Strategic Partnership

1
Evolving India-Vietnam Relations

Shantanu Chakrabarti

Introduction

The 40th anniversary of diplomatic relations between India and Vietnam in 2012 was celebrated as 'Year of Friendship'. Pre-colonial historical linkages provide a backdrop to the bilateral relationship which has evolved over a period of time. It is perhaps an appropriate time for a realistic analysis of the pattern of relationship as it has matured. Further, evolving internal and regional dynamics, in respect of both the countries, have acted as crucial factors in enhancing the relationship.

Vietnam's strong desire for autonomy led to intermittent conflict with the Asian Goliath (China) for more than 1,000 years and continued even after Vietnam's independence.[1] At another level, Vietnam's long nationalist struggle marks an important phase in the global history of decolonisation, which also received support from Indian nationalists. It has been argued, for instance, that only in Vietnam, 'has this force turned into a national purpose of depth and magnitude, sufficient to wage a lengthy struggle against two Western powers'.[2] This has increased the importance of Vietnam for Indian foreign policy makers, as India seeks to give a strategic hue to its Look East Policy in the phase-II period.

Historical Phase

India has geographical proximity to Southeast Asia and shares maritime boundary with three countries. The islands of Andaman and Nicobar in the Bay of Bengal are closer to Southeast Asia than mainland India. The southern tip of India is astride an important sea line of communication in the Indian Ocean, connecting Southeast Asia (and East Asia) with West Asia and Europe, through which nearly 40 per cent of the world trade passes.[3] This has given rise to civilisational contacts in various spheres and at different levels between the two regions over a period of time. Throughout history, pilgrimages, migrations, economic interactions, trade, voyages and even military missions like the Chola conquest of the Sailendra dynasty, had established bilateral relationship.

The Indian subcontinent was an integral part of the economic and cultural networks interconnecting the Asian continent. According to historian Sugata Bose, for instance:

> In early times, the thriving agrarian and urban economies of the Achaemenid and Mauryan empires provided the basis for the exchanges between the Middle East and South Asia, which predated the crafting of close links between South and Southeast Asia. By the beginning of the Common Era, there was a perceptible shift in the balance, from the earlier emphasis on luxuries, to staple goods in the commodity composition of the Indian Ocean trade. At key centres throughout this realm sprang up important expatriate communities of South Asian merchants, who appear to have been more direct agents of cultural diffusion in Southeast Asia than in the Middle East.[4]

Contacts between the Indian subcontinent and the kingdoms in Southeast Asia particularly flowered from the early centuries of the Christian Era (CE) to the early medieval period. The advent of Islam added another dimension to these patterns of contact. According to Fernand Braudel, for instance, in pre-colonial period the Far-East consisted of the three large and interconnected world economies:

(a) the Islamic world, overlooking the Indian Ocean from the Red Sea and the Persian Gulf, controlling endless chain of deserts stretching across Asia from Arabia to China; (b) India, whose influence extended throughout the Indian Ocean, both east and west of Cape Comorin; and (c) the Chinese empire, a great territorial power, striking deep into the heart of Asia, and a maritime power, controlling the seas and countries bordering the Pacific.[5]

By modifying the older view of 'Indianisation' of Southeast Asia, modern scholars unanimously agree on acculturation in this region, linking this to maritime trade and cultural networks. The central parts of Vietnam, particularly the fertile valley tracts of the Thu Bon River have yielded rich archaeological evidence of a 'civilisation' variously called 'Cham' or 'Champa.' The lower reaches of Mekong delta covering parts of southern Vietnam and Cambodia witnessed development of the state of Funan in the early centuries of the CE, which declined in the 6th and 7th CE. In Vietnam, the remains have been found in the famous site of Oc Eo, showing distinctly 'Indian' traits in the adoption of Brahmanical and Buddhist cults, political ideologies and a ritual language. Coins, seals, semiprecious stones, beads, glass, bronze vessels, ceramics have been found in archaeological sites providing evidence of long-distance trade networks between India and the Indo-China region.

Historical research has proven that though the advent of the colonial powers did to an extent disrupt the traditional linkages between South and Southeast Asia, but this did not happen to an extent as was once believed to be the case.[6] Modern analysts have shown that the colonial powers like the Portuguese, the Dutch, the French and the English had to make adjustments and co-opt the indigenous and traditional networks which survived and morphed into new ones to a large extent.

Post-Decolonisation Phase

Colonisation of South Asia and Southeast Asia with their divergent political, territorial and economic ambitions, with attendant tariff, travel barriers, varying administrative and educational patterns, led the colonial powers to be oriented towards their respective metropolitan powers than towards one another, which made a break in the earlier patterns of linkages.[7] Struggle for decolonisation, however, led to sporadic contacts during the colonial period. Jawaharlal Nehru, for instance, met Ho Chi Minh at the Congress of Oppressed Nationalities held in Brussels in February 1927. In 1929, Rabindranath Tagore, the first Asian Nobel Laureate, visited Vietnam, and in his speeches emphasised the age-old cultural ties between the people of India and Vietnam.

When India convened the Asian Relations Conference in 1947 in New Delhi, both the regimes of Ho Chi Minh and Bao Dai in Vietnam were given representation at the Conference.[8] In the post-1945 period, independent Indian government showed its preference for Vietnam as its policy became guided by the ideological considerations of anti-imperialism and support for decolonisation process in Asia and Africa. Nehru, for instance, visited Vietnam in 1954 after the historic victory of the Vietcong forces over the French at Dien Bien Phu. Ho Chi Minh paid a return visit to India in 1958. The Indian Vice-President S. Radhakrishnan visited Vietnam in 1957 followed by the first Indian President Rajendra Prasad, who visited Vietnam in 1959. India also maintained contacts with South Vietnam during this period. In fact, India's neutral role as a member of International Commission of Control and Supervision for Vietnam (ICC) which was critical of the North Vietnam sponsored subversive activities in the South, led to strains in India's relationship with North Vietnam. During the Sino-India conflict of 1962, North Vietnam adopted a neutral position like Soviet Union.

India's relations with North Vietnam, however, began to improve during 1970s as India became a more vocal critic of the US intervention in Vietnam. In January 1972, India and North Vietnam decided to upgrade their missions to the embassy level. This significant decision paved the way for closer contacts with North Vietnam. However, India did not upgrade the diplomatic representation with South Vietnam from the level of Consulate-General. Following the fall of the South Vietnamese government, India became one of the first countries to recognise unified Vietnam. After the invasion of

Cambodia by Vietnam in 1979 leading to the ouster of the Pol-Pot regime and installation of the Heng Samrin government, India was among the few countries to extend recognition to the new government in 1980. This was done to the displeasure of China and the US; and also at the cost of India's participation in Association of Southeast Asian Nations (ASEAN) as a dialogue partner.[9] At the same time, India's ties with Indo-China countries of Cambodia, Lao Peoples' Democratic Republic and Vietnam (CLV) became a prominent aspect of India's Southeast Asian policy during 1980s.

In 1979, China made a short but bloody incursion into northern Vietnam, ostensibly to punish Hanoi for its 200,000 troop intervention in Cambodia, which had deposed the pro Chinese Khmer Rouge regime. In 1988, China-Vietnam long-standing dispute over Spratly Islands led to naval clashes between the two countries. Although a treaty on the Vietnam-China border was reached at the end of 1999, China's claim over almost the whole of South China Sea led to the ongoing disputes with neighbours in the region including Vietnam. This has perhaps provided impetus to both Vietnam and India to forge a strategic relationship.

Vietnam has also greatly enhanced its regional participation in the post Cold War period, particularly since acceptance within the ASEAN in 1995. India and Vietnam collaborate closely in regional forums such as the ASEAN, East Asia Summit (EAS), Mekong-Ganga Cooperation (MGC) and Asia-Europe Meeting (AEM). Vietnam has also been a steady supporter of India's aspirations towards becoming an emerging global power. For instance, Vietnam supported India's nuclear tests in 1998 and is also committed to support India's entry as a permanent member in the United Nations Security Council (UNSC).

Strategic Dimension

India's strategic engagement with Southeast and East Asian countries has been expanding in the post Cold War period. Since the early 1990s, the East Asian states have actively engaged India to contribute to regional growth and peace.[10] India's unstated goal, beyond the promotion of its economic interests, seems to manage the rising Chinese influence that might both encircle and frustrate its aspirations to meaningful leadership role within the sub-continent and the region.[11] At a geo-strategic level, after the end of the Cold War, it became increasingly untenable, illogical and detrimental to India's long-term national interests to continue regarding South Asia and Southeast Asia as separate strategic theatres.[12]

India-Vietnam relationship, with memories of civilisational contact in the background, has certainly progressed to a large extent and into hitherto unchartered areas. Mutual exchanges and information sharing is taking place in the strategic sphere along with initiatives to improve economic ties which show signs of steady progress. India is also investing in Vietnam's capacity development programmes by investing in educational and other infrastructure development. India's relationship with Vietnam has its own trajectory and one should not only think of it in terms of any competitive race with China. It has been argued that, it is almost impossible for India to match China in economic assistance at this stage of economic development. Therefore, India needs to follow a careful thought out strategy for optimising its soft power leverage in the region. Financial limitations must be offset by cultural and educational advantages, with country-specific variations wherever required.[13]

One major indicator of India's growing strategic influence in the region is ONGC Videsh Limited's (OVL) exploration project in the South China Sea, which falls under Vietnam's Exclusive Economic Zone (EEZ), but contended by China. However, the OVL pulled out from Block 128 in South China Sea. The official reason given was that the block 128 had low prospects of producing hydrocarbons, as was the case with the adjacent block 127, which OVL returned to Vietnam three years ago.[14] OVL has paid US$ 15 million exit fee to Petro Vietnam for getting out of the block. Though it was a judicious economic decision, it has the danger of negating India's attempts to project her strategic importance in the region. It also strengthens to an extent the sceptical view that India's strategic capability in the region essentially still remains rather limited. Apart from India's participation in the ARF dialogues and occasional forays to combat piracy, India unfortunately is still an insignificant player in the security structure of the region.[15] But India can ill afford to neglect the importance of the South China Sea. Apart from naval competition with China, almost 55 per cent of India's trade with the Asia-Pacific region transits through the South China Sea. Moreover, OVL continues to have access to Lan Tray and Lan Do fields in Block 06.1, off the coast of Vietnam in the South China Sea. OVL would also continue to be engaged in the Nam Con Son basin (close to Natuna Sea) that OVL was awarded as a goodwill gesture to India. Currently, OVL has 45 per cent stakes in these blocks.[16]

In the field of IT training, NIIT, APTECH and Tata Infotech have so far opened more than 50 franchised centres spread all across Vietnam. India has also set up the Vietnam-India Entrepreneurship Development Centre and Vietnam-India Centre for English Language Training as part of its support to the Initiative for ASEAN Integration (IAI) providing technical assistance to the Government of Vietnam. In the ICT sector, India has set up the Vietnam-India Advanced Resource Centre in ICT.[17]

India's cooperation with Vietnam includes cooperation in the field of defence. Defence delegation visits during the 1980s were followed by signing of a defence cooperation agreement between India and Vietnam in 1994 which included provision for training of the Vietnamese defence personnel and supplying of military hardware spare parts. Defence exchanges continued and received a big boost during the visit of the India's Defence Minister, George Fernandes in 2000, in the course of which the two countries signed a comprehensive agreement for defence cooperation. Apart from expanding the scope of defence cooperation in various sectors, provisions for joint naval training to combat piracy, assistance in ship-building and upgrading of the Vietnamese Navy were important aspects of the agreement. The Indian naval ships have been regularly undertaking visits to Vietnam. Vietnamese Navy takes part in joint exercises in the region along with the Indian Navy.

Conclusion

In this backdrop, Strategic Partnership agreement was signed between India and Vietnam in 2007, giving a boost to the bilateral relationship. What makes India Vietnam relationship special is the close understanding that both countries share over the growing rise of China and its subsequent implication on the security of both countries. The changing dynamics in the region has made closer India-Vietnam relations imperative.

Still, one must remember that the media and the cultural field in Vietnam, continues to be state controlled, to a large extent. In spite of some relaxation, state controlled censorship exists and is enforced by a state bent on conforming information to its will in order to transform itself into something between a capitalist economy and a one-party state. There have been reports that dozens of activists, religious leaders, union members, opposition-party affiliates, journalists and professors have been systemically detained for years for being critical of the party or the state. Even social media like Facebook continue to be prohibited, though many still access it through proxy servers.

Given such realities, it seems that India's policy of enhancing engagement with Vietnam would continue to grow at a slow pace than it is desired. That, however, should not be construed as a failure of India-Vietnam relations. Both countries need to take account of their domestic realities for proper calibration of power in the changing regional and global realities.

NOTES

1. Andrew J. Pierre, Vietnam's Contradictions, *Foreign Affairs*, Vol. 79, No. 6, 2000, p. 84.
2. Helen B. Lamb, *Vietnam's Will to Live*, Monthly Review Press, USA, 1972, p. 2.
3. G.V.C. Naidu, Whither the Look East Policy: India and Southeast Asia, *Strategic Analysis*, Vol. 28, No. 2, 2004, p. 333.
4. Sugata Bose, A Hundred: *The Indian Ocean in the Age of Global Empire*, Harvard University Press, USA, 2006, p. 16.

5. Fernand Braudel, *The Perspective of the World Civilization and Capitalism: 15-18 Century*, Vol. 3, Fontana Press, USA, 1985, p. 484.
6. For a traditional viewpoint on colonial disruption see, for instance, K.M. Panikkar, India and Indian Ocean: An Essay on the Influence of Sea Power on Indian History, George Allen & Unwin, London, 1962; for an alternative viewpoint, see for instance, Michel Morineau, "Eastern and Western Merchants from the Sixteenth to the Eighteenth Centuries," in Sushil Chaudhury and Michel Morineau (eds.), *Merchants, Companies and Trade: Europe and Asia in the Early Modern Era*, Cambridge University Press, Cambridge, 1999, pp. 116-144.
7. D.R. Sardesai, *Indian Foreign Policy in Cambodia, Laos and Vietnam: 1947-1964*, University of California Press, Berkley, USA, 1968, p. 2.
8. C. Ravindranatha Reddy, *India and Vietnam: Era of Friendship and Cooperation, 1947-1991*, Emerald Publishers, Chennai, 2009, pp. 7-8.
9. S.D. Muni, The Turbulent South China Sea Waters: India, Vietnam and China, *ISAS Insights*, No. 140, Institute of South Asian Studies, National University of Singapore, October 2011, p. 6.
10. Sujit Dutta, Managing and Engaging Rising China: India's Evolving Posture, *The Washington Quarterly*, Vol. 34, No. 2, 2011, p. 139.
11. Archana Pandya and David M. Malone, India's Asia Policy: A Late Look East, *ISAS Special Report No. 2*, Institute of South Asian Studies (ISAS), National University of Singapore, August 2010, p. 39.
12 Rajiv Sikri, India's Foreign Policy Priorities in the Coming Decade, ISAS Working Paper No. 25, Institute of South Asian Studies (ISAS), National University of Singapore, 25 September 2007, p. 21.
13. Parama Sinha Palit and Amitendu Palit, Strategic Influence of Soft Power: Inferences for India from Chinese engagement of South and Southeast Asia, *ICRIER Policy Series, No. 3*, August 2011, p. 25.
14. Sandeep Dikshit, India finds oil drilling off Vietnam a losing proposition, The Hindu, May 11, 2012, at http://www.thehindu.com/news/national/article3405680.ece (Accessed November 12, 2012).
15. Baladas Ghosal, 'Some New Thoughts on India's Look East Policy', IPCS Issue Brief No. 54, Institute of Peace and Conflict Studies, New Delhi, October 2007, p. 1.
16. Teshu Singh, The Curious Case of India's Withdrawal from the South China Sea, International Relations and Security Network (ISN), at http://www.isn.ethz.ch/isn/Security-Watch/Articles/Detail/?lng=en&id=143966 (Accessed November 12, 2012).
17. 'India-Vietnam Relations', External Affairs Ministry, Government of India, at http://www.mea.gov.in/Portal/ForeignRelation/Vietnam-January-2012.pdf (Accessed November 12, 2012).

REFERENCES

Abbott, Philip and Finn Tarp (2011), '*Globalization Crises, Trade, and Development in Vietnam*', Working Paper No. 2011/20, UNU World Institute for Development Economics Research (UNU-WIDER), pp. 1-32.

Bose, Sugata (2006), '*A Hundred Horizons: The Indian Ocean in the Age of Global Empire*', Harvard University Press, USA.

Braudel, Fernand, (1985), '*The Perspective of the World Civilization and Capitalism: 15-18 Century*, Vol. 3, Fontana Press, USA.

Dutta, Sujit, (2011), '*Managing and Engaging Rising China: India's Evolving Posture*', The Washington Quarterly, Vol. 34, No. 2, pp. 127-144.

J. Pierre, Andrew (2000), '*Vietnam's Contradictions*', in Foreign Affairs, Vol. 79, No. 6, November-December 2000, pp. 69-86.

Lamb, Helen B. (1972), '*Vietnam's Will to Live*', Monthly Review Press, USA.

Libby, Samantha (2011), '*The Art of Censorship in Vietnam*', Journal of International Affairs, Vol. 65 No. 1, Fall/Winter 2011, pp. 209-218.

Muni, S.D. (2011), '*The Turbulent South China Sea Waters: India, Vietnam and China*', ISAS Insights, No. 140, Institute of South Asian Studies, National University of Singapore, October 2011, pp. 1-11.

Naidu, G.V.C. (2004), '*Whither the Look East Policy: India and Southeast Asia*', Strategic Analysis, Vol. 28, No. 2, April-June 2004, pp. 331-346.

Palit, Parama Sinha and Amitendu Palit (2011), '*Strategic Influence of Soft Power: Inferences for India from Chinese engagement of South and Southeast Asia*', ICRIER Policy Series, No. 3, August 2011, pp. 1-27.

Pandya, Archana and David M. Malone (2010), '*India's Asia Policy: A Late Look East*', Report No. 2, Institute of South Asian Studies (ISAS), National University of Singapore, 25 August 2010, pp. 1-39.

Sardesai, D.R. (1968), '*Indian Foreign Policy in Cambodia, Laos and Vietnam: 1947-1964*', University of California Press, Berkley, USA.

Sikri, Rajiv (2007), '*India's Foreign Policy Priorities in the Coming Decade*', ISAS Working Paper No. 25, Institute of South Asian Studies (ISAS), National University of Singapore, 25 September 2007, pp. 1-49.

2
Milestones in Vietnam-India Strategic Partnership, 1972-2012

Tran Viet Phuong

Introduction

Vietnam-India relationship has evolved and developed since historical time to the present day. In the present times, the relationship was established in the beginning of the 20th century, when both nations were under colonial rule, struggling to achieve independence. Throughout the course of Vietnam's resistance war against French colonialism and US imperialism from the middle to the end of the 20th century, Indian government and Indian people extended great support to Vietnamese people. History is witness to cordial relations between President Ho Chi Minh and Prime Minister Jawaharlal Nehru, the great leaders of the two nations. The late Prime Minister Pham Van Dong once said that the relations between Vietnam and India were like a 'clear cloudless sky'.

In 1954, with its active involvement, India contributed to the signing of the Geneva Accord for the restoration of peace in Vietnam, Laos and Cambodia. India was elected as the Chairman of the International Commission for Supervision and Control in Vietnam. After peace had been restored in Vietnam and following Vietnam's Capital Liberation Day, the Vietnamese people welcomed Indian Prime Minister Jawaharlal Nehru to Hanoi in October 1954. In February 1958, President Ho Chi Minh paid a return visit to India.

In this backdrop, in May 1956, consular relations were established between Vietnam and India. On January 7, 1972, Vietnam and India established full diplomatic relations. In 2012, Vietnam and India celebrated the 40th anniversary of the establishment of their diplomatic relations and the 5th anniversary of the Strategic Partnership. 2012 was also celebrated as Vietnam-India Friendship Year. The past 40 years have laid the foundation for the development of Vietnam-India relations.

Formative Years

After the establishment of diplomatic relations in 1972 and following the official visits to India by Vietnam's Prime Minister Pham Van Dong in 1978 and 1980, Vietnam-India relations entered a new phase. After Indian Prime Minister Indira Gandhi statement, India was willing to assist in post-war reconstruction in Vietnam; the two countries signed a number of agreements in economic, scientific, technological and cultural spheres. Some highlights of Indian financial assistance in the restoration of Vietnam were: (a) the establishment of the Rice Research Institute at Mekong Delta in O-Mon, Hau Giang Province; (b) the Buffalo Breeding Centre in Song Be province to which Indian government gifted 500 Murrah buffaloes; (c) locomotives for Gia Lam train station; and (d) equipment for Nam Dinh textile mill.

Receiving great support from India, Vietnam has taken active part in the Non-Aligned Movement (NAM) since the 1970s. At the third NAM Summit in Lusaka (Zambia) in 1970, the members agreed to the Observer status of Vietnam. At the fifth NAM Summit in Colombo (Sri Lanka) in 1976, Vietnam became an official member of the grouping.

The 1980s marked a high point in the history of Vietnam-India relations. Vietnam faced various political and economic difficulties during this period. To cope up with these, Vietnam launched the policy of Doi Moi. In this period of hardship, India aided Vietnam by sending tonnes of wheat and extending low-interest credits. Mechanism for cooperation between the two countries evolved in all spheres, i.e. politics, security-defence and socio-economics. In 1982, Vietnam-India Joint Commission for Economic Scientific and Technical Cooperation (the highest form of cooperation mechanism) was established. Vietnamese Minister of Foreign Affairs and Indian Minister of External Affairs were Co-chairmen of the Commission. In December 1982, the first session of the Joint Commission was held in New Delhi. Other important mechanisms such as joint missions and joint committees of specific spheres were also founded. Indian entrepreneurs were the first foreign partner to establish head offices in Vietnam and form joint ventures with Vietnamese partners. The visits to Vietnam by Indian Prime Minister Rajiv Gandhi in November 1985, April 1988 and December 1988 were timely encouragement for Vietnam. With the visits to India by General Secretary of the Vietnamese Communist Party Le Duan in September 1984 and by General Secretary of the Vietnamese Communist Party Nguyen Van Linh in January 1989, Vietnam-India relations reached a new height.

Dawn of a New Phase

The 21st century witnessed a new height in Vietnam-India relations and the two nations reached maturity and transformed it into a Strategic Partnership. Politics, security-defence, trade, culture and human resource training are five pillars of Vietnam-India Strategic Partnership. In December 1999, during the visit to India, Vietnamese President Tran Duc Luong stated 'Vietnam always considers the cooperative relations with India as of strategic and long-term importance'. Indian Prime Minister A.B. Vajpayee during his visit to Vietnam in 2001 asserted that India-Vietnam relations were strategic relations.

During the visits to India by General Secretary Nong Duc Manh in 2003 and by Prime Minister Nguyen Tan Dung in 2007, the two countries signed several important documents, i.e. Joint Statement on Comprehensive Cooperation Framework for the 21st Century and Joint Statement on the Official Establishment of Strategic Partnership. These documents facilitated the diversification of bilateral cooperation in field of economics, politics, culture, education, security-defence, science and technology, etc. The exchange of high-level visits deepened Vietnam-India strategic partnership, enhanced cooperation in specific fields, and created favourable environment for the achievement of efficiency and practicality in the relationship.

Other significant bilateral visits were by Vice President Nguyen Thi Doan in October 2009, Chairman of Vietnamese National Assembly Nguyen Phu Trong in March 2010, Prime Minister Truong Tan Sang in October 2011, and Deputy Prime Minister Nguyen Thien Nhan in April 2012. From Indian side, Lok Sabha Speaker Somnath Chatterjee visited Vietnam in 2007; President Pratibha Patil in 2008; Prime Minister Manmohan Singh for taking part in ASEAN-India Summit and East Asia Summit in Hanoi in 2010; Lok Sabha Speaker Meira Kumar in May 2011; and Vice President Hamid Ansari in 2013.

Cooperation between the two countries continues to develop and expand. In 2011, the bilateral cooperation between Vietnam and India was comprehensively evaluated and measures to promote cooperation in all fields were discussed at the meetings organised in Hanoi. These meetings included the 5th Political Consultations, the 2nd Strategic Dialogue in August 2011, the 14th session of Vietnam-Indian Joint Commission and the 6th Defence Policy Dialogue in September 2011. Vietnam and India have signed various agreements and memorandum in economic, science and technology, and socio-cultural fields.

India's recognition of Vietnam's market economy status and the implementation of ASEAN-India FTA and other economic agreements between the two countries, the bilateral trade in 2012 touched US$ 5.4 billion, increasing by more than 10 folds compared to 10 years ago. Both nations are striving to increase the bilateral trade to US$ 7 billion by 2015.

India's direct investment in Vietnam began in 1988 with the oil and gas exploration project of the Oil and Natural Gas Commission (ONGC) in the East Sea. India has had 61 investment projects in Vietnam with total registered capital of more than US$ 232 million.

Vietnam has also initiated a number of investment projects in India. Both Vietnamese and Indian enterprises are willing to expand their investment projects and commercial undertakings, as well as ventures in key areas such as oil and gas, high technology, computer technology, software technology, etc. India's renown cooperates like Tata and Infosys have penetrated into the Vietnamese market. Likewise, other Indian companies are also trying to invest in Vietnam.

India has provided Vietnam with Official Development Assistance (ODA) and preferential credits. These credits have brought practical results to Vietnam in medium and small scales industries sector, hydroelectricity, mechanics, agriculture and software technology, etc. Training is one of the main strengths of Vietnam-India relations. India has helped to establish training centres such as Vietnam-India Training Centre for Nuclear Energy in 2002, English Language Centre in Da Nang in 2008, Vietnam-India Advanced Resource Centre in Information and Communication Technology (ARC-ICT) in 2011, PARAM supercomputing facility in Hanoi in 2011, and forthcoming centres such as Centre for criminal evidence recovery to be established in Ho Chi Minh City, English Language Centre in Diplomatic Academy, Remote Sensing Centre in the ASEAN-India cooperation framework, etc. These facilities have contributed immensely to train Vietnamese human resources in economic fields, which in turn has enhanced cooperation in economics, investment, trade, defence-security, etc. India is going to increase the number of scholarship from 100 to 150 in the required domains in 2012.

Vietnam Airlines and India's Jet Airways plan to open direct flight route between Vietnam and India. The two countries' are cooperating in establishing an Indian Culture Centre in Hanoi and a Vietnamese Culture Centre in Kolkata, in restoring Cham temples in My Son, Vietnam; promoting commercial investments; increasing exchange of visits; cultural activities; performer exchange; promoting tourism, etc.

Vietnam and India have mutual understanding on various regional and international issues. In the 1990s, Vietnam's geo-strategic location and its role in the region, it became the bridge between

ASEAN and India. Vietnam supported India's Look East Policy, to develop connection between India and ASEAN. India became a sectoral dialogue partner of ASEAN in 1992 and a full dialogue partner in 2002. India then took part in East Asia Summit, ASEAN Regional Forum and many other forums. In 2009, India and ASEAN signed the Agreement on ASEAN-India Trade in Goods (AITIG). Indian leaders think highly of Vietnam's role in ASEAN, and appreciate Vietnam's support for India's Look East Policy and in the strengthening ASEAN-India relations. Vietnam supports India in becoming a permanent member of the United Nations Security Council (UNSC). The two countries coordinate closely in regional and international forums, sub-regional development plans, East-West corridor project, Ganga-Mekong Cooperation (GMC), etc.

In parallel with the process of developing traditional cordial relations and Vietnam-India Strategic Partnership, defence cooperation between the two nations has also been gradually strengthened. Vietnam and India established close ties in defence cooperation, conforming to the two nations' internal affairs and the regional and international situation. The aim is to create a stable, peaceful and prosperous milieu for both countries as well as for the region and the world.

Since 1980, Vietnam and India have exchanged Defence Attaché. The two nations have signed various agreements such as protocol on defence in April 1994, Memorandum of Understanding (MoU) on defence cooperation in November 2009, and a MoU on navy cooperation in June 2011. Both sides have effectively implemented the mechanism of Defence Policy Dialogue between Deputy Ministers of Defence, which has had six sessions till date.

India has agreed to assist Vietnam in promoting defence modernisation, training of defence personnel and developing Vietnam's military. India places emphasis on helping Vietnam in engineering, intelligence, defence industry, remote sensing, information technology and so on. Vietnam and India are striving to strengthen air force cooperation, specifically in supplying spare parts and repairing equipments and upgrading air force weapons, training pilots, and operating Mig-21, Su-27 and Su-30 aircrafts. Most notably, the two nations are currently putting efforts to implement the MoU on navy cooperation. India has agreed to assist Vietnam in training submarine crew, maintaining and repairing vessels, and enhancing capacity for coastal defence. On an average, Indian vessels call at Vietnam's ports twice a year. Vietnam and India send observers to each other's military training establishments and have started joint training such as fire fighting, rescue, etc. between the two naval forces. During the visit to India by President Truong Tan Sang in October 2011, Indian Prime Minister expressed willingness to provide Vietnam with credits to develop its defence industry especially warship-building.

Since the beginning of the decade, India has offered 30 scholarships for medium to high ranking officer training annually. In 2008, Vietnam admitted one Indian high-ranking officer to Vietnam's Academy of Defence and one Indian officer to Vietnamese language course at Vietnam's Academy of Military Science. India has been supplying free-of-charge equipment, weapons and spare parts to Vietnam, of which total value may be in million of US dollars. The two nations have also begun to establish relations in defence trade. At present, Vietnam and India are focusing on the installation of satellite receiving station in Vietnam which aims to enhance Vietnam-India cooperation in imagery sharing, for antiterrorism and anti-piracy activities.

Security cooperation also has new breakthroughs. Vietnam and India signed Mutual Legal Assistance Treaty in Criminal Matters in 2007, Memorandum on Crime Prevention Cooperation in 2008, MoU on Cooperation between Vietnam's Ministry of Public Security and India's Ministry of Home Affairs in September 2011.

India has expressed willingness to help Vietnam in training and modernising its police force, and in holding specialised courses on security in Vietnam. The two nations are directing their efforts towards implementing the MoUs, organising sessions on security issues at deputy ministerial level and completing the construction of Indira Gandhi Centre for criminal evidence recovery in Ho Chi Minh City. National investigating agencies of the two countries have cooperated effectively in crime prevention.

Suggestions for Further Enhancing Cooperation

To further enhance and deepen strategic engagement between Vietnam and India, the two countries need to:

(a) Maintain and further develop mechanisms for bilateral cooperation. Both countries should continue frequent exchange of visits, meetings between high-level officers, Ministers, and governmental officers at various levels.

(b) Intensify and realise five pillars of the Strategic Partnership cooperation, i.e. politics, security-defence, trade, culture and human resources training. They need to further cooperate and coordinate at regional and international fora.

(c) Implement thoroughly and effectively seven cooperation agreements in the fields of oil and gas, aviation, agriculture and culture, which were signed during President Truong Tan Sang's visit to India in October 2011; nine cooperation agreements and five projects in high-tech domains which were agreed during Deputy Prime Minister Nguyen Thien Nhan's visit to India in April 2012.

(d) Both countries need to strive to achieve bilateral turnover of US$ 7 billion in 2015, and to decrease Vietnam's trade deficit.

(e) Vietnam should create favourable conditions for Indian entrepreneurs. India should urge ONGC to maintain and promote oil exploration and exploitation in the East Sea (South China Sea).

(f) Vietnam should invite Indian corporate to take part in constructing high-tech centre in Vietnam and to invest in Vietnamese industries. Both should further cooperative ties in potential fields such as high technology, computer technology, computer software, human resources training, agriculture-forestry-fishery and culture coordination. They should utilise effectively the existing high-tech centres and initiate construction of new centres.

Concluding Remarks

Several historical challenges have proved that India is a traditional, loyal and trustworthy friend of Vietnam. Vietnam-India relations have constantly deepened in the past 40 years. The effective and expansive cooperative ties between the two countries are built upon mutual trust, whose foundation was laid by President Ho Chi Minh and Prime Minister Jawaharlal Nehru, which was continuously nurtured by various generations of leaders and people. The bilateral ties aim at attaining peace, stability and prosperous development in both nations, in the region and in the whole world.

SECTION II

Economic Relations: Trade, Investments and Cooperation in Conventional and Non-Conventional Sources of Energy

3
Four Decades of India–Vietnam Economic and Commercial Relations and the Way Forward

Shantanu Srivastava

Introduction

Vietnam's long and gallant struggle for freedom and subsequent determined thrust to undertake the gigantic task of economic reconstruction offer several important lessons in management to the corporate world. India and Vietnam celebrated 40 years of establishment of the full diplomatic relations and the Year of Friendship in 2012. Forty years have gone by 'like the beautiful water of the Ganges flowing through the Himalayas or the scenic waterfalls in the highlands of Vietnam', each year bringing with it a new challenge and a new opportunity. Therefore, it is important to look back at the past 40 years, introspect, and conceive a vision for the future so that India and Vietnam can together carve out an innovative and effective strategy for future cooperation. In order to set the ball rolling along these lines, this chapter is divided in two parts; four decades of India-Vietnam Economic and Commercial Relations (1972-2012); and the way forward for the next decade (2012-22).

Four Decades of India-Vietnam Economic and Commercial Relations

First Decade (1972–82): Early Days, Cold War Era, First Line of Credit and Setting Up of India-Vietnam Joint Commission

This was the period of the last phase of Vietnam's war for liberation of Saigon and thereafter national reunification and consolidation. The global scenario was dominated by the Cold War and there was a call for 'South-South Cooperation' to reduce dependence on the developed world. These were difficult years for Vietnam as it was emerging from 30 years of freedom struggle. India strongly supported and assisted Vietnam in its efforts for economic reconstruction since the liberation of Saigon. In 1978, India offered the first line of credit (LoC) to Vietnam worth Rs. 400 million and this credit was utilised for the import of 980 wagons, 1,000 bogies and 50 coaches from India. There was no other major activity by way of trade during this decade, but the two countries set up the Joint Commission in 1982 for economic, scientific and technical cooperation.

Second Decade (1983–92): Reconstruction of Vietnam's Economy and Introduction of New Economic Policies in Both Countries, Low Levels of Bilateral Trade

India offered the second LoC in 1983 against which 15 diesel locomotives were supplied. These locomotives were based in Ho Chi Minh City. This was followed by a third credit in 1984-85 which was utilised for the import of finished equipment and boiler for Nam Dinh Textile Mill and fabrics from India. The next credit in 1986 led to the supply of 300 coal hopper wagons for Hon Gai and Cam Pha coal mines located in the northeast of Hanoi.

Bilateral trade during this decade was mostly dependent on the LoC. There was very small amount of business outside the LoC which was mainly export of tea, machinery, yarn and textiles from India and, towards the later part of the decade, export of raw cashew, raw silk and timber from Vietnam to India.

During the 6th Party Congress in 1986, the Government of

Vietnam introduced a new economic policy, known as 'Doi Moi'. This open door economic policy proved to be a real success story for Vietnam. It is interesting to note that from 1988 to 1992, the repayment of old Indian credits were made in terms of rice which was purchased by a select few Indian and Thai companies. These companies exported rice to third countries and made payments to the Indian government based on certain discount formulas which were finalised before each deal.

The 7th Party Congress in 1991 adopted the programme on national reconstruction. In the same year, India also introduced its new economic policy which eventually led to a rapid growth of Gross Domestic Product (GDP) and transformed India into an important economic power in the world.

This decade witnessed the beginning of India's investments in Vietnam. In 1989 OVL (earlier known as Hydro Carbons India Ltd.) started their first overseas venture off the coast of Vung Tau, located to the east of Ho Chi Minh City.

Third Decade (1993–2002): Limited Growth in Bilateral Trade, Regional Economic Crisis in Southeast Asia, Rise in Investments from India, Establishment of Indian Business Chamber in Vietnam.

This was the phase of rapid growth for both countries, though there was a slowdown in Vietnam for a brief period due to the Asian economic crisis of 1997–98.

In Vietnam, two historic meetings, the 8th Party Congress in 1996 witnessed the ending of the socio-economic crisis and encouraged the country to boost industrialisation and modernisation, and the 9th Party Congress in 2001 that prepared a 10-year strategy for socio-economic development. These led to landmark decisions that hastened the process of international economic integration and transformed Vietnam into one of the fastest growing economies in the region and an attractive destination for foreign investment.

India offered a credit in 1993 which was used for tea machinery for Son La and Nghe An provinces and textile machinery for Vinh Phu province and Ho Chi Minh City. A complete sugar mill of 1,250

TCD capacity was set up in Can Tho Province under another LoC which was signed in the year 1995. This was a very successful project that not only created visibility but also provided opportunities for further export of sugar machinery to Vietnam outside the credit. Another credit was offered in 1998 for the supply of a fruit drink processing plant in Hanoi and a production line to manufacture adhesive tapes for packaging in Vinh Yen province.

This decade somehow did not witness much growth in bilateral trade. By 1996 the two way trade could reach only about US$ 100 million and even by 1999 it was a mere US$ 150 million. India's exports to Vietnam accounted for more than 90 per cent of total bilateral trade. By the year 2000, the figure rose to a little over US$ 200 million with Vietnam's exports to India still remaining in the range of 10 per cent.

However, during this period, India's investments grew rapidly as companies like KCP and Nagarjuna set up sugar mills in Phu Yen and Long An provinces, respectively. Ranbaxy set up a pharmaceutical plant in Ho Chi Minh City, and United Phosphorous and Godrej set up factories in Binh Duong province.

Another positive development of this decade was the setting up of the Indian Business Chamber in Vietnam in August 1998 which was formally licensed in February 1999, whose mandate was to provide a platform for smooth flow of information and facilitate interactions between the business communities of the two countries.

Fourth Decade (2003–2012): Period of Real Growth in Bilateral Trade, Sharp Rise in Vietnam's Exports to India, Global Economic Crisis, Signing of FTA.

The new decade brought fresh energy into bilateral trade and was the turning point in the bilateral relations, as the trade rose sharply during this period. During the visit to Hanoi in January 2001, then Prime Minister Atal Bihari Vajpayee expressed the desire to increase the bilateral trade from US$ 200 million to US$ 500 million in 5 years. This appeared to be a difficult target at that point of time. However, the trade actually grew more rapidly and the figure rose to US$ 1,000 million in 2006. At that stage the share of Vietnam's export to India in the overall trade relations between the two countries remained below 20 per cent. In 2009, bilateral trade exceeded US$ 2,000 million, with India's exports at 78 per cent and Vietnam's export to India at 22 per cent. The years 2010 and 2011 saw a very sharp increase in Vietnam's exports to India. Vietnam exports share rose to US$ 1.55 billion or 39 per cent out of the total bilateral trade of US$ 3.90 billion in 2011. During the first 5 months of 2012, the trade was worth US$ 1.52 billion, out of which Vietnam's exports were US$ 0.59 billion or 39 per cent of the total trade and India's exports were US$ 0.93 billion or 61 per cent of the total trade. Major items of export from India to Vietnam are engineering goods, chemicals, pharmaceutical formulations and raw materials, steel, non-ferrous metals, plastic resins, animal feed, agro-chemicals, textiles, cotton fibre and yarn, tobacco, maize, etc. Major items of export from Vietnam to India are black pepper, coffee, tea, cinnamon, cashew, rubber, sea food, coal, footwear, wooden furniture, mobile phones, computers, etc.

During this decade, India offered LoCs worth US$ 27 million and US$ 45 million which were mainly used for the import of Hydro Power projects from India. These Hydro Power projects have been highly successful and have created a large amount of visibility in Vietnam. They have also led to more imports of Hydro Power projects from India outside the credit lines.

IT companies like NIIT and Aptech were amongst the major investors from India in Vietnam during this decade. There were also investments from R.K. Marble, Alliance Mineral and Philips Carbon Black and some others. India-ASEAN Free Trade in Goods Agreement was signed in August 2009. High growth in bilateral trade, sharp rise in Vietnam's exports to India, and signing of the FTA were the main highlights of this decade.

The Way Forward for the Next Decade (2012–22)

Being amongst the fastest growing economies in the world, India and Vietnam have a vast potential for cooperation. While good progress has been made in the last 10 years, a lot still remains to be done. Bilateral trade which has risen from US$ 200 million in 2000 to nearly US$ 3.90 billion in 2011 has to cross the targeted figure of US$ 7 billion by the year 2015. In fact both countries need to achieve at least 10 per cent of India's total trade with ASEAN. This needs 'out of the box' thinking and an innovative approach. The general sentiment of friendship between the two countries needs to be translated into enhanced business cooperation in the same proportion. In this context, a few suggestions can be considered for enhancing business relations between the two countries:

Connectivity

Air: This is an important aspect for both business and tourism. It was encouraging to see Jet Airways sign an MoU during the visit of President Truong Tan Sang to India in 2011. It would give major boost to business and tourism once direct flights become a reality.

Sea: Trans-shipments are expensive and time consuming. It is therefore important that there are direct sea-connectivity between the major ports of the two countries.

Road: India, Thailand and Myanmar are cooperating to improve regional connectivity through initiatives such as India–Myanmar–Thailand Trilateral Highway and Asian Highway Network. It would be useful if this could be extended to Vietnam.

Eximbank Credit

Eximbank's offer of buyer's credit to finance project export from India is ridden with difficulties and tough conditions. The requirement of sovereign guarantee is difficult to meet and the repayment period is short. However, these conditions need to be modified subject to government's approval.

Line of Credit

The Indian LoC has played an important role in promotion of bilateral trade and cooperation during the past 40 years and it is necessary that it continues. India should ensure that LoCs are utilised for those areas that provide visibility, such as power and infrastructure.

Advantages of LoCs are:

(a) Contributes to capacity building in recipient country.
(b) Opens new and mutually beneficial areas of cooperation between the two countries.

Banking

Banking arrangements are an important facet of international business especially with regard to payment guarantees and other forms of guarantees. Bilateral trade and investment having reached the critical mass, it is now time that a bank from India opened a full branch in Vietnam. Bank of India, which has a representative office in Ho Chi Minh City, should take lead in this direction.

Partial Trade in Rupee

In order to minimise dependence on foreign exchange and also the risks arising out of exchange rate fluctuations, the two sides should consider doing a part of trade in Rupees. This could start with 50 per cent of the value of Vietnam's exports to India.

Tourism

Tourism can contribute substantially to the promotion of people-to-people contact and in turn influence business relations positively. Efforts should be made by both sides to increase tourism between the two countries. To promote tourism, there should be a number of direct flights between the two countries which can ease travel and facilitate competitive packages for the people.

Capacity Building

Both the countries need to promote cooperation in education, scientific research and human resource and skill development.

Visas

The two governments should consider giving long-term multiple entry visas to business-related visitors. Short-term visas create hurdles for regular travellers who have ongoing projects and who need to travel at short notices.

Bridge Information Gap

Despite the sharp rise in trade, there exists a major information deficit and efforts are needed to bridge this gap. Business Chambers can play a vital role in this and promotional activities and exchange of delegations can help in reducing the information gap.

Vietnamese Companies Should Open Offices in India

A large number of Indian companies have established representative offices in Vietnam. However, so far, no Vietnamese company has opened office in India. The successful Indian model in Vietnam should be replicated by Vietnamese companies. This will help in bridging the information gap and provide the much needed boost to the bilateral economic relations.

Adopt Innovative Approach to Boost Bilateral Trade

Business can consider new items and offer concessional prices to Vietnamese customers. They also need to pay attention to quality control and adopt a long-term view for the promotion of business in the country. Businesses can also consider softer payment terms for loans for the Vietnamese market.

Indian Investment in Vietnam

Indian companies should explore investment opportunities in the fields of renewable sources of energy, transport, telecom, healthcare, education, agriculture, forestry, mining and tourism. In this context,

Tata Steel's proposed investment project is important and both sides need to hasten the process for issuing the licenses.

Vietnam's Investment in India

While it is expected that investments from India would keep growing, a similar measure to promote Vietnam's investments in India should also be explored. The time is ripe and Vietnamese companies should come to India and explore investment opportunities. This will give them a competitive edge in India's large and lucrative market and also in export as all the raw materials are available in India at competitive prices.

Participate in Promotional Activities

This is important since there is limited information about each other's potential, culture and way of 'doing business' which often lowers comfort levels. Therefore, it is important to increase promotional activities like participation in trade fairs, seminars and frequent visits of business delegations to visit each other's country. Reaching out to the masses through the print and electronic media will create awareness and attract more companies to explore business opportunities.

Concluding Remarks

The last decade saw immense growth in economic cooperation between India and Vietnam. Bilateral trade grew many folds and Indian FDI witnessed a sharp increase in Vietnam. However, a huge reservoir of opportunities still remains untapped and it is necessary for both the governments and business communities of the two countries to explore new areas and widen the bandwidth of cooperation. India and Vietnam have a lot to offer to each other and they need to unleash their full potential to emerge as successful partners in the long run.

4
Strengthening India-Vietnam Trade and Investment Relations in the Current Global Financial Crisis

Vikash Ranjan

Introduction

India and Vietnam have shared cordial political and strategic relation since historical time. The launch of India's Look East Policy from 1992 led to increase in New Delhi's political and economic engagements with East and Southeast Asian countries. The admission of Myanmar in ASEAN in 1997 made India, ASEAN's contiguous neighbour.

After the end of the Vietnam War and the unification of Vietnam, trade and investment relations were established between India and Vietnam. India granted 'Most Favoured Nation' status to Vietnam in 1975, and signed a trade agreement in 1978. After the 'Doi Moi' reforms in Vietnam and the opening up of the Indian economy from 1991 onwards, India-Vietnam 'Double Taxation Avoidance Agreement' was signed in 1994, and the 'Bilateral Investment Promotion and Protection Agreement' (BIPPA) in 1997. In 2003, India and Vietnam announced the Joint Declaration on Comprehensive Cooperation, and signed Strategic Partnership agreement in 2007. After Vietnam's accession to WTO in 2007, India acceded to a longstanding demand from Vietnam for grant of Market Economy Status in 2009. The coming into force of ASEAN-India

FTA in goods in January 2010 (Vietnam signed in June 2010), further boosted trade and investment relations between the two countries.

However, in spite of these trade and investment agreements, the two countries are yet to realise their full potentials. It begs the question that why India and Vietnam have failed to unleash full potential in the economic sector and what steps they need to take to ameliorate the situation. To do so it is important to have a look at the growth and structure of the Vietnamese economy, and in that backdrop, try to understand India-Vietnam trade and investment relations. This would help in identifying challenges and opportunities inherent in the bilateral relationship.

Bilateral relationships develop as part of the regional and global milieu under which they exist, and therefore it is not possible to undertake a realistic assessment for future development of bilateral relationship. It is pertinent to mention that regional and global factors have direct or indirect impact on the relationship. As the world is passing through a recessionary phase in the form of global financial crisis its effects on the development of bilateral India-Vietnam economic relationship needs to be taken into account. Moreover, as security and economy issues are intertwined, Vietnam's security dilemma in the South China Sea may have repercussions on the overall relations between the two countries. Taking into account these factors, it is fair to suggest some ways and identify potential areas for cooperation, which may give fillip to the already burgeoning bilateral relationship.

Growth and Development of the Vietnamese Economy

Since the introduction of 'Doi Moi' (Renovations) reforms in 1986, Vietnamese economy has undergone relatively smooth period of structural adjustment and stabilisation. Vietnam's export-led growth centred on its wealth of raw materials, has transformed Vietnam from a closed economy to a market economy.

Vietnam's economy is predominantly agrarian; the Red River basin in the North and the Mekong Delta in the South are the principal agricultural regions and their primary agricultural products include rice, pepper, jute, rubber, sugarcane, coffee, tea, groundnut and tobacco. With a view to encouraging farmers to make long-term investments and increasing production, land reforms were adopted in 1993 in Vietnam wherein rights of farmers to exchange, transfer, rent and inherit allotted land were recognised. The land, however, continues to belong to the State in accordance with the Constitution of the Socialist Republic of Vietnam.

With the enforcement of contract quota system in the agricultural sector, coupled with more direct investment, tax incentives and higher purchase price of food by the State, there has been a significant boost in total food grain production since 1988. Production of tea, coffee and natural rubber has driven the strong export performance in the agriculture sector. Strong external demand also underpinned growth in the fisheries sector. Currently Vietnam is the largest producer and exporter of pepper in the world, the second largest exporter of rice (after Thailand), coffee (after Brazil) and cashew nuts (after India), the fourth largest of rubber and seventh largest of tea[1]. The Government is placing increasing emphasis on cash crops with export potential and on building agro-based industries.

The 'Monetisation' of the economy since 1989, helped Vietnam to limit the inflationary impact of radical price reforms and monetary expansion. The 1992 Constitution embodied the market-oriented reforms and recognised citizens' right to engage in private business. In 1993 the Land Law was promulgated allowing the transfer of land use rights, and in 1994, Labour Law was introduced. As a result of these reforms, rapid industrial growth of Vietnam has taken place. Increasingly agricultural lands are being used for industrial purposes, which reflect the changing economic structure of Vietnam. According to 2012 estimates agriculture's share of GDP has declined from 24.5 per cent in 2000 to 21.5 per cent in 2012, whereas the industry and services sectors accounted for 40.7 per cent and 37.7 per cent of GDP, respectively.[2]

In this backdrop, export led growth took place in Vietnam. Vietnam's trade policy can be characterised as 'export-led protectionism', whereby import substitution was encouraged with trade protection. Export industries were promoted by providing subsidies to counter balance the high relative costs of intermediary products. However, the export structure of Vietnam consisting of primary products and low value added goods, a major proportion of which consists of agricultural and mineral products, has changed very little over the years.

In the current global crisis scenario, the 'export led protectionism' policy of Vietnam may not reap rich dividend. As the prices for unprocessed export commodities are decreasing in the world market, it would have negative effects on continuously increasing exports of such commodities on the Vietnamese economy, because the lower export prices would mean greater costs for Vietnam in terms of resources to be sacrificed to maintain export growth and income level. Vietnam's export led protectionist policy will also get hampered due to open competition from global industries, once Vietnam opens its economy under WTO conditions from 2014.

India-Vietnam Trade and Investment Relations

India-Vietnam bilateral trade increased by 46.72 per cent to reach US$ 5.4 billion in 2012, from US$ 3.7 billion in 2011.[3] Out of India's total imports of US $ 489.3 billion, Vietnamese goods were worth only US$ 1.7 billion, accounting for only 0.35 per cent in India's total imports. Similarly, out of India's total export of US$ 305.9 billion in 2012, exports to Vietnam were worth only US$ 3.7 billion, accounting for only 1.22 per cent of India's total exports.[4] Though the percentage share of Indian exports and imports to Vietnam increased by 40.27 per cent and 62.78 per cent respectively, the absolute figures are abysmally low in the overall trade relations of the two countries. This shows that though the bilateral trade between the two is increasing, it is not exceptional in the light of overall trade volume of the two countries. The two countries have set the target of US$ 7 billion to be achieved by 2015.

India is currently the 10th largest exporter to Vietnam. Major commodities exported from India to Vietnam include animal feed ingredients, pharmaceuticals, machinery and equipment, yellow corn, cotton, plastics, ordinary metals, chemical, leather and textile materials. Major items exported by Vietnam to India mainly consists of mobile phones and accessories, machinery and equipment, steel and products thereof, rubber, computer hardware and electronics items, coffee, coal and pepper. Thus, one of the major factors behind the slow expansion of trade is the similarity of export items between the two countries.

In investment sector, both India and Vietnam are considered attractive investment destinations, but they have invested very little in each other. As of December 2011, India had only 62 investment projects in Vietnam with total registered capital of US$ 234 million. If investments by Indian companies from third countries are included, India has 86 projects with total investment capital of US$ 868 million.[5] Indian companies have invested in oil and gas exploration, mineral exploration and processing, sugar manufacturing, agro-chemicals, IT and agricultural processing in Vietnam. These include the Godrej plant for steel furniture, Mangalam Steel Ltd for steel strips in Bing Duong province, etc. JK Tyre and the Southern Rubber Industry Joint Stock Company (Casumina) have signed an off take agreement valued at US$ 36 million under which Casumina will produce 180,000 truck tyres for export using JK Tyre's brand name, and production in this project has begun. In April 2007, Hoa Sen Corporation, a leading private steel maker inaugurated a US$ 30 million cold rolled steel mill in Binh Duong province, for which an Indian company, Flat Products Equipments had supplied equipment worth US$ 8 million. This factory is one of the largest of its kind in Vietnam and is the first private project financed partly under a LoC from India. Phillips Carbon Black is setting up the first ever Carbon black plant in Vietnam with a total investment of US$ 84 million in southern Vietnam. Other notable investments include the project of Venkateshwara Hatcheries Group to set up a poultry feed producing factory in Tay Ninh Province and of CCL Products Group for biggest instant coffee manufacturing plant in Central highland. Marico, one of India's leading FMCG companies, picked up 85 per cent equity in International Consumer Products Corporation (ICP), a successful Vietnamese FMCG company. M/s Unispice, a joint venture between Bafna and a Vietnamese company have commenced spice processing plant in Vietnam.[6] Besides, Fortis Healthcare International has bought 65 per cent stake in Vietnam's Hoan My Medical Corp for US$ 64 million.[7]

Out of various Indian investment projects, proposal by Tata Steel to invest in Vietnam is the most important. Tata Steel plans to invest US$ 5 billion for setting up an integrated steel mill in Vietnam, the largest single Indian investment in Vietnam. The proposed steel complex with an estimated capacity of 4.5 million tons per year is supposed to be phased over 10 years to be built in Ha Tinh province. Tata Steel will also have a stake of 30 per cent in the Thach Khe Iron Ore Joint Stock Company which will undertake mining. However, this project has run into difficulties, particularly on two issues: first, the total amount of compensation for the acquisition of land estimated by Tata Steel is different from that sought by Ha Tinh province; and second, the Ha Tinh province has expressed its inability to pay this amount due to lack of resources even though as per law, they are supposed to provide the amount towards compensation. They have requested Tata Steel to pay the same. The project is stuck on these two issues. During the visit by External Affairs Minister of India Mr. S.M. Krishna in September 2011, Prime Minister Nguyen Tan Dung of Vietnam proposed that the Government of India may consider extending Official Development Assistance of US$ 100 million to finance the compensation amount. The request was reiterated when the Finance Minister of Vietnam Mr. Vuong Dinh Hue called on the then Finance Minister Mr. Pranab Mukherjee in New Delhi on October 12, 2011. The Indian government conveyed that it is ready to resolve all issues with regard to the project in consultation with the Government of Vietnam. Separately, India also conveyed its willingness to extend LoCs for infrastructure development. However, it needs to be noted that Indian LoCs cannot be offered for site clearance compensation in Vietnam as demanded in the case of Tata Steel. Since Indian LoCs require 75 per cent of the value of credit to be sourced from Indian public exchequer, it cannot be given for the purpose of promoting one company. During the visit of President Truong Tan Sang to India in October 2011, Indian Prime Minister Mr. Manmohan Singh raised the issue of Tata Steel during delegation-level talks. President Sang responded that this was a high-priority project; Vietnam is prepared to offer Tata Steel a higher stake in the Thach Ke Iron Ore mine; and that remaining issues should be resolved through discussions between the two governments. This shows that though both the countries want to implement the project, lack of resources with the provincial government of Vietnam and legality of extending ODA for site clearance purpose from the Indian government side has stalled the project.

Nevertheless, the two governments are extending their cooperation through LoCs and other mechanisms. At the government level, India has extended 14 LoCs totalling Rs. 561 crores to Vietnam since 1976.[8] This includes a LoC for US$ 19.5 million in 2011 to Vietnam for setting up hydropower projects and LoC for US$ 45 million for Nam Chien hydropower project which is being executed by BHEL. India has agreed to consider earmarking an amount of up to US$ 100 million under the Buyer's Credit under the National Export Insurance Account (BC-NEIA) for use by Vietnam,[9] subject to the approval process of the BC-NEIA at the most competitive terms prevailing at the time of project proposals. During Indian Vice President Mr. Hamid Ansari's visit to Vietnam in January 2013 for the closing ceremony to commemorate 40 year of diplomatic relations between the two countries, the two countries signed a MoU for cooperation in the field of micro, small and medium enterprises (MSME).

Taking all these into accounts, it can be inferred that though investments from India to Vietnam are increasing, and both the governments intend to further enhance the relationship, the legality and technical problems are hampering Indian investment into Vietnam.

India is one of the most sought after investment destinations in the wider world. Yet, no Vietnamese company has invested in India. In the current global financial crisis India and Vietnam need to invest in each other to make up for the reduced capital flows from western countries, embroiled in the crisis situation.

Global Financial Crisis and Its Effects

Vietnam is considered by investors as an attractive destination in the region. However, economic growth in Vietnam slowed in 2009 due to effects of global recession. Vietnam's real GDP growth fell from 6.2 per cent in 2008 to 5.2 per cent in 2009, the slowest pace of growth since 2000. However, it rebounded to 6.8 per cent in 2010 only to dip down to 5.9 per cent in 2011 due to Government's decision to sacrifice growth at the expense of inflation. To rein in inflation which rose to more than 20 per cent, government responded by tightening the monetary policy. This led to credit crunch leading to high interest rates which in turn affected overall economic engagements of Vietnam. Vietnam's inflation rate reached double digits at the start of 2010 and approached 20 per cent by the end of 2011, as food prices doubled.[10] In the face of rising inflation, growing trade deficit and a weakening currency, the export led growth of Vietnam is likely to suffer. Similar is the case with India. The slow growth, tighter external financing conditions, volatile capital flows, is likely to affect both Vietnam and India.

Vietnam received foreign direct investment (FDI) worth US$ 60.3 billion in 2008.[11] Out of this, 654 new foreign-invested projects were registered worth US$ 43.7 billion and 188 existing projects planned to put US$ 788 million into their already operating businesses. In reality, however, disbursed FDI was much less. The total committed FDI in Vietnam dropped to US$ 14.7 billion in 2011.[12] This shows the effect the financial crisis can have on the incoming capital of the developing countries.

In this era of globalisation, the rapid integration of world markets has generated a powerful force for change. It has led many countries to abandon their inward-looking policies and adopt forward-looking policies that can pave the way for greater avenues of growth. In this respect the less-developed countries that are short of domestic resources strive to attract external sources of finance to compensate for their meagre resources. Under conditions of perfect capital mobility, these flows help in equalising rates of return on capital across countries and narrow developmental gaps. However, the worsening of the sovereign debt default of some of the euro zone members is likely to affect Vietnam's economic situation. As Vietnamese economy is mainly trade dependent, severe crisis in Europe and slow growth in other developed countries, could put pressure on the balance of payments and incomes of countries heavily reliant on commodity exports and remittances flow from these countries. In association with reduced incoming capital, the growing depreciation of currencies would fuel inflation and reduce the margins of earnings for even better performing sectors. These are likely to increase the cost of servicing foreign debts, while limiting the scope for lowering borrowing costs. Rising borrowing costs and scarcer international capital will take a toll on investment and private consumption. If global financial markets freeze up, governments and firms may not be able to finance growing deficits. The sudden reversal in capital flows would prompt countries to intervene by selling off foreign currency reserves in support of their currencies. Therefore, if a new crisis occurs, or, present crisis continues, India and Vietnam will have less fiscal space to respond to the challenge.

The downturn in Europe and weaker growth in developing countries also raises the risk that the two developments reinforce each other, resulting in an even weaker outcome. Political tensions in the Middle-East and North Africa is likely to disrupt oil supply, and the possibility of a hard landing in one or more economically important countries. Similarly, any negative development in South China Sea is also likely to embroil both India and Vietnam, hampering their economic conditions.

Though Vietnam's economic relations with India has not realised its full vigour, Vietnam's economic exchanges with the neighbouring ASEAN countries, the US, the EU, Japan, South Korea, Australia, Singapore and China have been expanding at a rapid pace. A number of foreign banks have been given licence to open branches in Vietnam and many have already started operations in Hanoi and Ho Chi Minh City. Singapore, Taiwan, Japan and South Korea are the leading foreign investors in Vietnam.

Over the past decade the growth of the private sector has been a significant feature of Vietnam's economic development. The non-state sector accounts for more than half of GDP. Even though private businesses have accounted for most jobs created in the last few years, shortages of skilled labour have become apparent. Vietnam is trying to improve corporate governance and market regulation, particularly for state-owned enterprises (SOEs), the process has been rather slow.

Currency depreciation theoretically is argued to stimulate economic expansion by making exports more competitive, but, in the present recessionary phase it is likely to lead to increased budget deficit. Weaker currencies would wipe out the margins of earnings for even better performing sectors and would increase the cost of servicing foreign obligations. Therefore, the uncertainty and volatility associated with the current global crisis is the biggest concern.

Though both India and Vietnam are better prepared to tackle the global financial crisis than 1997 Asian financial crisis, as they have accumulated some foreign reserves to withstand deterioration in their current account balance; the weakening export demand and consumer spending in the two countries would raise the threat of job losses and possible unrest in the two countries.

In these conditions, India and Vietnam need to shore up growth by increasing bilateral engagements to mitigate any possible negative effects on their economies on account of the global financial crisis or change in the regional situation or just shore up growth of their economies.

On the global scale, as India's comparative advantage is more in services and software, and in knowledge based manufacturing than Vietnam's labour intensive manufacturing, both the countries can explore some potential new areas for cooperation.

Potential Areas of Cooperation

Capacity Building

In Vietnam, there are severe shortages of skilled labourers. The industrial park and exchange processing zone authority for Ho Chi Minh city has stated that the city's vocational schools can only supply about 15 per cent of the 5,00,000 workers that the city's industry needs. Moreover, as the ratio of people in the low income group in the two countries is still high, this makes 'poverty reduction' and boosting income bases of vulnerable groups a key mission relevant in any regional co-operation and integration initiatives and programmes. Without focussing on the most vulnerable, the critical gaps would likely turn out to be the 'critical points of crisis', which would then be destructive for the growth of the whole economy. For example, it was estimated that during the Asian crisis, around 50 million people were pushed into poverty. With these objectives, effective safety nets such as social welfare system for the poor and old and the capacity building of people needs to be done. Even in the 2008-09 global financial crisis, Asian Development Bank had warned that around 21 million people in some 24 developing Asian countries may be mired in poverty, if economic growth in 2009 and 2010 fell below that of previous year. The International Labour Organisation warned that the crisis could put 50 million people out of work worldwide this year, with unemployment rates rising rapidly in most regions, including in East Asia.

An appropriate social safety net not only has short-term effect of providing support to the poor, but also long-term effects could provide the country to absorb shocks and prepare it to take necessary risks to cope with changes in markets, and to promote productivity and economic growth by enabling poor people to invest in education and health services even during crises. India can cooperate with Vietnam through e-education, to reduce digital divide and prepare youth for modern IT based professions.

Science and Technology

As Vietnam's vision is to become a leading country in the area of IT and e-governance, and wants the industry to contribute 8-10 per cent of the GDP, India and Vietnam have opportunity to cooperate with each other. However, in order to achieve these targets, frameworks and regulations needs to be put in place, in areas of information security and infrastructure building. India can provide Vietnam assistance in the training of human resources and infrastructure development for the communications and IT industries. As Vietnam government wants to save up to VND 30 trillion (US$1.5 billion) annually, under the five-year plan, by providing public services online, India and Vietnam have great opportunity to cooperate with each other and meet these targets. India can also share its managerial experiences and applications of IT solutions in state management.

A proposal to set up a Centre for Tracking and Data Reception and an Imaging facility in Vietnam under ASEAN-India Cooperation mechanism is under consideration. The centre will be fully funded by India and ISRO will be the implementing agency. It will utilise data provided by Indian remote-sensing satellites and harness it for multiple developmental applications. Taking this as a cue, India's expertise in remote sensing and space technology can also be shared and jointly developed with Vietnam to obtain mutual beneficial goals.

Infrastructure Sector

Vietnam's high economic growth and the incoming flow of FDI in critical infrastructure sectors reflects that there are many business opportunities available to both local and foreign companies in this sector, which is expected to grow at the rate of 10-15 per cent annually. Vietnam has devised a 10-year strategy for the development of infrastructure, including electrical power, roads and sea-ports, which offer big opportunities to Indian companies. According to the Vietnam Construction Association, the construction industry will be implementing a programme to develop housing until 2020. A target has been set to have an additional 30-32 million square metres of housing in the nation and 12 square metres of living space per person. Vietnam also plans to develop 117 industrial zones by 2020, and invest US$ 79.9 billion in power generation and the development of the electricity network, according to the National Electricity Development Strategy for 2006-25. All these point to the fact that Vietnam's construction industry is on upswing, which will need associated investments in other industries. This is also a quick way to pump money into the economy in the current global financial crisis. With the increasing property prices in Vietnam many people are likely to see it as a favourable investment option than depositing in low-interest bank deposits. Here India and Vietnam can explore to cooperate with each other.

Healthcare

Healthcare spending in Vietnam is expected to grow at an annual rate of 10.3 per cent till 2015. Also, about 6.5 per cent GDP is spent on healthcare, which is higher than many other Southeast Asia countries. Overall, looking at the economic and healthcare indicators, this is the most opportune time to get into Vietnam's healthcare sector. Indian healthcare major Fortis announced to pick up a 65 per cent stake in Vietnam's HMC for Rs. 289 crores ($64 million), in August 2011. As India is a leading producer of generic drugs and provides high-quality medical services, the option of tele-medicine and medical tourism between India and Vietnam can be explored.

There are a number of other areas where both countries can cooperate with each other such as: electricity generation, high value manufacturing, electrical part production, steel manufacturing, high technology, entertainment complex development, transport infrastructure, urban development, oil and gas exploration and extraction, pharmaceuticals, knowledge based industries, agriculture techniques, research and biotechnology, etc.

Ways to Increase Trade and Investment Relations

One of the major factors hampering direct trade and investment relations between the two countries is the lack of connectivity. The two countries are yet to start a direct flight, and establish land and water connectivity. As Vietnam is a member of ASEAN and there are various infrastructural projects to connect India with neighbouring countries of ASEAN, if these projects fructify they are likely to resolve the land based connectivity issue. For example, the New Delhi-Hanoi rail link was proposed at the ministerial meeting at Phnom Penh in June 2003. Even though rail networks exist in India, Myanmar, Thailand, Cambodia and Vietnam, missing links need to be laid out for the completion and operationalisation of the link from Delhi to

Hanoi. The route of ASEAN-India Car rally can be followed to make up for the lack of infrastructure connectivity between the two countries. Earlier, national governments provided most of the capital outlay for infrastructure development. However, a hybrid model of public-private partnership for infrastructure financing may be explored to expedite the connectivity.

The process of ASEAN Economic Community brings with it the prospects for increased intra-regional trade which needs to be increased to at least 40 per cent from a current level of 25 per cent. This is 68 per cent among the 27 EU members. The availability of good physical infrastructure can increase intra-regional trade and investments by improved resource sharing, and can contribute to regional integration by narrowing development divide. ASEAN leaders endorsed the Master Plan on ASEAN Connectivity (MPAC) in 2010. The MPAC represents an in-depth plan of action based on (a) a list of priority projects for ASEAN connectivity, (b) requirements for institutional and policy coordination and (c) recommendations for financing key projects. In addition to the MPAC, a number of other ASEAN initiatives that promote infrastructure development exist, including those that are supported by ADB such as the ASEAN Infrastructure Fund (AIF). Based on equity investments from ASEAN and ADB, the AIF is designed to provide an innovative financing instrument to address the ASEAN sub-regional connectivity constraints. In doing so, the AIF will support the MPAC as a key driver towards realising the vision for an ASEAN Economic Community by 2015. This technical assistance will provide complementary support to realise the MPAC. AIF which began operations in May 2012 is the largest ASEAN-led initiative in the association's history with a planned start up capital of US$ 485.2 million.[13] However, ASEAN cannot just depend on AIF to fund its infrastructure financing as its fund size of US$ 485.2 million is too small and is not sufficient to finance major projects. According to ADB and ADBI's study, ASEAN needs about US$ 60 billion a year for infrastructure development purpose for the 2010-2020 period.[14] Nevertheless, various ASEAN and sub-regional groupings like BCIM, BIMSTEC, Mekong-Ganga Cooperation, related infrastructural projects, if fructified is likely to change the issue of connectivity between the two countries.

As in exports and imports, only export competitiveness of supplying country and import demand of importing country is being looked into, which needs to be changed. The potential of trade creation and trade diversion between the two countries should also be taken into account.

As Vietnam's reliance on export sector is more acute, in the absence of a well-developed domestic market, they need to become more competitive in marketing by increasing the quality of their products, by partnering with India in respective areas of strength.

Given volatile global political and economic climate, the need for enhanced economic activity and integration between India and Vietnam will help in promoting growth and stability in the region. Both countries would stand to gain with Indian FDI investments and expertise in services sharing in the long run. A coordinated approach in competitive areas may provide high dividend to both the countries. For example, Vietnam was the undisputed leader of the world rice market, exporting eight to 10 metric tonne yearly. In 2011, Vietnamese rice was priced higher than that of India. As India started dropping its rates, Vietnam had to follow suit to stay in the competition. Indian rice was priced at US $360-450 a tonne (FOB), while that of Vietnam was priced at US$ 450-550, Thailand at US$ 575 a tonne and Pakistan sold at US$ 480 a tonne. As the price differentials were almost US$ 100-150 per tonne between the two countries, any coordinated pricing would have helped both the countries.

As the global crisis affects the most vulnerable sections of the society, government's focus may be shifted from attracting big companies to Small and Medium Enterprises (SMEs), as they absorb maximum work force in the industrial sector, rather than import substituting capital intensive industries. India and Vietnam have not been able to sell themselves to the common audiences in each other country and their partnership is limited to government and strategic community, limiting cooperation in SMEs and tourism sector, which have vast potentials.

The lack of direct financial mechanism is another lacuna for the limited trade and investment relations between the two countries. Language and lack of information are other barriers for the growth of economic activities between India and Vietnam. There is lack of awareness about possible tourist destinations of Vietnam in India. A mechanism of information dissemination between the two countries for economic opportunities and tourism needs to be provided. If some of these suggestions can be incorporated it would help in increasing trade and investment relations between India and Vietnam.

Conclusion

It can be said that while bilateral trade and investment relations between India and Vietnam is increasing, it is not exceptional in the light of overall trade and investment activities of the two countries. The major factor behind the slow expansion of trade is the similarity of export items of both the countries, which needs to be rectified. The overall balance of trade is in favour of India; nevertheless, it is increasingly becoming much more balanced. In the trade of goods, while tariff reduction is on, non-tariff barriers are on increase, which may nullify the benefits of tariff reductions. As the share of exports in the foreign-invested sector of both countries has increased, it is likely to be affected due to the financial crisis and slow growth in developed countries. Similarly, in investment it can be concluded that though both the countries want to enhance bilateral investment relations, lack of resources, information deficit and legality of extending ODA for enhancing private investment has hampered the investment relations. It can only be hoped that some of these problems associated trade and investment relations can be resolved with improved infrastructure and connectivity between the two countries and the region.

NOTES

1. Vietnam Economy: An Overview, Embassy of India, Vietnam, at http://www.indembassy.com.vn/tabid/240/default.aspx, (Accessed 5 September 2012).

2. CIA World Factbook, Vietnam, at https://www.cia.gov/library/publications/the-world-factbook/geos/vm.html (Accessed 18 May 2013)
3. Ministry of Commerce and Industry, Government of India, Export Import Data Bank at http://commerce.nic.in/eidb/iecnt.asp, (Accessed 15 May 2013)
4. *Ibid.*
5. CSEINDIAPORTAL, at http://cseindiaportal.wordpress.com/2013/03/08/india-vietnam-relations-backgrounder/ (Accessed 18 May 2013)
6. India Vietnam Broadening Frontiers 2012, Extraordinary and Plenipotentiary Diplomatist Special Report at http://www.peopleandmanagement.com/diplomatist2012august/Vietnam2012.pdf, (Accessed 7 September 2012)
7. Fortis to pick up 65 per cent stake in Vietnam co for $64 m, The Hindu Business Line at http://www.thehindubusinessline.com/companies/fortis-to-pick-up-65-stake-in-vietnam-co-for-64-m/article2342620.ece, (Accessed 10 July 2012)
8. Ministry of External Affairs of India, India-Vietnam Relations, January 2013 at http://www.mea.gov.in/Portal/ForeignRelation/Vietnam_Feb_2013.pdf, (Accessed 27 February 2013)
9. *Ibid.*
10. Vietnam Profile at http://www.bbc.co.uk/news/world-asia-pacific-16567315 (Accessed 29 January, 2013)
11. According to General Statistics Office of Vietnam, (Accessed over a period of time from July 2012 to May 2013)
12. Vietnam FDI at http://www.vietnam-report.com/vietnam-fdi/, (Accessed 14 September 2012)
13. Joint Ministerial Statement of the 17th ASEAN Finance Ministers' Meeting (AFMM) Bandar Seri Begawan, Brunei Darussalam, 3-4 April 2013, Theme: Our People, Our Future Together, at http://www.asean.org/news/asean-statement-communiques/item/joint-ministerial-statement-of-the-17thasean-finance-ministers-meeting-afmm-bandar-seri-begawan, (Accessed 7 May 2013)
14. Meeting ASEANs Infrastructure Financing Requirements, at http://www.adbi.org/working-paper/2009/05/27/3011.infrastructure.dev.asean.economic/meeting.aseans.infrastructure.financing. requirements/ (Accessed 21 September 2012)

REFERENCES

According to General Statistics Office of Vietnam, (Accessed over a period of time from July 2012 to May 2013)

Asia Development Bank (2012), *Vietnam: Confronting Rising Inequality in Asia*, Asia Development Outlook 2012, pp. 223-27.

CIA World Factbook, Vietnam, at https://www.cia.gov/library/publications/the-world-factbook/geos/vm.html (Accessed 18 May 2013)

CSEINDIAPORTAL, at http://cseindiaportal.wordpress.com/2013/03/08/india-vietnam-relations-backgrounder/ (Accessed 18 May 2013)

Fortis to pick up 65 per cent stake in Vietnam co for $64 m, The Hindu Business Line at http://www.thehindubusinessline.com/companies/fortis-to-pick-up-65-stake-in-vietnam-co-for-64-m/article2342620.ece, (Accessed 10 July 2012)

Global Finance, Vietnam Country Report, http://www.gfmag.com/gdp-data-country-reports/146-vietnam-gdp-country-report.html#axzz2R00DOEkB, (Accessed on 10 May 2013)

Ha, Ngo Trinh (2004), *Catching-up Industrial Development of East Asian Economies and its Application to Vietnam*, Working Paper No. 11, Tokyo: Centre of Excellence, Contemporary Asian Studies, (COE-CAS), Waseda University.

Husain, Ishrat and Kwang W. Jun (1992), "*Capital Flows to South Asian and ASEAN countries: Trends, Determinants, and Policy Implications*", Policy Research Working Paper Series 0842, The World Bank.

India Business chamber in Vietnam, http://incham.vn/resource-center/india-vietnam-economic-and-commercial-relations.html, (Accessed 25 September 2012)

India Vietnam Broadening Frontiers 2012, Extraordinary and Plenipotentiary Diplomatist Special Report at http://www.peopleandmanagement.com/diplomatist2012august/Vietnam2012.pdf, (Accessed 7 September 2012)

India, Vietnam to forge strong economic and trade ties, says Ranjit Rae, http://automotivehorizon.sulekha.com/india-vietnam-to-forge-strong-economic-and-trade_newsitem_5880, (Accessed on 5 February 2013)

India-Vietnam Relations, *Ministry of External Affairs, India, August 2012,* http://meaindia.nic.in/meaxpsite/foreignrelation/vietnam.pdf, (Accessed 27 February 2013)

Joint Ministerial Statement of the 17th ASEAN Finance Ministers' Meeting (AFMM) Bandar Seri Begawan, Brunei Darussalam, 3-4 April 2013, Theme: Our People, Our Future Together, at http://www.asean.org/news/asean-statement-communiques/item/joint-ministerial-statement-of-the-17thasean-finance-ministers-meeting-afmm-bandar-seri-begawan, (Accessed 7 May 2013)

Meeting ASEANs Infrastructure Financing Requirements, at http://www.adbi.org/working-paper/2009/05/27/3011.infrastructure.dev.asean.economic/meeting.aseans.infrastructure.financing.requirements/ (Accessed 21 September 2012)

Ministry of Commerce and Industry, Government of India, Export Import Data Bank at http://commerce.nic.in/eidb/iecnt.asp, (Accessed date 15 May 2013)

Ministry of External Affairs of India, India-Vietnam Relations, January 2013 at http://www.mea.gov.in/Portal/ForeignRelation/Vietnam_Feb_2013.pdf, (Accessed 27 February 2013)

Morley, James W. and Masashi Nishihara (eds.), (1997), '*Vietnam Joins the World*', M.E. Sharpe, U.S.A.

Taylor, Philip (ed.), (2004), '*Social Inequality in Vietnam and the Challenges to Reform*', ISEAS, Singapore.

The World Bank (2012), *Global Economic Prospects: Uncertainties and Vulnerabilities*, Volume 4, January 2012.

Tsuboi, Yoshiharu (2005), *Corruption in Vietnam*, Working Paper No. 20, Tokyo: Centre of Excellence, Contemporary Asian Studies, (COE-CAS), Waseda University.

Tsuboi, Yoshiharu (2005), *Government, Party, Military and business Relations in Vietnam: Focusing on a Comparison with China*, Working Paper No. 18, Tokyo: Centre of Excellence, Contemporary Asian Studies, (COE-CAS), Waseda University.

Vietnam Development Report (VDR) 2012: Market Economy for A Middle-income Country, The World Bank, http://www-wds.worldbank.org/external/default/WDSContentServer/WDSP/IB/2011/12/13/000333037_20111213003843/Rendered/PDF/659800AR00PUBL0elopment0Report02012.pdf, (Accessed on 10 May 2013)

Vietnam Economy: An Overview, Embassy of India, Vietnam, at http://www.indembassy.com.vn/tabid/240/default.aspx, (Accessed 5 September 2012).

Vietnam FDI at http://www.vietnam-report.com/vietnam-fdi/, (Accessed 14 September 2012)

Vietnam Profile at http://www.bbc.co.uk/news/world-asia-pacific-16567315 (Accessed 29 January 2013)

5
Vietnam–India Economic and Trade Cooperation

Ly Quoc Hung

Vietnam and India share good political relations which have been constantly improving and strengthening for the past 40 years. Since the establishment of Strategic Partnership in 2007, the cooperative ties between the two nations have flourished to new heights.

Bilateral Trade

The Vietnam-India bilateral trade relation is the highlight of the Strategic Partnership between the two countries. At present, India is among the top 10 trading partners of Vietnam. The bilateral trade turnover rose by 3.9 times, from US$ 1.01 billion in 2006 to US$ 3.9 in 2011. The export turnover of Vietnam also increased tenfold from US$ 138 million to US$ 1.55 billion despite the fact that the composition of exports from Vietnam to India does not consist of Vietnam's major export commodities like crude oil, rice, high-value machinery, etc. In the first-half of 2012, bilateral turnover touched US$ 1.85 billion in which exports reached US$ 755 million, up by 23 per cent, and import was at US$ 1.09 billion, which is a fall of 18 per cent over the corresponding period in 2011. The major export commodities from Vietnam to India include mobile phones, computers, electronic products and components, coal, rubber, ore, plastic materials, chemicals, peppercorns, etc. Vietnam's major imports from India are animal feed, pharmaceuticals, machinery, equipment, and raw materials. Although the balance of trade is still in favour of India, the trade deficit is on the decline. In 2011, the trade deficit reduced from US$ 1.2 billion to US$ 794 million.

There is a good legal framework for trade exchanges between Vietnam and India. With India's recognition of the market economy status of Vietnam, a series of agreements were signed between the two nations. The most significant among these was the ASEAN-India Trade in Goods (AITIG) Agreement, which has created favourable conditions for the signatories to further develop their competitive advantages in each other's market. Since the official commencement of this Agreement in Vietnam in June 2010, many new products from Vietnam like rubber, computer hardware, electronic goods, cinnamon and spices, garment and textiles, etc. have penetrated into the Indian market. This has contributed to a shift in export structure from Vietnam to India, an increase in export value and a fall in trade deficit. Apart from trade benefits, under AITIG, Vietnam has attracted more investments from India. Until now, Vietnam has received 61 investment projects from India with total registered capital of US$ 258 million, mainly in manufacturing and mineral extraction.

The AITIG Agreement and grant of market economy status to Vietnam by India, have important economic and political implications. These events mark a new shift in the multifaceted friendly and cooperative ties between Vietnam and India. They will help in strengthening economic and trade cooperation, foster economic growth, maintain stable and prosperous milieu for development in the Asia-Pacific region, consolidate the faith of Vietnamese and Indian entrepreneurs and investors, and create favourable and stable environment for trade in ASEAN–India FTA.

Opportunities for Investment

The Vietnam-India cooperative ties in industry have also been constantly expanded, especially in the fields of oil and gas, energy, chemicals and industrial steel. Many investment and cooperation projects have been initiated in these fields. The joint venture to explore gas and oil resources between Indian Oil and Natural Gas Cooperation Videsh Limited (OVL) and PetroVietnam, the joint project between Vietnam Steel General Corporation and TATA Group of India to invest in the building of Ha Tinh Conjugate Steel Company, are concrete proof of expanding partnership.

In essence, both countries possess immense potential in economic and trade development. With a population of 86 million and improved per capita income, the demand for raw materials and consumer goods are on the increase in Vietnam. Similarly, India with a population of 1.2 billion with 28 states and 7 union territories, create a variety of clients and markets. However, at the moment, exports from Vietnam to India make up only 0.3 per cent of Indian import turnover. The exports of both countries have not been able to deeply penetrate into each other's market. The main reasons are: (a) Entrepreneurs of both nations still do not consider each other as target market. This is especially the case of Vietnamese entrepreneurs; (b) Products from both countries have not been able to compete in regard to price, quality, design and delivery timing; and (c) Indian protective tariffs remain high (despite the fact that the rates have been reduced in recent years, India is still among countries having high tariffs in the world).

Conclusion

To overcome the above-mentioned constraints as well as to strengthen and foster comprehensive economic and trade cooperation, Vietnam and India need to further improve the legal frameworks for economic and trade activities between the two countries in the coming years. Vietnam and India can also enhance their cooperation through research, discussion, agreements on finance and banking, legal assistance, maritime transport, mutual agreements on animal and plant quarantine regulations and standards of food hygiene and safety. Both countries need to establish a joint Trade Committee for removing obstacles affecting bilateral trade relations, so as to enhance bilateral trade. The two countries can conduct research to propose economic areas which need to be prioritised and focused on for cooperation.

Priority should be given to finance, banking, telecommunications and construction of seaport, etc. India and Vietnam should assign concerned Ministries and governmental organisations, to consider the possibility of mutually beneficial cooperation in trading agricultural products which the two countries has leverage in the world market by limiting fruitless competition and still maintaining favourable prices for their farmers. Finally, ASEAN and India need to complete the signing of agreement on free trade in services and investment at the earliest, which will help in enhancing economic relations between the two countries.

6
Prospects for India-Vietnam Economic Relations

Nguyen Van Lich

Over the last 40 years, Vietnam-India relations have witnessed a strong growth in various areas including commercial sector. There have been lots of opinions over the success, difficulties and shortcomings in bilateral cooperation. This chapter will point out the basis of bilateral cooperation on which the prospective Vietnam-India commercial relations can flourish.

Ever-Blossoming Political Relations

Vietnam and India enjoy age-old relationship, starting with exchanges of culture, religion and trade. In modern time, this relationship was fostered by President Ho Chi Minh and Prime Minister Jawaharlal Nehru and nurtured by generations of leaders and people from the two countries. The late Prime Minister Pham Van Dong once said during his visit to India in 1980 that India-Vietnam relations are as clear as cloudless blue sky.

The regular exchanges of high-level visits have helped consolidate and develop the bilateral relations. Vietnam supports India's Permanent membership to the UNSC and India supported Vietnam's candidature to be a non-permanent member of UNSC for 2008-09 period.

Till date, both sides have exchanged visits from the Presidents, parliamentarians, government and parties' officials. Visits from Government of Vietnam include the visits of Prime Minister Pham Van Dong to India in 1955, 1978, 1980 and 1983; Vo Van Kiet in 1997; President Trần Đức Lương in 1999 and Trương Tấn Sang in 2011; Vice-President Nguyen Tan Dung in 2007 and Nguyen Thi Doan in October 2009. Visits of party officials to India included the visits by General Secretary Le Duan to India in 1984; Nguyen Van Linh in 1989; Do Muoi in 1992 and Nong Duc Manh in 2003. Deputy Prime Minister Pham Gia Khiem paid an official visit to India to Chair the 13th Joint Commission Meeting in February 2007. With an objective to add greater substance to the strategic partnership, Deputy Prime Minister Nguyen Thien Nhan visited India to promote the effective implementations of agreements reached during the visit of Prime Minister Nguyen Tan Dung and President Truong Tan Sang to India, in April 2012. These visits have helped promote bilateral cooperation, especially when both countries have established strategic partnership marking 'Vietnam-India Friendship Year 2012' to commemorate 40th anniversary of the establishment of full diplomatic relations and 5th anniversary of Vietnam-India Strategic Partnership.

For India, Vietnam holds an important position in its Look East Policy especially in trade relations. There has been a strong consensus among political parties of India in fostering good relations with Vietnam. Visits from India included the visits by President R. Venkataraman in 1999 and Pratibha Devisingh Patil in 2009, Vice-President K.R. Narayanan in 1993; Prime Minister Rajiv Gandhi in 1985 and 1988, P.V. Narasimha Rao in 1994, A.B. Vajpayee in 2001; Lok Sabha Speaker Somnath Chatterjee in March 2007 and Meira Kumar in May 2011. Foreign Minister of India S.M. Krishna visited Vietnam in September 2011.

The geo-political and strategic location of Vietnam has provided it with several advantages in relations with powers in East Asia. Similarly, the strategic location of India in South Asia has helped New Delhi become an important factor in strategic calculations of many powers in the Indian Ocean region. Vietnam and India share the same problem with China over territorial and border affairs. This fact has generated commonalities of interest in foreign policies of both the countries.

Economic Relations

Both India and Vietnam are experiencing robust economic growth, therefore, economic and commercial cooperation has received the highest priority in building bilateral ties. Vietnam and India have established various mechanisms for the observance and promotion of economic-commercial cooperation. This includes a comprehensive legal framework covering various aspects such as: Bilateral trade Agreement signed in 1978, which was amended in 1997; Agreement for Avoidance of Double Taxation in 1994, Agreement for Investment Protection and Encouragement in 1997, Agreement on Science and Technology Cooperation signed in 1976 and extended in 1996; Agreement on Tourism Cooperation in 2001, Agreement on Civil Aviation, which was signed in 1999 and amended in 2004, etc. These agreements along with Agreements on Consular Affairs, Cultural Exchanges and Mutual Legal Assistance among others have facilitated the development of bilateral trade relations. Both countries have also established the Joint Commission for Economic, Scientific and Technical Cooperation in 1982, which meets twice a year, the Joint Business Council (JBC), the Joint Committee on Science and Technology, and other mechanisms for cooperation in different areas of speciality. Agreement on financial cooperation was signed in 2007. The two nations are in the process of implementing the agreed terms. India promised to increase ODA and preferential credits for Vietnam. Most markedly, on 25 October 2009, Vietnam and India signed the MoU on the recognition of Vietnam's full market economy status[1]. This is of crucial importance for expanding the bilateral commercial relations which will help in expanding the legal framework to enable entrepreneurs from both countries to penetrate into each other's market, and for deploying the competitive advantages of the two nations more efficiently. In order to enhance commercial ties, the two nations established Vietnam-India Business Forum in 2009. This forum facilitates meetings, exchange of information, business opportunities, which have boosted investments and trade relations between the two countries.

In bilateral trade, Vietnam is facing trade deficit with India. If this continues, bilateral trade between Vietnam and India cannot be durable. However, this deficit is in decline. According to statistics, Vietnam's trade gap fell from US$ 1.7 billion in 2008 to US$ 1 billion in 2009, to US$ 770 million in 2010 and stood at US$ 700 million in 2011. In the first five months of 2012, Vietnam's export to India touched US$ 589.66 million, up by 15 per cent compared to the corresponding period in 2011. This has contributed to narrowing the balance-of-trade between the two nations. Vietnam's trade deficit in the first 5 months of 2012 was at US$ 342.6 million, down by 39 per cent[2]. The decreasing trade deficit brings stability and balance to the bilateral trade between Vietnam and India, as well as contributes to better growth of trade.

The future export prospect of Vietnam seems to be full of promise. The common trend is that the export turnover will be more balanced. This is also Vietnam's priority in bilateral trade ties with India. Vietnam wants to increase and diversify its exports to India. Apart from its traditional exports like rice, peppercorn, tea, footwear, rubber, an increase in its major exports such as crude oil and coal will generate greater turnover for Vietnam and make trade deficit decline *vis-à-vis* India.

On the other hand, Indian investments in Vietnam are increasing. This will help in bringing about a more balanced trade and closer economic ties. In reality, Vietnam has given Indian enterprises many substantial opportunities to invest in areas like agriculture, forestry, food processing, oil exploration and exploitation, all of which India has an advantageous edge. Products from joint projects are not only for use in Vietnam and India but also for export to other countries.

In recent years, on the basis of traditional cordial cooperative relations which are constantly consolidated and developed, Vietnam-India trade relationship has grown remarkably, from US$ 50 million in the middle of the 1980s to US$ 1 billion in 2006. The current bilateral trade turnover has grown 20 per cent on an average annually. In 2011, despite the global recession, the growth rate of Vietnam-

India bilateral trade reached 42 per cent. The total turnover was US$ 3.9 billion in which India's export increased by 33 per cent and Vietnam's export surged 57 per cent[3]. Both nations are aiming to achieve bilateral trade turnover of US$ 5 billion in 2012 and expect that this figure will rise to US$ 7 billion by 2015. Considering the potential and the demands of both nations, these aims are possible.

Since 2008, India is among the top 10 countries for Vietnamese imports. The major items of imports are equipment, spare parts, medical devices, pharmaceuticals, food, cotton, computer components, consumer goods, animal feed, raw materials, steel, metals, plastics, new medicine, machinery, textile materials, pharmaceutical materials, chemicals, insecticide, etc. These products are essential for the process of industrialisation and modernisation as well as to satisfy consumer demands in Vietnam.

Vietnam's products have also gradually gained a foothold in the Indian market. Stones and handicrafts (lacquered products, mother-of-pearl inlaid products, etc.) are two products of Vietnam which have recently made their presence in India, and have gained popularity. Vietnam's commercial strengths include marine products, handicrafts, processed food and textiles. Vietnam can increase its export of rice, footwear, ceramics, rubber and rubber products, vegetable oil, tea, cashew nut, etc. to India. Moreover, both countries are big players in producing and exporting agricultural products. Enhancing commercial cooperation will help both nations in improving efficiency in agricultural sector.

India's commercial strengths are pharmaceuticals, animal feed, automobile components and plastic products. One notable feature of the Indian market is its diversity which enables the consumption of products of various categories and quality. This feature has made Indian market attractive for countries exporting to India, including Vietnam. In the coming years, India's demand for raw materials and energy will increase immensely, which its domestic supply cannot meet. As the result, India will have to import strategic raw materials and fuels like crude oil, coal, natural rubber, building materials, etc. These products are within Vietnam's supply capacity. A number of Vietnam companies in fruit beverages consider that India is a promising market for their products due to its huge population, taste for sweet dish and a long and extreme summer.

In addition to bilateral mechanisms, Vietnam-India commercial relations are also based on multilateral mechanisms, such as ASEAN-India Free Trade Agreement, and Mekong-Ganga Cooperation, which was initiated in 2000. These mechanisms are also likely to bolster Vietnam-India commercial relations.

Mechanisms for Promoting Cooperation

Over the past few years, the Indian economy has registered a high rate of growth, which is among the highest in the world. In the last 17 years, the average annual growth rate of India stood at 7 per cent. India has also accumulated a large amount of foreign currency reserves. The increase of foreign investments in India is record-breaking, ranking second in the world. Rise in exports is also promising. With these achievements, the Indian economy is highly valued internationally and ranked among the most potential economy in the world. In addition to its current achievements, Indian economy has immense potential to develop further. Hence, the term 'India's economic boom' is often reiterated worldwide.

Economic reforms have greatly upsized the scale of the Indian economy, expanded its trade and opened up new possibilities for its partners. In the coming years, the Indian market is likely to open up more and its tariffs lessen, which will provide a great prospect for Vietnam to advance its trade ties with India.

Various international economic organisations like International Monetary Fund (IMF) and World Bank (WB) have evaluated that India is on its way to becoming one of the major economic powers in the world. Furthermore, possessing a large area, a population of 1.2 billion, a large proportion of high-income class, and a high growth rate, India is a huge market in which purchasing power is growing and demand is being diversified. Fifty-four percent of Indian population is under 25 years old; about 300 million Indian people belong to the middle class or higher, of which 70,000 hold property of approximately US$ 1 million value. Coupled with constantly improving living standards and incomes, consumer demand is on the rise. It has been predicted that this value will further increase and about 40 million Indian people have higher 'consumer power'. At this pace, India will become a massive consumer market in the next few years. This is a great opportunity for Vietnamese entrepreneurs to penetrate into the Indian market. Today, India has emerged as one of Vietnam's top 10 commercial partners and as the gateway to the South Asian market for Vietnam's exports.

Concluding Remarks

In addition to the above mentioned scope for cooperation, India is also an important partner of Vietnam in the spheres of Science & Technology. India has assisted a number of Vietnam's IT projects such as project to develop human resources for software technology in Vietnam, and project to establish a high quality human resources centre in Hanoi. Besides, Vietnam and India are cooperating in the use of atomic energy for peaceful purposes, biotechnology, plant and animal cross-breeding, etc. In the education and training domain, India provides Vietnam annually more than 100 scholarships in various subjects such as economics, commerce, biotechnology, IT, medicals and atomic energy. These indirect links are vital for promoting the growth of bilateral trade.

On these foundations, Vietnam-India trade relations are likely to develop more robustly in the near future. The great achievements of the past 40 years have not only heightened strategic cooperation between the two countries, but will also serve as an important base for the strengthening of bilateral trade relationship in the coming years.

NOTES

1. VNExpress, ngày 26/10/2009.
2. http://www.baomoi.com/Tham-hut-thuong-mai-Viet-Nam—An-Do-giam-39/45/8748697.epi, (Access date N.A)
3. http://www.dangcongsan.vn/cpv/Modules/News/NewsDetail.aspx?co_id=30106&cn_id=371034, 11/11/2009.

REFERENCES

Enhancing Vietnam-India bilateral trade, at http://www.baocongthuong.com.vn/p0c194s196n21997/tang-cuong-thuong-mai-song-phuong-viet-nam-an-do.htm (Accessed 11 May 2012)

Exchange of trade between Vietnam and India in the first 5 months of 2012, athttp://www.ttnn.com.vn/nuoc-lanh-tho/-1/tin-tuc/34719/trao-doi-thuong-mai-viet-nam-an-do-5-thang-dau-nam-2012.aspx (Accessed 21 June 2012)

Expanding India-Vietnam relations to match the framework of strategic partnership, http://www.cpv.org.vn/cpv/modules/news/newsdetail.aspx?cn_id=417290&co_id=30094#, (Accessed 14 August 2010)

Further trade promotion between Vietnam and India, at http://www.bsc.com.vn/News/2010/6/24/100216.aspx (Accessed 24 June 2010).

India: the gateway to South Asia for Vietnam's products, http://www.vitas.org.vn/Pages/Index.asp?ProgID=3&LoaiTin_ID=14&BanTin_ID=1140, (Accessed 11 May 2012)

The 14th session of Vietnam-India Joint Commission, at http://www.dangcongsan.vn/cpv/Modules/News/NewsDetail.aspx?co_id=30106&cn_id=479263 (Accessed 16 September 2011)

Tighten Vietnam-India bilateral trade relations, at http://www.thuongmai.vn/tin-tuc/su-kien/co-hoi-hop-tac/26999—tht-cht-quan-h-hp-tac-thng-mi-vit-nam-n—.html (Accessed 5 August 2010)

Vietnam-India relations are further consolidated and developed, http://www.vietpeace.org.vn/express/express_detail_v.aspx?id1=21&id2=143&id3=510, (Accessed 14 August 2010)

Vietnam-India trade increased by nearly 20 folds, at http://www.vietnamplus.vn/Home/Thuong-mai-giua-Viet-NamAn-Do-tang-gan-20-lan/20122/126385.vnplus (Accessed 16 February 2012)

7
India-Vietnam Energy Cooperation

Lydia Powell

Introduction

Energy security strategies of non-OECD (Organisation for Economic Co-operation and Development) countries in general and India and China in particular have become a matter of global interest. Non-OECD countries led by China and to a lesser extent India are expected to account for over 70 per cent of global economic output, 90 per cent of the increase in population and 90 per cent of the global increase in energy demand by 2035.[1] China is expected to become the world's largest energy oil consumer and importer, and account for over 50 per cent of global coal production by 2035. Overall China is projected to consume 70 per cent more energy than the United States by 2035. Though India's energy demand is unlikely to match that of China in scale, growth in energy demand is expected to be faster in India. India is projected to become the world's largest coal importer by 2020 and China and India together are expected to account for over 50 per cent of global increase in power generation. Vietnam's energy consumption is much smaller in comparison to India but its strategic location and future energy potential make it a very attractive partner for India.

The growing presence of China in the global market for traded energy (oil, gas and coal) will necessarily mean an increase in the price of globally traded oil, gas and coal on which both India and

Vietnam depend. Apart from this, both India and Vietnam along with the rest of the world need to address the challenge of moving towards a low carbon energy profile. This chapter will essentially address the key challenges of energy import dependence and shift towards low carbon energy sources that both India and Vietnam face and identify how both countries can work together in meeting these challenges.

Energy Profile: India

Energy demand in India was higher than that of Russia in 2009, making it the third-largest energy consumer in the world. India's energy demand is currently about 700 million tonne oil equivalent (mtoe). India's energy demand is more than 20 times that of Vietnam's which stands at 30 mtoe.

Coal continues to dominate India's primary energy basket accounting for over 42 per cent, followed by non-commercial energy sources such as fuel wood and dried animal dung which accounts for 25 per cent. Oil which is primarily used in transportation accounts for 24 per cent while natural gas accounts for 7 per cent. All other forms of energy such as several nuclear, hydro-power and renewable energy make less than 1-2 per cent contribution to India's primary energy basket.

In 2010, India consumed roughly 3.2 million barrels per day (bpd) of oil and produced roughly 950,000 bpd of total liquids of which 750 bpd was crude oil. India's primary oil consumption in 2006 was 3 per cent of the world's total consumption and it is predicted that in 2030, India's oil consumption will rise to 7.5 per cent of the world's total oil consumption.

In 2010, India consumed roughly 47.51 billion cubic metres (bcm) of gas. The gross production of natural gas in India was 46.49 bcm during 2009-10. This was 44.63 per cent higher than the production of 32.85 bcm during 2008-09. India's primary gas consumption in 2006 was 2 per cent of the world's consumption. This percentage is predicted to rise to 5.4 per cent in 2030. On average, natural gas accounts for 24 per cent of the world's primary energy today while in India it accounts for only 7 per cent of the primary energy basket. Demand has outstripped supply in the natural gas sector and India has been a net importer of gas since 2004. In 2010 India imported 12 bcm of gas.

Figure 7.1: India's Primary Energy Basket 2010

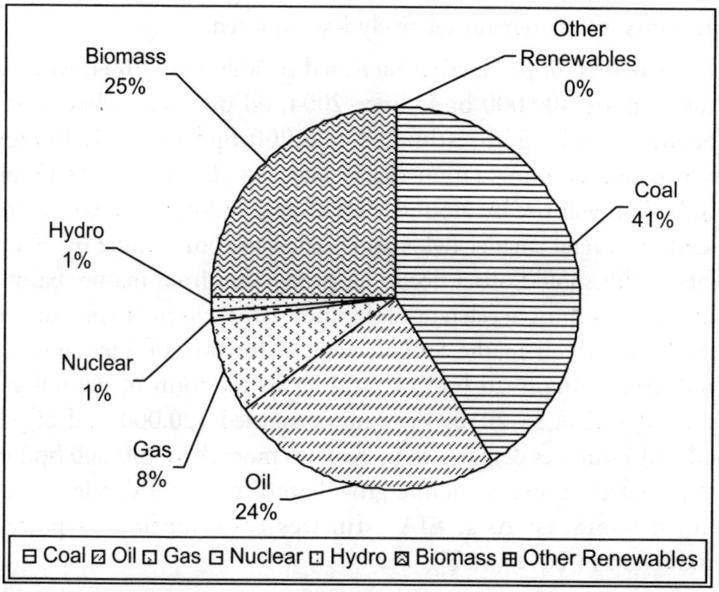

Source: Prepared from World Energy Outlook 2012, International Energy Agency.

Energy Profile: Vietnam

Vietnam is endowed with energy resources such as natural gas, oil, coal, hydropower, biomass, wind and solar energy. The estimated potential of oil and gas is about 4 billion tonne oil equivalent and coal is about 6 billion tons. There is a potential of about 20,000 MW of hydropower. Gas and crude oil are being exploited in the southern offshore areas, and coal is exploited in the northern region. From 1990, Vietnam began exporting energy, mainly coal and crude oil.

According to Oil & Gas Journal (OGJ), Vietnam now ranks third in terms of proven oil reserves for the Asia-Pacific region. Vietnam held 4.4 billion barrels of proven oil reserves as of January 2012, which was significantly higher than 0.6 billion barrels of oil in 2011. This increase is in part a result of Vietnam's efforts to intensify exploration and development of its offshore fields. Ongoing exploration activities could increase this figure in the future, as Vietnam's waters remain relatively less explored.

Vietnam's oil production increased steadily until 2004, when it peaked above 400,000 bpd. Since 2004, oil production has slowly declined, reaching an estimated 326,000 bpd in 2011. Energy Information Administration (EIA) forecasts that the country's oil production will rise by around 50,000 bpd within the next 2 years, based on several smaller fields anticipated to come online by 2015. These fields should offset declining production from mature basins, but Vietnam must accelerate exploration efforts to maintain current production levels in the longer term. A fraction of Vietnam's oil production, almost 20 bpd in 2011, is in the form of natural gas liquids (NGLs). In 2010, Vietnam consumed 320,000 bpd of oil, and EIA estimates demand to increase to more than 400,000 bpd in 2013, reflecting the economic growth and industrial developments within Southeast Asia. EIA estimates consumption surpassed production in 2011 (*see* Fig. 7.2).

All oil production in the country is carried out by PetroVietnam's (PVN) upstream subsidiary, PetroVietnam Exploration and Production (PVEP) or through joint-ventures (JVs) or production sharing contracts (PSCs), in which the national oil company (NOC) has at least a 20 per cent equity interest. Vietnam's oil production has decreased over the last 7 years primarily as a result of declining output at the Bach Ho (White Tiger) field, which accounts for about half of the country's crude oil production. After reaching peak output of 263,000 bpd in 2003, the field's production dropped to an average 92,000 bpd in early 2011. It is expected that Bach Ho's production decline rate will range from 20,000 bpd to 25,000 bpd through 2014. Vietsovpetro intends to boost oil production by using water injection

Figure 7.2: Vietnam's Primary Energy Basket

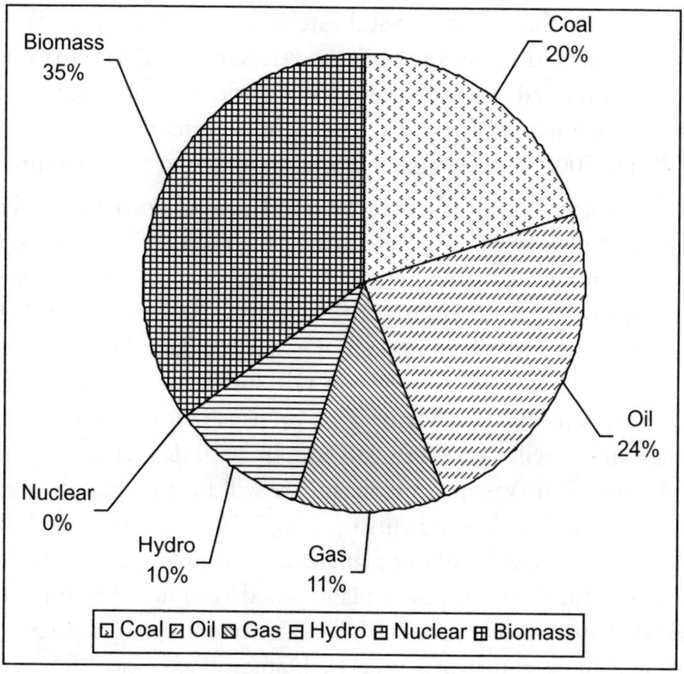

Source: Prepared from Energy Information Administration (Country Brief).

to stem declines of aging fields and by investing US$ 7 billion on exploration activities over the next 5 years.

Vietnam currently has one operating refinery, but hopes to expand capacity within the next decade in the interest of reducing import dependency for oil products and fostering economic development in the north and central regions of the country where the proposed projects are located. However, the projects have encountered several delays stemming from financial, contractual and land-clearing challenges.

Vietnam has a short history for gas development. Its gas industry emerged through the development of associated gas from the Bach Ho oilfield in mid-1990 and an offshore gas field in Nam Con Son in 2001. Vietnam features a large number of small gas fields, forcing a great number of wells to be dug at higher costs. However, Vietnam's gas prices are the lowest in Southeast Asia excluding Malaysia that has implemented a policy to limit gas prices. At the Bach Ho oilfield for Vietnam's first gas utilisation, PVN's price of associated gas for sales to the Vietnam Electricity (EVN) was estimated at US $ 2-3/ mmBtu in 2007. Such low gas prices have worked to curb investment.

According to OGJ, Vietnam held 691 bcm of proven natural gas reserves as of January 2012. Reserves have risen considerably since 2007 as a result of Vietnam's aggressive policy to attract investment and issue exploration contracts for its offshore acreage. In 2010, Vietnam produced 8 bcm of natural gas, more than double of 2005 production. Vietnam is currently self sufficient in Natural gas. Vietnam's National Gas Master Plan projects that gas consumption in the country will increase from 8 bcm in 2010 to over 12.8 bcm by 2015. Also, PetroVietnam predicts there will be a gas supply gap of 13 bcm by 2025 as demand outstrips supply in the country. Domestic coal and gas prices for power plants are set at lower levels. In 2006, coal prices for domestic power plants stood at some US$ 20 per ton against export prices around US$ 35. Associated gas prices are separated from natural gas process. Domestic gas prices for power plants were far lower than the international standards of US$ 7-8/ mmBtu (million metric British thermal units). Domestic coal prices for power plants, though planned to shift to market levels, are now 30 per cent lower than domestic market prices and 50 per cent less than export prices. Electricity prices are limited under government policy to as low as $0.05/kWh on average.

Vietnam uses the greater part of coal supply for electricity generation. The remainder is used at cement, brick, paper and fertilizer plants. Vietnam, though exporting coal at present, will become a coal importer around 2015 onwards as demands in electricity increases. Coal prices for power plants are 30 per cent less than domestic market prices and 50 per cent less than export prices. The Vietnam National Coal-Mineral industries group, known as Vinacomin, is required to provide coal to power plants at lower prices. In the Finance Ministry's report no. 191, given to the government for submission to the Standing Committee of the National assembly in January 2009, electricity, coal and clean water prices as well as bus fares were planned to remain as it was, subject to the market mechanism.

While commercial energy consumption in Vietnam has been increasing over recent years, conventional renewable energy consumption for non-commercial purposes has still been accounting for nearly 40 per cent of total energy consumption. This means that commercial energy demand has great growth potential. From 1995 to 2007, primary energy supply expanded at an average annual rate of 11 per cent. Particularly, associated gas consumption for power plants increased. Coal and petroleum products are consumed mainly in the industrial and transportation sectors.

Vietnam has reached a turning point regarding energy prices. Although energy prices had long been controlled under the communist ideology, last year's high crude oil prices forced Vietnam to set petroleum product prices at levels close to market levels because of its full dependence on imports for petroleum product supply. The fast energy demand expansion over the past years is forcing Vietnam to become a net importer of oil and coal in the near future. Unless coal and gas prices as well as petroleum product prices are raised to international market levels, Vietnam may lose its competitiveness in energy security. Vietnam will also have to promote energy conservation and new energy in order to curb energy consumption and maintain the environment while keeping high economic growth. In Vietnam, many relevant laws and regulations have been approved but, reportedly have not been enforced effectively. In the future, Vietnam will be urged to come up with an enforceable energy policy for meeting its energy security.

Energy Imports: India

India's net imports of energy (petroleum, coal and gas) increased from 129 mtoe in 2006 to 191 mtoe in 2010 representing a growth of 10 per cent per annum. This is likely to increase to about 227 mtoe in 2011-12. Supply and demand projections for the 12th Five Year Plan indicate that imports will further grow to about 366 mtoe in 2016-

17 i.e. energy imports would nearly triple in just over a decade from 2006. India's Planning Commission also projects that the country's dependence on imports could almost double; rising from about 33 per cent today to about 53 per cent of commercial energy needs by 2031-32.

Figure 7.3: India's Energy Imports in MTOE (2010)

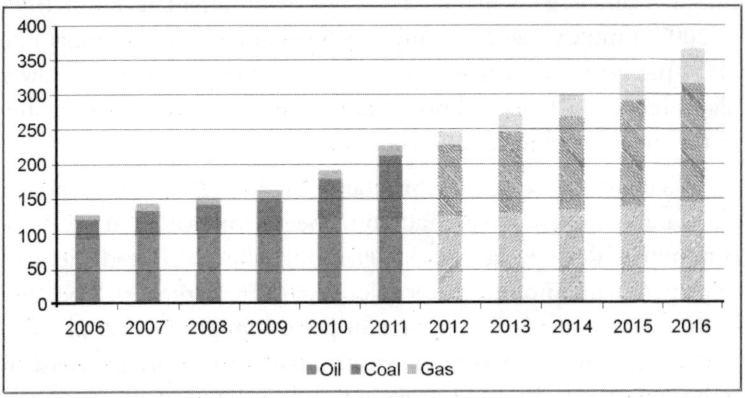

Source: Planning Commission, (12th Plan Document).

Despite having the world's fifth largest coal reserves with over 77 billion tonnes of proved reserves, India's coal imports are growing.[2] In 2011 India is estimated to have imported more than 100 million tonnes of coal and by 2020 India is expected to be the largest coal importer in the world.[3] India's coal import dependence has increased from 6 per cent to 13 per cent in the last 5-6 years. Till 2005-06, coking coal used to dominate coal imports (about 50 per cent) but now its share has declined to 33 per cent. Demand-supply gap for coal is expected to grow from the current average level of about 50 MT to more than 250 MT by 2025.[4] Coal now accounts for over 55 per cent of installed power generation capacity and over 69 per cent of actual generation (2010-11).[5] India's current fossil fuel dependence coupled with limited domestic oil reserves and lower-than projected coal resources is generating increasing reliance on energy imports.

India's ultimate oil reserves have declined from 1646 million metric tonnes (mmt) in 2008 to 1544 in 2010.[6] With probability of large hydrocarbon discoveries in Indian onshore and offshore prospects declining, Indian upstream oil and gas companies, irrespective of whether they are owned by the State or by private actors, are acquiring assets outside India. India imports about 79 per cent of its crude needs.[7] India's oil imports are likely to increase from the current 4 million barrels per day (mbpd) to over 7 mbpd by 2035.[8]

The International Energy Outlook projects that India's oil production will grow at the rate of less than 1 per cent on an average by 2035. The combination of rising oil consumption and relatively flat production has left India increasingly dependent on imports to meet its petroleum demand. In 2010, India was the world's fifth largest net importer of oil, importing more than 2.2 million bpd or 70 per cent of its hydrocarbon requirements.

In 2000, the Hydrocarbon Vision 2025 commissioned by the Prime Minister of India to address the issue of energy security in the context of the hydrocarbon sector (Oil & Gas) was released. The report recommended 'intensification of exploration efforts and securing acreages in countries having 'high attractiveness for ensuring sustainable long-term supplies' such as Russia, Iran, Iraq and North Africa.[9] The recommendations were repeated with some variations in subsequent documents. The Integrated Energy Policy Report released in 2006 redefined energy security from the perspective of the 'Individual' as well as that of the 'Nation' for the first time and highlighted the need for equitable access to energy within the nation.[10]

With regard to the latter perspective where supplies to the nation as a whole are considered, the Report commented that 'obtaining equity oil, coal and gas abroad do not represent adequate strategies for enhancing energy security beyond diversifying supply sources'[11] but also recommended 'investing in equity oil' to enhance energy security in subsequent sections (*see* Fig. 7.4).[12]

The report argued that energy security was about managing risks and identified three broad types of risks: (a) supply risks mainly arising from disruptions in the supply of imported energy but also of domestic energy (such as a strike in Coal India Limited which may disrupt the domestic supply of coal); (b) market risk which concerns

Figure 7.4: Oil Production and Consumption in India 2010

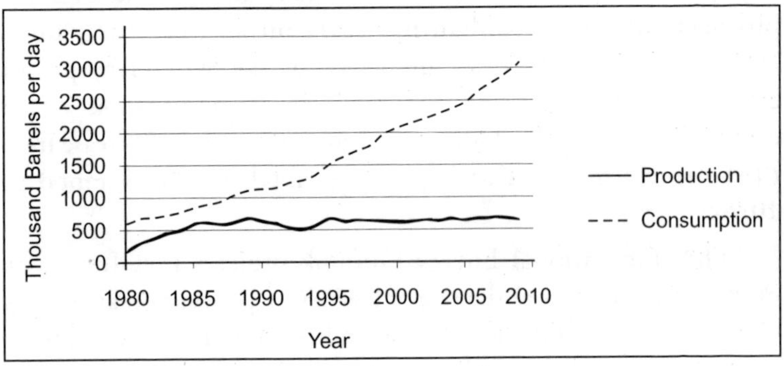

Source: BP Statistical Review 2012.

price volatility of imported energy and the consequent to the economy and terms of trade; and (c) technical risk arising from threats to domestic energy infrastructure. Maintenance of reserve coal stocks and oil diplomacy were among solutions recommended in the report.

Energy Imports: Vietnam

Vietnam is currently a net exporter of crude oil but remains a net importer of oil products. According to EIA, oil demand has nearly doubled in the past decade from 175,000 bpd in 2000 to an estimated 320,000 bpd in 2010. Vietnam still needs to import about 70 per cent of refined products and petrochemicals since the output from the Dung Quat refinery does not satisfy domestic demand. As more refineries are scheduled to come online, PetroVietnam anticipates meeting 50 to 60 per cent of the domestic product demand by 2015.

However, some concerns have emerged recently about the maintenance of crude oil production levels and natural gas coal supply meeting rising demand. Meanwhile, Vietnam is considering the expansion or construction of hydroelectric and nuclear plants, thermal power generation using imported coal and electricity import. Vietnam is expected to become a net importer of coal and oil around 2015. It will have to start energy imports as electricity demand increases. If distorted domestic energy prices are left untouched, Vietnam may have great turmoil on its commencement of energy imports around 2015.

India's Hydrocarbon Equity Investments Around the World

OVL was created with the mission to pursue 'equity oil' investments. Barring a few exceptions, it has so far made equity investments in countries like Vietnam, Myanmar, Russia, Kazakhstan, Iran, Iraq, Syria, Libya, Nigeria, Sudan, Brazil, Columbia and Venezuela.

In Vietnam, OVL has invested US$ 114 million in exploratory assets and US$ 244 million in a producing asset which gives OVL 2.249 bcm of gas and some condensate. In Myanmar, India has invested US$ 160 million in natural gas assets from which production is anticipated next year. Russia has the largest OVL equity investments at US$ 4 billion yielding 1.4 million metric tonne (mmt) of oil and 0.415 bcm of gas. In Iran and Iraq, OVL has exploratory assets worth US$ 38 million. In Syria, OVL has two assets, one producing and one exploratory accounting for an investment of US$ 277 million with 0.662 mmt of 'equity oil' in 2010-11. In Libya, OVL has invested US$ 50 million in three exploratory assets out of which formal letters on relinquishment are awaited on two, while force majeure notice has been served and operations suspended on the third. In Nigeria, OVL has invested US$ 257 million in exploratory blocks out of which US$ 25 million has already been written off. OVL's US$ 2.5 billion investment in the Greater Nile Project in Sudan gives ownership of about 1-2 mmt of 'equity oil' each year. Another producing asset in Sudan assigns OVL about 0.226 mmt of equity oil for an investment of US$ 428 million. In Venezuela, OVL has a producing asset in which it has invested US$ 191 million and has the right to about 0.757 mmt of crude. In Cuba, OVL has invested US$ 69.7 million in exploratory assets and in Columbia it has invested US$ 9.5 million in exploratory assets and a producing asset in which it has invested US$ 437.5 million with right to 0.468 mmt of crude. In Brazil, OVL has a US$ 548 million investment to give about 0.573 mmt of crude and 0.013 BCM of gas. It also has an investment of US$ 81 million in exploratory assets in Brazil. These investments add up to an investment of US$ 1.1 billion in exploratory assets and US$ 8.7 billion in producing assets yielding about 5.3 million tonnes or 38.8 million barrels of equity oil. This is about 3 per cent of India's total annual consumption.

Low Carbon Energy Sources: India

India is one of the fastest growing countries in terms of energy consumption. Currently, it is the fifth largest consumer of energy in the world, and will be the third largest by 2030. At the same time, the country is heavily dependent on fossil fuels for meeting most of its energy demand. This has necessitated the country to start aggressively pursuing alternative energy sources, such as solar, wind, bio-fuels, small hydro and others. Sustainable energy investment in India went up to US$ 3.7 billion in 2008, up by 12 per cent since 2007 and this is likely to increase much more in the coming years. It included asset financing of US$ 3.2 billion, up by 36 per cent (*see* Figure 7.5).

Venture capital and private equity saw an increase of 270 per cent to US$ 493 million. India has a total renewable potential of around 90,000 MW for power generation from different renewable energy sources in the country, including 48,561 MW of wind power, 14,294 MW of small hydro power and 26,367 MW of biomass. In addition, the potential for solar energy is estimated for most parts of the country at around 20 MW per square kilometre of open, shadow free area covered with solar collectors, which would add to a minimum of 657 GW of installed capacity.

India is the 4th largest country with regard to installed power-generation capacity in the field of renewable energy sources. India intends to provide a reliable energy supply through a diverse and sustainable fuel mix that addresses major national drivers. These include security concerns, commercial exploitation of renewable power potential, eradication of energy poverty, ensuring availability and affordability of energy supply and preparing the nation for imminent energy transition.

Figure 7.5: Share Break-Up of Renewable Energy Sources

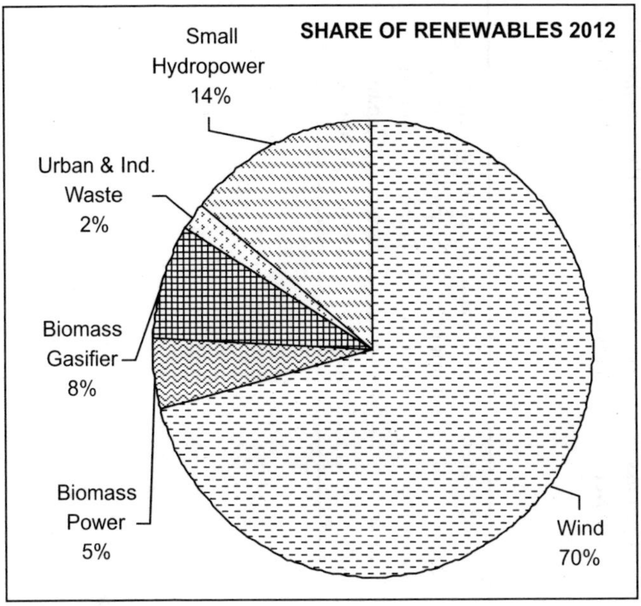

Source: Ministry of New and Renewable Energy.

The market in India for the Renewable Energy (RE) business is growing at an annual rate of 15 per cent. The scope for private investment in RE is estimated to about $3 billion. This growth is expected to continue in the coming years as stricter environmental norms and regulatory pressure are placed on Indian industries.

Solar energy development is supported by Government of India incentives and, more recently, is spurred by the high fossil fuel prices. Generation of electricity from sun is a flagship programme of the climate programme of the Government of India. India has one of the world's largest programmes in solar energy which include research and development, demonstration and utilisation, testing & standardisation, industrial and promotional activities. Processed raw material for solar cells, large capacity Solar Photovoltaic (SPV) modules, SPV roof tiles, inverters, charge controllers all have good market potential in India as do advanced solar water heaters, roof integrated solar air heaters; and solar concentrators for power generation (above 100 KW).

Table 7.1: India's Global Position in Renewable Energy Capacity

Top Five Countries-Existing Capacity as of end-2010	Renewables Power Capacity (not including hydro)	Renewables Power Capacity (including hydro)	Wind Power	Biomass Power	Geothermal Power	Solar PV	Solar Hot Water/Heater
1	United States	China	China	United States	United States	Germany	China
2	China	United States	United States	Brazil	Philippines	Spain	Turkey
3	Germany	Canada	Germany	Germany	Indonesia	Japan	Germany
4	Spain	Brazil	Spain	China	Mexico	Italy	Japan
5	India	Germany/India	Sweden	Italy	United	States	Greece

Source: REN 21 (Renewables 2011: Global Status Report).

The onshore wind power potential has been estimated at about 48,500 MW, assuming 1 per cent land availability in potential areas for setting up wind farms @ 12 ha/MW in sites having wind power density greater than 200/W/sqm at 50 metre hub-height. Thus far only 21.6 per cent of India's potential is being generated. The growth of wind energy in India has been consistent with the global trends. In 2008 India added 1800 MW taking the total wind energy installed capacity to 9645 MW, making it fifth top country in the world, after USA, Germany, Spain and China. For wind energy installed capacity India is implementing the world's largest wind resource assessment programme comprising wind monitoring, wind mapping and complex terrain projects. This programme covers 800 stations in 24 states with around 200 wind monitoring stations in operation at present. Wind Electric Generators are being manufactured in the country by nearly a dozen manufacturers through: (a) joint ventures or under licensed production; (b) subsidiaries of foreign companies under licensed production; and (c) Indian companies with their own technology. The current annual production capacity of domestic wind turbine is about 3,000 MW. The Indian Renewable Energy Development Agency (IREDA) sponsored wind power development programme provides financial assistance for the project and extends equipment financing.

Globally, India is in the fourth position of generating power through biomass and with a huge potential, is poised to become a world leader in the utilisation of biomass. Biomass power projects with an aggregate capacity of 773.3 MW through over 100 projects have been installed in the country. For the last 15 years, biomass power has attracted annual investment of over Rs. 1 billion, generating more than 9 billion unit of electricity per year. More than 540 million tons of crop and plantation residues are produced every year in India and a large portion is either wasted, or used inefficiently. By using these surplus agricultural residues, by conservative estimates, more than 16,000 MW of grid quality power could be generated through biomass. In addition, about 5,000 MW power can be produced, if all 550 sugar mills in the country switch over to modern techniques of cogeneration. Thus the estimated biomass power potential is about 21,000 MW.

With numerous rivers and their tributaries in India, small hydro-power energy sources have an excellent opportunity to be developed in India with an estimated potential of 15,000 MW. Out of the total potential only 17 per cent has been exploited so far. As on 12 December 2009, over 674 projects aggregating to about 2558.92 MW generating capacity have been set up in the country. Of the estimated potential of 15,000 MW of small hydro power in the country, 5415 potential sites with an aggregate capacity of 14,292 MW have been identified. Most of the potential is in the Himalayan States as river-based projects and in other States as irrigation canals. The Government of India (GoI) is encouraging the development of small hydro projects and aims to double the current growth rate that leads to a capacity addition of 500 MW per year with total installed capacity of 4,000 MW by the end of 2012. The GoI is providing concessions for existing hydro projects including financial support for renovation, modernisation and capacity upgrading of aging small hydro power stations.

The rising piles of garbage in urban areas caused by rapid urbanisation and industrialisation throughout India represent another source of non-conventional energy. An estimated 50 million tonnes of solid waste and approximately 6,000 million cubic metres of liquid waste are generated annually in the urban areas of India. Good potential exists for generating approximately 2,600 MW of power from urban and municipal wastes and approximately 1,300 MW from industrial wastes in India. A total of 48 projects with aggregate capacity of about 69.62 MW equivalents have been installed in the country thereby utilising only 1.8 per cent of the potential that exists.

The Indian government recently mandated the blending of 10 per cent fuel ethanol in 90 per cent gasoline. This mandate has created an approximately 3.6 billion-litre demand for fuel ethanol in the entire country. This significant demand growth creates a tremendous manufacturing opportunity for the fuel ethanol industry seeking to expand its investments internationally.

Low Carbon Energy Sources: Vietnam

Vietnam is rich in renewable energy resources. Renewable energy resources suitable for electricity generation include small hydro, solar, biomass, wind and geothermal. The potential for small hydro-power resources is estimated to be about 1600 MW; total capacity of geothermal is estimated at 200 MW; wood and agricultural residues and by-products are about 50 million tonnes per year. Wind, solar and biogas potential in Vietnam is relatively abundant. About 75 per cent Vietnam's 82 million population is living in rural areas with currently about 8.5 per cent of households in these regions having no access to electricity.

The Vietnam Electricity (EVN) will spend Vietnamese Dollar (VND) 3.1 trillion (about US$194.7 million) for building 37 small-scale hydroelectric power stations in the Northern provinces bordering China. Of these, 10-13 stations, with a maximum capacity of 5 MW each will be built in the bordering districts of Lai Chau, Lao Cai, Ha Giang and Lang Son provinces. Since the 1980s, Vietnam has reviewed the implementation of wind turbines for power generation in islands and remote grid-connected areas. Some of the recent wind power developments are: 15 kW solar PV-wind power hybrid systems in one of the smaller village with 40 households. This project was implemented by Institute of Energy (IE) with a grant from Tohoku Electric Company of Japan. The 800 kW wind power generator in Bach Long Island was financed completely by the Government of Vietnam. Future wind energy developments in Vietnam aims at a total installed capacity of about 120 MW including the following projects: Ly Son Island (2 MW); Phuong Mai wind farm in Binh Dinh Province (15 MW); Wind Power Project in Phuong Mai (84 MW), the main investor is Grabowski Renewable Energy Company. Phu Quoc Island (2.5 MW); Wind farm in Phu Yen Province (15 MW) and Con Dao Island (2.5 MW).

Potential for Cooperation

Taking into account all these aspects of areas for cooperation between India and Vietnam can be explored in Research and Development in low carbon energy sources, joint bidding for hydrocarbon assets, joint investments and sourcing of coal, leveraging India's low cost small and safe nuclear reactors, investment in each other's energy sectors, exchange of lessons in energy subsidy and pricing reform.

NOTES

1. International Energy Agency, 2011, *World Energy Outlook 2011 (WEO 2011),* all projections for future energy demand in this section are from the WEO 2011.
2. *World Energy Outlook 2011*, International Energy Agency.
3. Import figure for 2011-12 from Reuters (http://in.reuters.com/article/2011/02/03/idINIndia-54617620110203) and import projection from the World Energy Outlook 2011, International Energy Agency.
4. Presentation by ICF International at the 5th India Energy Summit on 28-29 November 2011.
5. Central Electricity Authority, 'Operating Performance of Generation Stations in the Country during the year 2010-11, Figures correspond to utility based generation.
6. Delloite, Background Paper for the 3rd India-Africa Hydrocarbons Conference, New Delhi quoting Directorate of Hydrocarbons, Government of India.
7. Petroleum Planning and Analysis Cell, Government of India.
8. *World Energy Outlook 2011*, International Energy Agency.
9. Hydrocarbon Vision 2025, Government of India.
10. Integrated Energy Policy, Expert Committee of the Planning Commission, Government of India, 2006, pp XXIV: 'Energy security: 'ensuring the continuous availability of commercial energy at competitive prices to support India's economic growth and meet the lifeline energy needs of its households with safe, clean and convenient forms of energy even if that entails directed subsidies'.
11. Integrated Energy Policy, Expert Committee of the Planning Commission, Government of India, 2006, pp. XXIV.
12. Integrated Energy Policy, Expert Committee of the Planning Commission, Government of India, 2006, pp. 9 and 57.

8
Conventional and Non-Conventional Sources of Energy in India

Jesudas Bell

India and Vietnam have much in common in the energy sector. Economic growth in both countries are relatively high, with a demographic boom, leading to high expectations and demands for better quality of life and increased material prosperity. It is a common saying in India that when politicians go to the countryside to ask for vote in their support in elections, people ask for 'bijlee, pani aur sadak' meaning electricity, water and roads. It is to be noted that electricity comes as first demand. The nature of modern daily life across the globe requires electricity, for basic sustenance, to food security, to industrial usage.

India's Energy Profile

India has an energy policy which calls for availability of electricity to every household in the country in the next five years. Given the fact that in 2001, 44 per cent of households in India did not have access to electricity, this is a huge task. Thermal plants provide the bulk of about 66 per cent of electricity in India, in which coal contributes about 56 per cent of electricity needs, gas about 10 per cent and oil about 0.5 per cent of the total energy needs. Hydropower accounts for about 19 per cent of generation, nuclear power about 2.5 per cent and renewable sources of energy like solar, wind, small hydropower and biomass units contribute around 12 per cent of the total energy needs.

India's electricity generation capacity is currently estimated to be 203,000 MW. To meet India's energy security, India will have to increase the generation capacity by another equivalent amount i.e. adding another 200,000 MW capacity by 2035. This is a massive undertaking which needs investment of the order of US$ 200 billion. In the current global scenario of rising prices of fossil fuels such as coal, oil and gas, it is very expensive to add energy capacity and then to pay for the inputs for its daily operations.

In spite of the rise in prices, India for the immediate future will have no option except to rely on coal-based power plants to augment capacity in energy generation. As India imports coal from Indonesia, Australia and South Africa, it will need to develop coal-based power plants in coastal areas where imported coals can be landed and used.

Gas turbine based plants consume about 40 per cent of the natural gas output in India. Gas powered capacity is expected to increase to 16 per cent of installed capacity by 2035 in India. This could increase with new discoveries in various basins in India once the price mechanism to exploit these resources gets resolved.

Nuclear power will also be expanded in India with six reactors being in the process of building, in addition to the 20 reactors already operating. The combined capacity is expected to reach 20,000 MW by 2020.

As far as large hydropower is concerned, India may not be able to expand this too much as a large number of possible sources have already been tapped and there are considerable environmental and land acquisition problems for new projects.

Non-Conventional Sources of Energy

The government of India is actively pursuing alternative and non-conventional sources of energy. To this end, India has set up a new and dedicated Ministry to enhance capacity in alternative and non-conventional sources of energy, called the Ministry of New and

Renewable Energy (MNRE). The chief sources of energy being looked at under this Ministry are wind, solar, small hydropower and biomass. At present wind accounts for about 17,500 MW, solar about 980 MW, small hydropower about 3400 MW and biomass about 3100 MW, of energy needs in India. Smaller projects based on waste are also being used. The investment in non-conventional energy is about US$ 10 billion a year.

Both in the conventional and non-conventional energy sectors, the Indian government places tremendous emphasis on involvement of the private sector. While large power projects were earlier managed by state owned giants such as the National Thermal Power Corporation (NTPC), National Hydropower Corporation (NHPC), and others, most new projects using both fossil fuels and renewable sources are being built by the private sector. Governments at the central and state level are concentrating more on transmission and distribution of power. Gradually, these are even being handed over to the private sector in some larger cities and also in distribution between cities and states. The aim is to develop an efficient market for energy with prices being set between supplier and consumer rather than arbitrarily by the government.

The result of these initiatives has resulted in the growth of a large number of companies in India for power manufacturing equipments like wind mills, solar panels, small hydropower and biomass generators, etc. Some of these equipment manufacturing companies have become world renowned.

Possibilities for India–Vietnam Cooperation

There is a huge scope for cooperation between India and Vietnam in both conventional and non-conventional sources of energy, and in other sectors including generation, transmission and distribution of power. Indian manufacturers including multi-national companies are actively looking at the Vietnam market, given that Vietnam also needs to increase electricity production substantially in the years to come. These include manufacturing of hydropower, wind power, solar and biomass generation equipments.

Apart from the manufacturing of equipments, project developers who have successfully developed energy generation projects in India are now looking for opportunities abroad including in areas like solar power, wind power and hydropower. Hydropower is the largest contributor to the generation of electricity in Vietnam. It would be ideal if they could partner with Vietnamese companies or the government to invest in and develop power either in Vietnam itself or in the neighbouring countries of the region such as Laos and Cambodia, with the aim of supplying to the Vietnamese market. It is hoped that Indian companies will find fertile ground in Vietnam, if actively assisted by the governments of the two countries.

9
Peaceful Utilisation of Atomic Energy in Vietnam and Scope for Vietnam-India Cooperation

Hoang Anh Tuan

Introduction

Vietnam has been utilising atomic energy for peaceful purposes since 1960s and has been actively preparing for the introduction of nuclear power in the country. Although Vietnam's endeavour to procure atomic energy is a recent phenomenon, Vietnam upgraded Dalat Nuclear Reactor disbanded by the US before it left Vietnam in 1975, with the help of erstwhile Soviet Union. Vietnam established the Nuclear Research Institute in Dalat in 1976. In 1984, it restored Dalat Research Reactor and established National Atomic Energy Institute (VAEC, now VINATOM). Since mid-1970s, Vietnam has been endeavouring to build nuclear capacities for scientific research. It has taken help from a number of countries including India to construct its nuclear power capabilities. Vietnam aims to build first unit of 1,000 MW of nuclear power by 2020, and 10 units producing total of 10,700 MW of nuclear power by 2030. In 2011 'Planning for National Electricity Development for the Period of 2011-20' was passed with a 'Vision for the Development of Nuclear Energy up to 2030 (Master Plan VII)'. In this backdrop, this chapter will deal with Vietnam's national policies, infrastructure development, IAEA assistance, and key facilities for developing nuclear energy, besides, scope for Vietnam-India cooperation.

National Policies on Atomic Energy

In 1994, Vietnam established Nuclear Regulatory Department under Ministry of Science and Technology (MOST), in which Vietnam Agency for Radiation and Nuclear Safety and Control (VARANSAC) and Vietnam Agency for Radiation and Nuclear Safety (VARANS) was established in 2003 and 2008, respectively. In 2010, Vietnam Atomic Energy Agency under MOST was established.

In 2006, Vietnam adopted 'Strategy on Peaceful Utilisation of Atomic Energy up to 2020' with the objective to put its first nuclear power unit into operation by 2020. The 'Master plan to Implement the Strategy on Peaceful Utilisation of Atomic Energy up to 2020', and 'Atomic Energy Law' were passed in 2007 and 2008, respectively. In 2009 by Resolution No. 41/2009/NQ-QH12, the National Assembly of Vietnam passed the 'Investment Policy on Ninh Thuan Nuclear Power Project' to produce nuclear power in Vietnam. In 2010, 'Master Plan for the Peaceful Development and Utilisation of Atomic Energy up to 2020' was passed, in which detailed 'Planning for Agriculture' was adopted in 2010, 'Planning for Medicine' was adopted in 2011, 'Planning for Industry' was adopted in 2011 and 'Planning for Geological Science and Environment' was adopted in 2010.

To build capacities in the nuclear field, 'Master Plan for Human Resource Development' for the development of atomic energy was adopted in 2010; 'Project on Capacity Building for Security Purposes' was adopted in 2011; 'Project on Capacity Building of State Management' was adopted in 2012; and 'Project on Capacity Building for Research and Development and Technical Safety Organisation (TSO)' was adopted in 2012. 'National Project for Human Resource Development' is currently under implementation by MOST, MOET, EVN.

Infrastructure Development for Utilising Atomic Energy

Vietnam is now actively preparing 19 issues relating to nuclear infrastructure for the introduction of nuclear power in the country. It is developing the regulatory framework and amending Atomic Energy Law of 2008 for this purpose. Various critical issues are developed by different ministries in this regard. For example, legal and regulatory framework is being examined by Ministry of Science and Technology, Ministry of Industry and Trade, etc.; human resource development issue is looked after by Ministry of Education and Training, Ministry of Science and Technology, MOIT, etc.; National Project on Public Information & Communication is prepared by Vietnam Atomic Energy Agency, which has to be submitted to the Prime Minister for approval. To deal with the nuclear waste 'Plan on Disposal Site' was adopted in 2010. Cooperation with International Atomic Energy Agency (IAEA) and bilateral cooperation with Russia, Japan, France, Republic of Korea and other countries in nuclear power infrastructure development has also been intensified.

IAEA Assistance in Infrastructure Development

Three Technical Cooperation (TC) Projects relating to nuclear infrastructure development (7 national TC Projects and 41 regional/ interregional TC projects) was agreed to be implemented in the period 2009-11; VIE/9/011 (managed by VINATOM) on 'Improving the Capability for Site Characterisation and Evaluation of New Nuclear Installations', was agreed; VIE/9/013 (managed by VARANS) on 'Strengthening the Technical Capacity of the Radiation and Nuclear Safety Regulatory Body', was signed; and VIE/4/015 (managed by VAEA) on 'Developing Nuclear Power Infrastructure' (main project) was agreed. In 2012-13, five TC Projects relating to nuclear power infrastructure were agreed. Regional Cooperation Agreement (RCA), Regional Cooperation Projects (RAS) and other funding measures are sought for the development of nuclear power infrastructure.

Vietnam needs assistance in organising workshops, review meetings, training courses, expert missions, scientific visits, fellowships, purchase of equipments, etc. There is need for better coordination and planning of TC activities. For effectiveness of TC activities, there should be focus on current critical issues, with broader involvement of stakeholders. In 2011, the total numbers of activities undertaken from TC Projects were: 16 expert missions, 19 scientific visits and 18 foreign exchanges.

Atomic Energy Applications: Key Facilities

Key facilities of atomic energy applications in Vietnam are in Hanoi, Dalat, Ho Chi Minh City, etc. Dalat Nuclear Research Reactor, 30 MeV Cyclotron in Tran Hung Dao Hospital, Pelletron-5 SDH-2 Electrostatic Accelerator in Hanoi University of Science, and Hanoi Irradiation Centre, are some of the well known centres dealing with atomic energy. In Hanoi, VINATOM exists under Ministry of Science and Technology with institutions like, ITRRE, NDE, HIC, NTC, etc. Vietnam Academy of Science and Technology (VAST) has Nuclear Research Centre in the Institute of Physics. There are hospitals like, Tran Hung Dao with a 30 MeV Cyclotron, Bach Mai, Universities like, HUST, HUS, EPU, which have atomic energy application units. In Dalat, Nuclear Research Institute (NRI) has Dalat Research Reactor of 500 kW, in Dalat University (DLU). In Ho Chi Minh City, there are Nuclear Centre, VINAGAMMA, Hospitals like Cho Ray, Universities like HCMUS, HCMUT which deal with atomic energy applications. Besides, Ninh Thuan-1 nuclear reactor is located in Phuoc Dinh province and Ninh Thuan-2 nuclear reactor is located in Vinh Hai province. Apart from these various hospitals have radiation facilities, and radioactive sources are used by various companies in different places.

Ninh Thuan Nuclear Power Project

In November 2009, Vietnam's National Assembly approved the investment in the Ninh Thuan Nuclear Power Project. In May 2010, State Steering Committee of the Ninh Thuan Nuclear Power Project was established and was chaired by Mr. Hoang Trung Hai, Deputy Prime Minister of Vietnam. Vietnam is now working on the Feasibility

Studies (FS) and Site Approval for the development of the Ninh Thuan Nuclear Power Project. In April 2011, 'Ninh Thuan Nuclear Power Project Management Board' under Vietnam Electricity (EVN) was established.

In October 2010, Vietnam-Russia Agreement on the construction of Ninh Thuan-1 nuclear power project was signed. Ninh Thuan-1 will be built with Russian support in Phuoc Dinh which will have two reactors generating 1,000 MWe power each. It is expected to start operation by 2020-21. In November 2011 there was official signing of the EVN-Consortium E4 Group (Russia) consulting contract for 18 months on Site Approval Dossier Development & Feasibility study for the Ninh Thuan-1 nuclear power project. In November 2011, official signing of the Vietnam-Russia Agreement on Credit Support for the construction of Ninh Thuan-1 nuclear power project took place.

In November 2011, Vietnam-Japan bilateral agreement on the construction of Ninh Thuan-2 nuclear power project was signed. Ninh Thuan-2 will be built in Vinh Hai, which will have two reactors generating power 1,000 MWe each. It is expected to start operation by 2021-22. In September 2011 EVN and Japan Atomic Power Company (JAPC) signed 'Consulting Contract for 18 months on Site Approval Dossier Development and Feasibility Study for the Ninh Thuan-2 Nuclear Power Project'. EVN is the investment owner of the projects, which will use Light Water reactor (LWR) of advanced and proven technology. Sea water will be used for cooling the reactors and fuels for the reactors are likely to be imported.

Vietnam-India Cooperation

On 25 March 1986, Vietnam-India Agreement on Cooperation in the Development and Peaceful Uses of Nuclear Energy was signed. In 2002, Vietnam-India Nuclear Science Centre (VINSC) in Dalat was established with the support of the Government of India. In 2002, a MoU between MOST of Vietnam and Department of Atomic Energy (DAE) in India was signed, which was again renewed in 2007. In 2008, Tri-party Agreement between IAEA, Vietnam and India on the donation of Bhabhatron-II tele-therapy unit by Indian Government to the Can-Tho General Hospital in support of IAEA's PACT initiative was signed. Board of Radiation and Isotope Technology (BRIT) of India has supported VINATOM with Co-60 source for the Research and Development Centre for Radiation Technology (VINAGAMMA) in Ho Chi Minh City.

In the field of human resource development, Vietnamese scientists have been trained in different establishments under the DAE of India. India has provided 1 year training at Bhabha Atomic Research Centre (BARC) for NRI's staff on nuclear physics and electronics. Training of staff of ITRRE (VINATOM) on nuclear fuel and materials, NDT technician training programme of BARC for staff of NRI (VINATOM), training of staff of VINAGAMMA (VINATOM) on installation and utilisation of Co-60 source, scientific visits of Indian experts to Vietnam and vice versa, have taken place over the years.

Future Vietnam-India Cooperation

India has great potential, experience and expertise in the peaceful utilisation of atomic energy. Vietnam and India have a long history of successful cooperation in atomic energy applications for peaceful purposes. Vietnam needs the international cooperation and expertise, including the cooperation of India for the safe, secure and successful introduction of nuclear power. The cooperation between Vietnam and India in the field of atomic energy should cover both power and non-power applications, especially in exchanging experience in professional training. Possibilities should also be explored for technology transfer between the two countries. Vietnam and India can cooperate in education and training of nuclear work force for regulatory bodies, research and development institutions, technical support organisations, programme management, etc. This is the right time for strengthening cooperation between Vietnam and India in the energy field in general and in the peaceful utilisation of atomic energy in particular.

Section III

Evolving Security Architecture in the Asia-Pacific Region: Political, Security and Defence Co-operation

10

Rising India-Vietnam Ties in the Emerging Security Architecture of the Asia-Pacific Region

Tridib Chakraborti

Introduction

Indian foreign policy in the post-Cold War era has drastically altered the perception and outlook of global power politics. India has shown resilience in the economic reforms and weathered global economic crisis, demonstrates its economic prowess. Since 1991, through Look East Policy as well as New Economic Policy (NEP), India has tried to concentrate on Southeast Asian region and beyond. In the last 21 years, India's promotion in the ASEAN orbit from sectoral dialogue partner in 1992 to summit partner in 2002, and as a founding member in the East Asia Summit in 2005, is reflective of India's growing stature. It has become a stakeholder and a balancer in the emerging power politics in the region.

What would be India's role in the emerging geo-economic and geopolitical architecture of the Asia-Pacific region is a question to be pondered upon. India has realised that its means of entering the Asia-Pacific region lies through Southeast Asia. It has also realised that multi-polarity in the region may be the best choice for India. In this context, India's membership in a number of regional and sub-regional organizations is a major triumph for Indian foreign policy. An interesting point to be noted in this context is that one country happens to be member of other organizations in different capacities. As a result, these meetings facilitate bilateral relations taking 'strategic' overtones. For example, India and Vietnam are meeting each other in the ARF, MGC, East Asia Summit, India-ASEAN Summit meetings etc. in various capacities, on diverse issues.

In this backdrop, India's strategic cooperation with Vietnam is crucial in making its presence felt in the Southeast Asian region and beyond. India's growing economic profile as well as its Look East Policy, coincided with Vietnam's economic growth and Look West Policy. The strategic partnership was officially declared, when Prime Minister of the Socialist Republic of Vietnam, Nguyen Tan Dung visited India from 4-6 July 2007, at the invitation of Indian Prime Minister, Manmohan Singh. During the visit the two countries agreed to boost political ties, strengthen security and defence cooperation and establish a strategic dialogue mechanism at the level of deputy foreign ministers. In an interview with the Vietnam News Agency, on 8 July 2007, Mr. Dung said that he hoped that India will become one of Vietnam's leading partners in politics, economics, trade, investment, security, national defence, science and technology, education and training in the near future"[1].

The purpose of this article is to highlight the growing security cooperation between India and Vietnam, and to analyse how the mutual understanding between the two can be strengthened in the evolving security architecture of the Asia-Pacific region.

Cold War Period

The strategic cooperation between India and Vietnam was not a sudden incident. It has gradually evolved over the Cold War period, and augmented its space in the post-Cold War era, spearheaded by growing economic rise as a result of the series of economic reforms both countries pursued in the last 21 years. India's relations with Vietnam have been governed by their common enemy China, on account of war and other experiences: India with reference to Pakistan, and Vietnam because of the 1979 war and the South China Sea issue.

As a result, New Delhi's military relations with Hanoi developed slowly but steadily in the Cold War period.

During the Cold War period, a number of bilateral visits took place and defence cooperation started between the two countries, with exchange of a few military delegations and naval ships. Among these visits, from Indian side, a military delegation, headed by the Indian Chief of General Staff, General K.V. Krishna Rao, in May 1983, after the Sino-Vietnam War of 1979, to study how Vietnamese border troops resisted attacks by China's regular army formations; the goodwill visit of Indian Navy Flotilla to Ho Chi Minh City, led by Rear Admiral S. Jain in May 1982; the visit of Army Chief, General K. Sundarji in March-April 1987 to analyze the defence strategy followed by Vietnam along its China border, are pertinent. The Air-Vice Marshal, S.D. Mohan led a military delegation to Vietnam in July 1987; the Air Chief Marshal S.K. Mehra[2] on February 1989, etc. Similarly, from the Vietnamese side, the visit of military delegations led by Lt. General Hoang Minh Thao in December 1982 and Chief of General Staff of the Vietnamese People's Army, General Le Trong in April 1984 were quite important. Besides, the visits of Vietnam's Defence Minister, Van Tien Dung in March 1985, Air Force Chief, Pham Thanh Ngan in March 1990 and Chief of General Staff, General Doan Khue in November 1990 were significant in its entirety. During all these visits, both countries discussed in detail the future of joint military, air and other spheres of strategic cooperation.[3]

However, the most striking event, which took place between India and Vietnam, during the Cold War period, was New Delhi's initiative to assist Hanoi to develop its alternative energy sources through peaceful use of nuclear energy. Since late 1982, Vietnam has paid attention to building the strategy and policy for national energy development. The peaceful use of nuclear energy is an important feature in this endeavour. Vietnam is a signatory to the International Atomic Energy Agency's (IAEA), Regional Cooperation Agreement (RCA) and South Asian Frameworks for Environmental Data-Sharing.

Although Vietnam's endeavour to procure energy is a recent phenomenon, its mindset about the utility of this resource dates back to 1980s, when it wanted to upgrade Dalat Nuclear Reactor with the help of erstwhile Soviet Union, which was disbanded by the US before it left Vietnam in 1975. Therefore, since the mid-1980s, besides the former Soviet Union, Vietnam took help from many other countries including India to construct its nuclear power plants for scientific research. During Pham Van Dong's visit to India in February 1978, Indian Prime Minister, Morarji Desai, offered to assist Vietnam in developing peaceful usage of nuclear energy. The process of Indian assistance started in August 1988, when a delegation of Indian Atomic Energy Commission, led by its Chairman, M.R. Srinivasan, visited Vietnam on 15 August 1988, and signed an accord on peaceful usage of atomic energy. Under the protocol and work plans signed under this agreement, a number of Vietnamese scientists and experts have received training in India. This nuclear accord, described as a 'memo of cooperation in the use of atomic energy for peaceful purposes',[4] is a milestone in India-Vietnam ties. India, owing to its cordial historical ties substantially helped Vietnam in this scientific endeavour. The kind of nuclear technical aid that New Delhi agreed to provide to Hanoi was initially not made public. The Vietnamese said that they planned to bring the Dalat nuclear research reactor back into operation with technical assistance from both India and the former USSR. It should be noted here that the Dalat nuclear reactor was built by the US in 1963, and in March 1975, Washington dismantled its main parts before withdrawing from South Vietnam, thus making it completely inoperative. From March 1982, with erstwhile Soviet assistance, restoration and expansion of this nuclear reactor had begun. This nuclear research reactor, with a capacity of 500 MW would be used for training scientific personnel for Vietnam's future nuclear power generation programme, for analysing mineral or biological samples, and for producing necessary isotopes for medical and agricultural research institutions.[5] Thus, from March 1982, with the assistance of erstwhile Soviet Union and India, restoration and expansion of this nuclear reactor was initiated. This initiative was however temporarily stopped owing to the sudden fall of the former Soviet Union and the adjustment of the economies of both India and Vietnam in the context of the New Global Order. Summarily then, it can be argued that India had evolved a strategic understanding with Vietnam during the Cold War period. During this time, India, with its limited capacity, had substantially contributed credit and other resource assistance to Vietnam to restructure its war-shattered economy. This specific pro-Vietnam policy, as followed by India mainly during the last two decades of the Cold War years, amply reflects New Delhi's focus on this country, rather than other ASEAN countries. Therefore, in the last two decades of the Cold War period, India's political and economic strategies while de-linked it from ASEAN countries; India carved out a niche for itself in the Indochina states, mainly Vietnam.

Post-Cold War Period

The sudden fall of the Soviet Union, followed by the changing dynamics of India's overall foreign policy towards the Southeast Asian region, reactivated the strategic importance of Vietnam for several reasons. First, the new economic policy of India in 1991, followed by its Look East Policy, coincided with Vietnam's transformation from a centralized planned economy to an open, liberalized market-oriented economy in 1986 through Doi Moi (renewal) reforms, brought the two countries economically and geo-politically closer to each other. Indian policy-makers foresighted that the global security situation of the 21st century will be more focused on the Asia-Pacific region, and where it has a role to play, along with other key players like China, United States, Russia, Japan, Australia, Vietnam, Singapore etc. on security issues.

New Delhi's growing involvement in the regional military-security framework, particularly through naval deployment and the Maritime Doctrine initiated in 2004 and modified later in 2009, amply demonstrates the fact that the New Delhi would not like the region to be dominated either by China, the US or Japan, individually or in conjunction with each other. Moreover, the safety of the sea-lanes, the coastal offshore areas, ports and harbours, through which over 70 per cent of India's oil is imported and 95 per cent of its overseas trade passes, remains vital for India's national interests.[6] The new Indian Maritime Doctrine visualized expansion of naval activities to the east, and a shift from coastal defence to operations in the wider Indian Ocean region, as the Indian Navy's 'legitimate areas of interest'. India's growing strategic interest in the region resulted in the conduct of a large number of regular bilateral and multilateral naval exercises with various ASEAN countries, such as Singapore (largest number), Myanmar, Thailand, Indonesia, Malaysia, Vietnam and the Philippines. Presently, Indian naval vessels move from Indian Ocean to the South China Sea. Apart from collaborating with the Southeast Asian countries, the Indian Navy has also started collaborating with the US Navy in patrolling the northern end of the Malacca Straits. In 2004, the Indian Navy conducted 'Operation Gambhir', for tsunami relief efforts in Indonesia's Aceh province. These remain clear examples of Indian naval presence in the region. Moreover, India has also been trying to diversify its energy resources, for which Indian Navy has been holding regular discussions with regional navies, making port calls and participating in international naval symposia.[7] In April-May 2007 India performed bilateral naval exercises with Vietnam, the Philippines, Malaysia, Singapore, and Indonesia. India's credible maritime profile, the absence of any maritime dispute with any of the ASEAN countries and its benign image has helped to develop strong maritime ties between South and Southeast Asian regions. India's strategic involvement in the region was demonstrated in 2000 through its bilateral and unilateral naval exercises in the South China Sea, an area next to China and claimed by it, but, disputed by Vietnam, Malaysia, Brunei and the Philippines. Consequently, 'by extending its area of operation into the South China Sea, India has presented a direct challenge to China' and 'promises...a redefinition of the naval balance of power in the region'.[8]

Second, at the multilateral level, New Delhi has become party to a series of institutions which bring it into greater contact with Southeast Asian countries. In 1996, India joined the ASEAN Regional Forum (ARF), the greater Asian region's first multilateral security institution. In 1995, New Delhi was promoted as a full dialogue partner and in 2002, a Summit level partner of ASEAN. In 2003, India's accession to ASEAN's Treaty of Amity and Cooperation and thereby agreeing not to interfere in the internal affairs of the Association's member states, further strengthened its position within the ASEAN orbit. Finally, with the support from ASEAN members, notably Singapore and Indonesia, India joined the ASEAN-led East Asian Summit (EAS) in 2005. The growing economic and strategic status of India bolstered its position, as along with economic matters, security issues became imperative for ASEAN as a grouping. For example, at the second ASEAN-India Summit in 2003, the two sides signed not only an agreement on comprehensive economic cooperation aimed at establishing a free trade area within 10 years (which was ultimately signed for trade in goods in 2009 but it has not been signed in services yet), but also ASEAN-India Joint Declaration for Cooperation to Combat International Terrorism, which accepted their mutual counter-terrorist interests in the contexts of increasing links between violent extremist movements, suffered by them.

Third, the burgeoning multi-directional defence diplomacy in Asia, on account of steering away from exclusive focus on economic issues in Phase-I to a broader agenda in Phase-II that involved security cooperation through India's Look East Policy, brought India closer to Vietnam. The military diplomacy, which India started with ASEAN countries on a low level in the early 1990s, has expanded into full-fledged defence cooperation with them (including Vietnam), and thereby gave New Delhi enough space as a major security player, which could offer a balancing role against the escalating Chinese military strength in the region.[9] India's growing prowess resulted in the regular defence exchanges and signing of a number of defence agreements with Southeast Asian countries and beyond. Since then, India's defence ties with the countries of Southeast Asia and beyond have reached a new height both at bilateral and multilateral level, with ASEAN as a regional bloc.[10]

Fourth, strategically placed on the eastern fringe of Southeast Asia, Vietnam figures prominently in the strategic calculus of both the US and China, in their approaches to East Asian security. India views Vietnam as the principal balancer to China's southward expansion. Convergence of geo-strategic interests on account of

China's emerging economic and naval strength, with reference to the pivotal location astride the sea-lanes of East Asia and South China Sea, has brought India and Vietnam together. Both countries are hesitant about China's entry into the Indian Ocean and the South China Sea. China has successfully exerted strategic pressure over India by bringing Myanmar and Pakistan within its sphere of influence. China has been insensitive to India's strategic imperatives, and has helped in building up of Pakistan's nuclear weapons and nuclear-capable missile arsenal. Then why should India be receptive to what China perceives with reference to Vietnam? India can play a vital role in the capacity-building of Vietnam's military, which will provide India an opportunity to pressurize China. In relation to Southeast Asia, India perceived that convergence in security perspectives and commitment to peace and stability in the region, and for maintaining security of sea-lanes of communications, assistance in capacity-building to the regional armed forces to deal with maritime challenges would be conducive for its own overall economic and social growth. Keeping these in mind, New Delhi initiated capacity-building of the Vietnamese armed forces, as Vietnam's pivotal location makes it extremely important for the emerging security architecture in the region. This strategic thinking was also endorsed by Vietnam in principle. Therefore, converging interests are compelling both India and Vietnam to establish a strong bond partnership, because both feel that the growing Chinese influence in the region is a major threat to the existing power structure in Asia, and to counter balance this, it is crucial for them to work together, as well as lend a helping hand to other players, to restrict China's ambitions to seek a hegemonic role in the region in future. Thus, the 'China factor' plays a major role in the emerging strategic calculus of both India and Vietnam.[11]

Finally, owing to its geo-strategic location in the neighbourhood of China, Vietnam holds the key to any future strategy of containing Beijing's hegemonic rise. It is significant to note that the US opted for a policy of rapprochement (since 1995) with Vietnam after a long period of isolation. In recent years, the two countries have expanded their political and security exchanges through commencement of dialogues on economic and regional security issues.

Although both the US and Vietnam emphasize that the budding bilateral strategic relations is not aimed at China, Hanoi is a major offshore oil producer in the South China Sea and it has an incentive to involve as many foreign powers as possible to reinforce its claim in the region. From Vietnam's point of view, strengthening strategic cooperation with India is in their mutual interest. Furthermore, the drastic improvement in relations between India and the US following Indo-US civil nuclear cooperation agreement in 2008 has further boosted New Delhi-Hanoi relations. As against such background, the Prime Minister of the Socialist Republic of Vietnam, Nguyen Tan Dung visited India from 4-6 July 2007, and signed an agreement on Vietnam-India Strategic Partnership.[12]

Defence Cooperation

Historically and geopolitically, India's association with the Southeast Asian region has been governed by two important links, land and sea. The peninsular Southeast Asia was a geographically contiguous region with India connected by land routes. In this backdrop, their common adversary i.e. China, with whom past bitter experiences have governed both countries relations, brought them closer to each other. Given such a common outlook, New Delhi's military ties with Hanoi developed slowly but steadily since the Cold War era. That position gathered thrust in the post-Cold War period, following the defence agreement signed between New Delhi and Hanoi, during Indian Prime Minister Narasimha Rao's visit to Vietnam in September 1994. The main focus of this agreement was to encourage cooperation between the defence establishments of the two countries, centred on safeguarding and preserving military equipments, supplied to Vietnam by the erstwhile Soviet Union. This agreement was not planned against any third country.[13]

In August 1997, at the Eighth India-Vietnam Joint Commission meeting in Hanoi, India offered to supply spare parts to Vietnam, apart from providing its service of Soviet-origin defence equipments on a commercial basis. The documents, which were finalized after the meeting, clearly stated that, 'cooperation in defence is an important aspect of bilateral relations between India and Vietnam.'[14] It was also decided that New Delhi and Hanoi would take essential steps to execute the provisions of the 'Protocol on Defence Cooperation' signed during the visit to Vietnam by Narasimha Rao in 1994, and agreed that periodic exchange of visits of defence personnel, exchange of information, transfer of relevant technologies and repair, maintenance and up-gradation of defence equipments were all 'important elements' of Indo-Vietnamese defence cooperation. Following this meeting, in late March 2000, India's Defence Minister, George Fernandes paid an official visit to Hanoi, which became the first ever visit by an Indian Defence Minister to Vietnam. As the most remarkable facet of this visit, a 15-point agreement was signed between the two countries and among them, the two Navies, the Indian Coast Guards and the Vietnamese sea-police agreed to cooperate with each other in combating piracy. After the signing of this agreement, the Indian Defence Minister hailed Vietnam as India's 'most trusted friend and ally', and clearly mentioned that Hanoi 'stood by us after the nuclear tests because they understand that if [India] went nuclear there were good security reasons for it', and thereby implied the 'China threat' was unmistakable. Finally, the Indian Defence Minister described this cooperation as the beginning of a 'periodical security dialogue', and agreed to assist Vietnam in the process of setting up its defence industry and opened its doors to the research conducted by the Defence Research and Development Organization (DRDO) of India. These steps were taken to help Vietnam in building its armed forces, and thereby institutionalising military relations between the two countries. It paved the way for regular meetings between the Defence Ministers of the two countries to discuss matters relating to shared threat perceptions, and the way for visits of Indian ships to Vietnamese ports and greater collaborations through naval exercises.[15] Therefore, this defence accord established the space for regular meetings between the Defence Ministers as well as for visits by Indian naval ships to Vietnamese ports and extensive collaboration through bilateral naval exercises.

Historically, Vietnam had an adverse relation with China, having fought its last war with China in 1979. Although Vietnam has been able to resolve most of its land border dispute with China skilfully, the mutual confidence between the two countries has not yet been fully restored. Presently, India and the US are primarily considering Vietnam's importance vis-à-vis their anti-China stance, as a result of Hanoi's past bitter relations with Beijing and its geo-strategic location, in terms of its proximity to the Sea Lines of Communication (SLOC) and to China. Axiomatically, the imperative of India's strategic endeavour to support in building Vietnam's armed forces to be militarily sturdy has been justified. During Nguyen Tan Dung's visit to India, on 6 July 2007, both countries agreed to promote cooperation in seven areas to improve regional security, including a pledge to strengthen cooperation in defence supplies, joint projects, training and intelligence exchanges. They also agreed to enhance cooperation in capacity building, technical assistance and information-sharing between their relevant agencies for ensuring security of sea-lanes, by combating piracy, preventing pollution and conducting search and rescue operations.[16]

Following this visit, India and Vietnam agreed on a plethora of measures to further expand relations in defence, when the Indian Defence Minister, A.K. Antony visited Vietnam in December 2007. During his meeting with his Vietnamese counterpart, Gen. Phung Quang Thanh in Hanoi, Antony agreed to transfer 5,000 spare parts belonging to Petya class of ships to infuse life into many of the Vietnamese ageing vessels. The Indian leader suggested increasing the frequency of goodwill visits by naval ships, application of information technology in defence, e-technology and technical support to the Vietnamese navy. Additionally, India agreed to dispatch a four-member army team to conduct training for UN peacekeeping operations. Finally, the two sides agreed to set up a Joint Working Group to facilitate the signing of a Memorandum of Understanding on defence cooperation including national defence, navy, air defence and personnel training. The Indian delegation visited defence industries in Ho Chi Minh City, while the Vietnamese Defence Minister sought Indian support in training of defence personnel, enhancing the exchanges of delegations, expanding training cooperation, increasing the frequency of goodwill visits by naval ships, application of information technology, e-technology and technical support for the Vietnamese navy. So far, 49 Vietnamese officers have attended various army and navy courses in India and 64 officers have attended English language courses.[17] Before that, at the 3rd India-Vietnam Security Dialogue meeting held in New Delhi in November 2007, both countries had agreed to exchange visits for better appreciation of the other country's requirements and problems, greater cooperation in the field of training of service personnel, particularly junior level officers, security dialogue at least once a year, sharing of expertise on issues of common concerns such as maritime security, border management and counter-insurgency, conduct of training for Vietnamese officers for UN Peacekeeping operations, invitation to Vietnamese officers to Indian military exercises as observers etc, aimed at providing greater impetus to their growing relationship.[18] These agreements reiterated India's desire to fortify common understanding, friendship and cooperation with Vietnam in the region.

Meanwhile, in continuation of this defence cooperation, in the succeeding years, a number of visits and counter-visits took place between India and Vietnam. Among these visits, the Indian Army Chief, General V.K. Singh's July 2010 visit was quite significant. Like the Cold War period, this was the first time in the post-Cold War years that an Indian Army Chief had visited Vietnam to implement the roadmap of the 2009 MoU between Ministries of Defence between the two countries. Nevertheless, the most striking event, which took place in 2010, was the First ASEAN Defence Ministers' Meeting Plus Eight (ADMM+8) held in Hanoi in October. This ADMM+8 is a gathering of ASEAN Defence Ministers and other stakeholders in the region including Australia, China, India, Japan, New Zealand, South Korea, Russia and the US, to collectively handle security issues such as terrorism, piracy, disaster relief and transnational crimes. In this meeting, the Indian Defence Minister, A.K. Antony held discussions with Vietnamese leadership and agreed to provide support for enhancing and upgrading capabilities in defence services in general, and Navy in particular.[19] He assured that India would help Vietnam in capacity building for repair and maintenance of its platforms. The Armies of the two countries would cooperate in areas like IT, English Training of Vietnamese Army personnel and joint training for both the armies in conducting mountain and jungle warfare in India next year. While expressing satisfaction on India-Vietnam defence cooperation, the Vietnamese Prime Minister, Dung asserted that 'Vietnam-India strategic partnership is a good model. Our traditional and friendly co-operation has been consolidated by generations of two countries' leadership.'

However, the growing defence understanding between India and Vietnam slightly reduced its tempo, when Hanoi expressed its dissatisfaction on India's lack of commitment to supply some of the missile systems as agreed by India earlier for modernising Vietnam's military. It has to be noted that during the tenure of BJP government it was decided that India would gift the Prithvi and Brahmos missile systems to Vietnam, to counter Chinese naval dominance in the South China Sea, by aiding Vietnam in sea denial strategy and coastal defence. Unfortunately, India failed to maintain its commitment due to two important reasons and they were: first, the Congress government has increasingly focused on economic rather than military cooperation with Vietnam, and thereby, has tried not to antagonize its immediate neighbour, China, with which New Delhi is building better ties; and second, some analysts feel that the Brahmos should be first fully inducted into the Indian Armed Forces, before a surplus can be generated for friendly countries such as Vietnam.

Vietnam procured 100 SMG-PK 9 mm submachine guns and 50 sniper rifles from the state-run Pakistan Ordnance Factories (POF) in Rawalpindi in 2007, in a veiled but significant expression of its displeasure with New Delhi.[20] This misunderstanding however withered away when India in September 2011 entered into negotiations with Vietnam to sell its first Brahmos cruise missiles to a foreign country. Brahmos stealth missile is capable of being launched from submarines, aircraft, or land, and is the fastest supersonic missile in the world. This decision was taken after an Indian Ship was halted by the Chinese after leaving port, and following China's admonition that India best stay away from exploring in the South China Sea. The Brahmos missiles are the result of a joint venture between Russia and India, and will be of immense value in boosting Vietnam's defence preparedness. This move of New Delhi further underscores importance in ongoing strategic ties between India and Vietnam in the face of China's assertiveness in the South China Sea region.[21] The growing security understanding between India and Vietnam was further strengthened in October 2009, when both countries agreed to hold regular 'Strategic Dialogue'. The First Strategic Dialogue and the Fourth Political Consultative meeting between the two countries were held on 15 October 2009 at New Delhi. Subsequently, regular biennial dialogues on security issues at various levels have been held and institutionalized. Among these regular meetings, the visit of the President of Vietnam, Truong Tan Sang to India from 11-13 October, 2011, remains quite outstanding. It is notable that President Sang chose India for his first official visit to a non-ASEAN country after assuming office. At the time of his visit, among other things, defence and security, energy, oil and gas, agriculture, science and technology, information and communications technology etc. were discussed in detail, and several agreements were signed. Among these agreements, the Extradition Treaty, Agreement on Cooperation between PetroVietnam and ONGC Videsh Limited, Work Plan for the years 2011-2013 in the fields of agriculture, fishery research and education etc are most striking. Also, since defence cooperation has emerged as a significant pillar of India's strategic partnership with Vietnam, new initiatives were taken in defence industry, research and development, and 'think-tanks' related areas.[22] The growing defence dialogue and cooperation between India and Vietnam continued its rhythm when the two countries exchanged views on the security situation in the region and the rest of the world, regional security structures and bilateral defence ties, at the 7th Vietnam-India Defence Strategy Dialogue, held in New Delhi on 26 September 2012. In this meeting, the Vietnamese Ministry of National Defence, led by Deputy Minister, Senior Lieutenant-General Nguyen Chi Vinh, and the Indian Defence Ministry, led by Deputy Secretary Shashi Kant Shamar, held discussion mainly on security issues affecting both countries and agreed to accelerate future cooperation in the context of existing Vietnam-India Strategic Partnership, in some fields, including the national defence industry, military techniques, training and practicing, and all-round cooperative ties in various fields between the two armies.[23]

It is to be mentioned here in this connection, that in recent times, a number of security dialogue and defence agreements are taking place in South, Southeast and East Asian region among regional countries as well as with extra-regional powers. The security dialogue, related to various agreements and joint naval exercises between India and Vietnam, Vietnam and the United States, China and Vietnam (since 2009), China and South Korea, United States and Bangladesh, United States and India, China and Sri Lanka, United States and China (started since 2003), Vietnam and Australia and Japan, United States and the Philippines etc. are remarkable. Following these trends, Vietnam has conducted frequent defence dialogues at various levels with ASEAN member countries, and other countries such as China, Russia, the United States, Japan, France, India and so on. This new dynamics of Vietnamese defence policy, as mentioned in the Vietnam Defence White Paper of 2009, clearly stated that the 'guideline of not using force or threatening of using force in international relations; solved differences and disputes with other countries by peaceful means. Vietnam advocates the gradual modernization of Vietnamese Army and enhancing defence potential only to maintain its military power, sufficient for its self-defence. Vietnam opposes arms race and opposes the military use of force in international relations, but is ready to resolutely fight against all aggressive acts'.[24] This White Paper also mentioned that, 'Defence cooperation is one of the most important factors for maintaining peace and stability in the region and the world. It is also important for achieving Vietnam's defence goals. Therefore, Vietnam advocates expanding defence diplomacy and actively participating in defence and security cooperation in the regional and international community to reinforce the friendship, mutual understanding, confidence building, and conflict prevention.'[25] In such backdrop, over the last few years, Vietnam has consciously pursued a balanced and 'omni-directional foreign policy.' Vietnam has been moulded by a national interest in protecting the basis for a more constant, focused, and market-driven economic growth, and of the need for a broader regional recognition and global respect in trade and aid linkages. In this way, Vietnam has become efficient in making strategic judgments, collaborating with big powers, sustaining links with neighbours, and developing capacities to execute as a member of numerous multilateral communities.[26] With this mindset, like India, Vietnam since 2010 has started strategic defence dialogue with China, 'to strengthen trust between the two countries'. affirm Vietnam's unchangeable standpoint in defence relations with China and push the implementation of high-level declarations and agreements on bilateral defence ties, as well as to affirm its standpoints relating to territorial sovereignty on sea issues', as stated by the Deputy Defence Minister, Senior Lieutenant-General Nguyen Chi Vinh, at the Third Defence Dialogue between Vietnam and China on 3 September 2012, in Hanoi.[27] Regarding the East Asia sea dispute, the Vietnamese Lieutenant-General, Nguyen Chi Vinh, at the Second Defence, Security Dialogue meeting held on 31 August 2011 in Beijing mentioned that this issue 'has three closely-related aspects, namely the declaration of sovereignty by concerned countries, solving issues related to the ties between Vietnam and China, and solving issues at multilateral forums'[28] and thereby signalled clearly its strategic position on the issue. The signing of a joint patrol agreement in the Tonkin Gulf area in October 2005 was a clear highlight in the relations between the Vietnamese and Chinese navies. Within the framework of this agreement, the joint naval patrols regularly organized different activities including joint training, search and rescue and handling of non-traditional security issues at sea. The annual meeting of the two naval delegations in Hai Phong city in 2011 clearly exhibited the ongoing cordial ties between them.

Like China, strategic cooperation between Vietnam and the United States started since 2003. This growing security understanding has evolved on account of three important reasons: first, both countries have common complex relationships with China; second, the US wants greater access to Vietnamese ports for its warships and Vietnam wants the US to remove restrictions on arms sales; and third, Vietnam can be a better strategic space for the US to counter the growing Chinese presence in the Southeast and Asia-Pacific region. US-Vietnam relations is mainly centred on four pillars: first, bilateral relations like people-to-people exchanges; second, major international security issues like non-proliferation, counter-terrorism etc; third, emerging global issues like, health, development, energy, climate change, environment, and global institutions; fourth, humanitarian response to civil and natural incidents; and finally, regional security and stability issues in Afghanistan/Pakistan, Iran, North Korea, Human Rights, military to military relations, as well as peacekeeping.

Interestingly enough, on 20 September 2011, the Deputy Assistant Secretary of Defence for South and Southeast Asia and Vietnam's Deputy Defence Minister signed an MoU for 'advancing bilateral defence cooperation', and both countries identified five areas to expand cooperation in maritime security, search and rescue, United Nations Peacekeeping Operations (UNPKO), humanitarian and disaster relief (HADR), and collaboration between defence universities and research institutes. From the Vietnamese point of view this expanded defence and security cooperation with the U.S. can partly be explained as Vietnamese attempt to hedge bets in a contest with a vigorously assertive and aggressively inclined China, and encouraging economic relationships that will contribute to modernization. It also sees the acceptance of the formality of a defence relationship with Washington as one way of coping with China's strategic intentions of increasing its influence in East Asia.[29] However, this posture of Vietnam to develop defence dialogue with various countries could be interpreted as a balancing role in the Southeast Asian region and beyond and thereby not to antagonize any power of the globe, against the backdrop of its 'omni-directional foreign policy.' Meanwhile, on 18 April 2012, India launched Agni-V missile to boost the country's rocket hitting capability of over 5,000 kms. This two-stage missile, equipped with an advanced high-accuracy navigation system and guided by a novel state-of-the-art command and control system, is powered by a solid rocket propellant structure. It can strike targets across China, potentially freeing up other short and intermediate-range missiles for use against Pakistan and much of West and South-central China. The Chinese reaction with reference to this testing was not favourable. The Global Times, on 19 April 2012, wrote: 'India should not overestimate its strength. Even if it has missiles that could reach most parts of China that does not mean it will gain anything from being arrogant during disputes with China. India should be clear that China's nuclear power is stronger and more reliable. For the foreseeable future, India would stand no chance in an overall arms race with China. India should also not overstate the value of its Western allies and the profits it could gain from participating in a containment of China. If it equates long range strategic missiles with deterrence of China, and stirs up further hostility, it could be sorely mistaken'.[30] However, this event was only highlighted by Vietnamese media. Chinese thought that their bullying regional policy will eventually have the entire Asia-Pacific region under their sway. But in practice, the result has been the opposite, driving Japan, the Philippines, Vietnam and even Myanmar closer to the US as a countervailing regional power.

Therefore, in a nutshell, while exploring the history of victories in wars against powerful states, Vietnam wants to present itself with economic competence and military strength in the emerging security architecture of the Southeast Asian region and beyond. For Vietnam, India rationally appears to be a suitable partner at this point of time, since military doctrine of both countries is defensive in nature. For India, expanding defence ties with Vietnam would create a dependable, committed partner in Southeast Asia and thereby emphasize the larger role it visualizes through its Look East Policy framework. Moreover, New Delhi looks towards Vietnam as a counter-weight to China, on account of the latter's increasing presence in the Indian Ocean, South and Southeast Asian regions. Thus, the emerging security architecture in the Asia-Pacific region makes Vietnam an ideal partner for India. So as a first step for a meaningful and sustained engagement with Vietnam, India requires broad-based involvement with continuous pro-active defence cooperation as an important tool to keep its presence felt in Southeast and East Asia along the Asia-Pacific rim region.

Naval Cooperation

The ongoing defence understanding had a spill over effect on the development of naval cooperation between India and Vietnam. The importance of the Indian Navy in New Delhi's foreign policy was propelled as early as late 1980s, when build up in the Andaman and Nicobar island bases on account of securing the sea lines of communication (SLOCS) in the Indian Ocean and the Arabian Gulf. This Mahanian naval interest evolved with India's trade with East and Southeast Asia, especially following its Look East Policy in early 1990s, which got amplified with the formation of ARF in 1994. The emergence of regional security architecture and establishment of ARF as a regional institution evolved on account of multiple security challenges, namely, competitive military spending, territorial disputes, growing ethnic and religious disputes, terrorism and piracy. These security challenges generated a great deal of uncertainty about the prospects of regional peace and stability. Although this region has witnessed growing economic collaboration and some progress in institution building, the risk of armed conflict remains grave in many areas. To overcome these challenges led to the formation of ARF, which provided a base for cooperation on these issues. The naval cooperation between India and Vietnam was further accelerated after Vietnam's joining ASEAN in 1995. So, India's Look East Policy and Vietnam's entry into ASEAN brought the two countries closer to each other, leading them to embark upon a mission to strengthen their naval ties and establish sustainable maritime cooperation between them.

The Indian naval manoeuvrability reached its height following New Delhi's Maritime Doctrine in April 2004, which was modified in 2009.[31] Through this Doctrine, the Indian navy can move in the Indian Ocean region and further east, thereby becoming a Pacific player. The Indian intention to expand its naval activities was reiterated at the Fifth Shangri-La Dialogue, held in Singapore in 2006, where then Minister of Defence, Pranab Mukherjee, spelt out India's defence policy to safeguard its territorial integrity and sovereignty; to promote durable peace in the immediate neighbourhood, including the Indian Ocean region; and to promote economic and social development. India hoped to become a key strategic player in Asia by virtue of its strong economy.

The summary of the speech clearly outlines certain agendas. These are: first, India sought to enhance its existing political, economic and security ties with countries in the South, Southeast, Northeast and Central Asia. This would enable India to increase its diplomatic influence and reduce tensions between China and India, allowing scarce resources to be channelled into developing India's economic and technological capabilities. Second, India sought to increase its strategic influence over key maritime and energy routes passing through the Indian Ocean, Arabian Sea, Bay of Bengal and the Straits of Malacca. Its role and importance in the energy supply chain, would lead to a concomitant rise in India's influence in the world stage, especially as energy security has become key to global politics. India hopes to use its influence to prevent any disruption in supplies of energy and raw materials that are vitally needed to drive its economy. To counter attempts by potential rivals to project power against India by gaining footholds in India's immediate neighbourhood. It is against this backdrop that the growing defence relations between India and ASEAN member countries should be understood.[32] Interestingly enough, before the Maritime Doctrine was announced by New Delhi, after Indian Defence Minister, George Fernandes's official visit to Vietnam in March 2000, a number of Indian naval ships visited Vietnam and tested the future viability and strategic cooperation in the naval domain between the two countries. For example, the Naval Ship 'INS-Rajput' undertook a goodwill visit to Ho Chi Minh City from 28 September to 1 October 2000.[33] In 2001, an Indian Coastguard vessel 'Sangram' made a goodwill visit to Ho Chi Minh City from 7-9 June, on its way back after participating in the 'Coastguard Fleet Review' in Japan. This was the first ever stopover by an Indian Coastguard ship in Vietnam. In the same year, two Indian naval ships 'INS Mumbai' and 'INS Jyoti' paid three-day goodwill visit to Ho Chi Minh City from 29-31 October.[34] Similarly in November 2004, three Indian naval ships namely, 'INS Ranvijay', 'INS Sukanya' and 'INS Kirch' paid goodwill visits to Ho Chi Minh City and this trip was commanded by Rear Admiral S.K. Damle, Flag Officer Commanding-in-Chief (FOC) of the Eastern Naval Fleet.[35] As a follow up action of the ongoing naval venture, from

9-13 June 2005, the Indian naval vessel 'INS Magar' again paid goodwill visit to Vietnam.[36] Like previous years, from 8-11 June 2006, three Indian naval ships, 'INS Rajput', 'INS Kulish' and 'INS Kirpan', led by Rear Admiral D.K. Joshi, FOC, Eastern Fleet visited Tien Sea Port at Da Nang City of Vietnam.[37] The continuity of defence exchanges and regular Indian naval vessels to Vietnam exhibited further momentum, when two Indian Navy ships, namely 'INS Mysore' and 'INS Ranjit' and a Coast Guard ship 'ICGS Sagar' docked at a port in Ho Chi Minh City from 7-11 May and 12-14 May 2007 respectively, and India supplied free equipment to the Vietnamese navy to repair its facilities.[38] So all these naval visits by India clearly demonstrates its strength, subsistence and mobility, primarily considering Vietnam's importance for its anti-China stand, due to past experiences and geo-strategic location in proximity to the SLOC area.

India's importance for Southeast Asia, especially for Vietnam became apparent in 2007, when both countries agreed to play an important role in the promotion of regional security and pledged to fortify cooperation in defence supplies, joint projects, training cooperation and intelligence exchanges. They agreed to work closely between defence and security establishments, enhance cooperation in capacity building, technical assistance and information-sharing for ensuring security of sea-lanes, including combating piracy, preventing pollution and conducting search and rescue operations.[39]

The evolving naval cooperation between India and Vietnam was further strengthened on account of India's announcement of Maritime Doctrine in April 2004. On 21 April 2008, the Flag Officer Commanding-in-Chief of the Indian Eastern Naval Command visited Hanoi with two naval ships, 'INS Kora' and 'INS Kirpan', thereby reiterating India's craving to buttress mutual understanding, friendship and cooperation between the two naval forces. Following this visit, in succeeding years, a number of visits and counter-visits took place between India and Vietnam. Among these, the Indian Army Chief, General V.K. Singh's July 2010 visit is quite significant. In the meantime, the first ASEAN Defence Ministers' Plus Eight Dialogue Partners Meeting (ADMM+8) was held in Hanoi in October 2010, and where the Indian Defence Minister, A.K. Antony held discussions with Vietnamese leadership and agreed to support to enhance and upgrade the naval and defence capabilities of Vietnam. It also guaranteed that New Delhi would help Hanoi in its capacity-building for repair and maintenance of its platforms. The Armies of the two countries would cooperate in areas like Information Technology (IT), English Training of Vietnamese Army personnel and conduct joint training in mountain and jungle warfare in India in 2011.[40] The most conspicuous event on the ongoing naval cooperation took place in 2011, when the Indian naval warships were granted permission to drop anchor at the Na Trang port in southern Vietnam. This Vietnamese move assumes significance due to the fact that the Indian Navy is the only foreign navy to have been granted such a privilege at a port other than Halong Bay near Hanoi. It was to facilitate the presence of Indian Navy in the South China Sea, to enable India to play greater strategic role in Southeast Asia. India and Vietnam are wary of growing Chinese military capacity as well as their increasing assertiveness in the region. The decision to give India this privilege was done following the visit of Vietnamese Naval Chief, Nguyen Van Hien to India in late June 2011. At the time of this visit, Nguyen Van Hien visited the public sector shipbuilder, Mazagon Dock Limited in Mumbai and Hindustan Shipyard Limited in Vishakhapatnam. He realized Indian naval ship-building capacities and functioning of the defence shipyard[41], and decided to secure Indian assistance for augmenting the size and capabilities of the Vietnamese navy. The Indian Navy dropping anchor in Na Trang port is important from a larger Indian effort to counter Chinese activities in South Asia, to monitor the South China Sea side of the Straits of Malacca, and securing India's energy and commercial shipping originating in East Asia. In September 2011, India and Vietnam agreed that India would train the Vietnam in submarine operations, mainly in 'intensive' submarine and underwater warfare training, as part of the expanding military ties.[42] The proposed training programme for Vietnamese sailors will take place at Indian Navy's submarine school INS Satavahana in Vishakapatanam, which is equipped with advanced training aids and other facilities. Also, India concurred to continue to train Vietnamese naval personnel and help maintain any equipment that Vietnam sources from Russia, in addition to providing aid to Vietnam to increase its naval strength by building ships and other necessary training facilities.

While defending India's stand on docking rights for its warships and facilities to post naval instructors in Cam Ranh Bay on Vietnam's south-central coast, and at Na Trang, 60 km north of the bay, which are on a busy commercial route cutting through South China Sea, Vishnu Prakash, the spokesperson of the Ministry of External Affairs, Government of India, in an interview said: "What I know is that security and defence co-operation are again important facets of co-operation with Vietnam. We have a memorandum of defence co-operation that was concluded in 2009. We have regular high-level exchanges, both military to military, as well as at the political and official levels visits. Our ships regularly pay port calls in Vietnam and vice versa. We have joint training. We have exchange of information."[43] Therefore, in a nutshell the growing defence cooperation between India and Vietnam has been centred on a number of important factors, which are as follows: First, the long-pending territorial disputes with China, in which India and Vietnam have been the common sufferers. Second, China's recent muscle flexing with reference to the South China Sea is another problem. It was felt by the Indian policy makers that, Vietnam's location is ideal to prevent China's expansion and thereby, to deny Beijing's total domination in the South China Sea. Both feel that growing Chinese influence is a threat to the existing power structure in Asia and to counterbalance Beijing's escalating military prowess in the region, it is imperative to work together as well as lend a helping hand to major powers involved in the region's security dynamics. Finally, a number of emerging non-traditional security threats, in the Straits of Malacca and the Indian Ocean Region, provide India an opportunity to upgrade its naval strength through its Maritime Doctrine. Presently, like Vietnam, India has also started security dialogue with Japan, South Korea and the US to safeguard the SLOCs for making this route free from the control of any power. A point to be mentioned in connection of India's growing naval deployment in the Asia-Pacific region is the month-long deployment of a flotilla of Indian warships, which visited Australia, Indonesia, Singapore and Vietnam and sounded an indirect alarm over China's increasing forays into the Indian Ocean region, which is poised to become the new playground for the Great Game of the 21st Century in the coming years.[44] Moreover, it was felt by the Chinese leadership that the proposal to outline a new quadrilateral alliance in the Asia-Pacific region, consisting of the US, Japan, India, Vietnam and Australia in a soft, 'values-based' containment initiative (the Quad Initiative), was directed against China. The Chinese government identified this plan as a direct threat to its naval deployment since it centred around China's national interest, defined in terms of its economic survival and empowerment. To develop a presence in the South China Sea region, which connects the hydrocarbon-rich Persian and Arab states to the Chinese coastline, and to maintain larger naval deployments in the Spratly archipelago, and eastern approaches to the Straits of Malacca, China enhanced its defence budget and modernised its existing equipment, focusing on building of new classes of conventional, nuclear and ballistic missile submarines[45]. As against this backdrop, both India and Vietnam felt the necessity of building strategic partnership, based on convergence of interests.

Nuclear Cooperation

Vietnam has no nuclear power plant and it is preparing for nuclear power electricity generation, to reduce its dependence on hydro and fossil fuel resources. Although the State-owned EVN (Electricity Vietnam) has done a feasibility study on nuclear energy, concluding that the country has the capability for nuclear power, concerns remain about experience, safety, technology and management of such a plant. For the peaceful use of nuclear energy, since the 1980s, Vietnam has paid attention to building the strategy and policy for national energy development, and called for international support and cooperation. Based on Vietnam's adherence to international nuclear transparency, it took help from many other countries including India besides the former Soviet Union, to develop its nuclear power plants for scientific research. India's assistance in this scientific endeavour stemmed from its cordial historical ties, and that process started in the Cold War period. This Cold War proposal between India and Vietnam was revived in the post-Cold War years and presently, Vietnam has drawn plans to harness nuclear energy for electricity generation to diversify and also lessen its reliance on hydrocarbon-based energy resources. Vietnam plans to build eight nuclear power plants in five provinces by 2030 with a total capacity of 15 Gigawatts, or 10 per cent of all electricity produced in the country. Vietnam's first nuclear power plant is expected to be built between 2015 and 2020 in Ninh Thuan province and for that, it is looking towards a plethora of nuclear technology capable countries such as Canada, China, Russia, France, Japan, South Korea, India and the US for cooperation and assistance. So far, Vietnam has signed two agreements in 2010 with the US and Russia for acquiring nuclear reactors. The Russian agreement visualizes building two power units with an ability of 1.2 Gigawatts each and also loan for the nuclear power plant construction. However, Vietnam needs trained human resources to handle the nuclear infrastructure, draft national legislation and for conceptualization of nuclear safety and security arrangements. Furthermore, in the wake of the Fukushima nuclear disaster in Japan, the Vietnamese Government is paying greater awareness to the safety of the nuclear power plants and has established a special committee for training the scientists.[46]

As a part of the earlier understanding, on 23 April 1999, the Indian Atomic Energy Commission (a part of the IDAE) and the Vietnam Atomic Energy Commission (VAEC) signed agreement for cooperation in the field of nuclear power, exchange of scientists and assistance in setting up a training centre in Vietnam. Under this agreement, around 30 Vietnamese nuclear scientists have received training at the Bhabha Atomic Research Centre (BARC) in Mumbai and few Indian scientists have visited Dalat in order to complete Vietnam's nuclear energy programme by 2015. Furthermore, in January 2001, the Indian Prime Minister, Atal Behari Vajpayee paid an official visit to Vietnam. During his stay in Hanoi, the two countries signed a MoU between the Department of Atomic Energy and Ministry of Science, Technology and Environment of Vietnam.

The basis of this MoU has been the agreement between the two governments for the cooperation in Utilization of Atomic Energy for Peaceful Purposes signed in 1988, which was valid till May 2002. It also accorded continued cooperation in the field of human resource development and exchange of expertise.[47] This agreement was an extension of the earlier MoU signed by New Delhi and Hanoi on 23 April 1999. Moreover, in 2005, India supplied, under international nuclear regulatory norms, cobalt, a critical source for a nuclear unit, to Ho Chi Minh City built by the Hungarians in the 1980s. India with a rich experience in nuclear energy operations can offer Vietnam its capacities in training skilled nuclear human resources to pave the way for bilateral cooperation in nuclear trade and fuel reprocessing. In the wake of the 1999 agreement, so far, more than twenty-five Vietnamese scientists have received training at BARC and four Indian scientists have visited Dalat to complete Vietnam's nuclear energy programme by 2015. Moreover, in February 2006, the Vietnamese government announced that a 2000 MW nuclear power plant would be on line by 2020[48], and where the feasibility study of this would be completed by the end of 2008, with a target to start construction in 2011 and commissioning by 2017. India-Vietnam nuclear energy cooperation has not been operating effectively, on account of US's non cooperative attitude both towards India and Vietnam. However, in recent times, the US has relaxed its earlier outlook towards Vietnam, in the backdrop of growing Chinese presence in the South China Sea region. Therefore, in a nutshell, it can be said that the issue of civil nuclear cooperation has been a major event in the bilateral trajectory between New Delhi and Hanoi and a clear manifestation of a major thrust in India's Look East Policy in the post-Cold War era.

Energy Cooperation

Another major issue in the emerging global politics is the procurement and conservation of energy, since the demand for energy sources has been deeply connected with economic development. Like China and India, Vietnam, as a leading producer of oil and gas, is crucial for India's quest to diversify its energy supply sources. India has been looking for overseas exploration rights and Vietnam has been a success story in this regard.[49] The ONGC Videsh Ltd. (OVL) was selected as the successful bidder in the global competitive bidding for nine offshore exploration blocks in Vietnam in 2004, and signed a petroleum sharing contract with Petro-Vietnam for three blocks-06, 12E and 19 in Nam Con Son basin, about 370 km offshore. Moreover, it also signed a MoU with Petro-Vietnam Investment and Development Company (PIDC) on 9 January 2001 for collaboration between OVL and PIDC in the exploration and production of hydrocarbons in Vietnam.[50] Also, on 24 May 2006, OVL signed another production sharing contract with Vietnam Oil and Gas Corporation (PetroVietnam) for Blocks 127 and 128, off shore Vietnam in the Phu Khanh Basin.[51] With this agreement, it is believed that the energy cooperation between the two countries has been strengthened gradually, following the process of refining facilities of oil developed in India. The major rationale for India's oil and gas exploration is based on the ground that, 'collaboration with China would be on the Chinese terms and will also help China strengthen and legitimise its extensive claims once it is present in these areas even if for developmental purposes'.[52] Unfortunately, this growing India-Vietnam cooperation for oil exploration, in the sovereign territory of Vietnam, is not looked at by China favourably.

Unfortunately, in recent years there have been diplomatic rows between the two countries on the issue of gas exploration by Petro-Vietnam and British Petroleum (BP) in the planned US$ 2 billion gas field and pipeline venture, Southeast of Vung Tau on the southern coast, which is close to the Lan lay-Lan Do project in which ONGC is a partner. China does not want ONGC in the South China Sea and has been trying to allure Vietnamese oil companies into joint exploration so that Indian companies will face competition in coming years.[53] Moreover, the BP, which is raising capital to cover the cleanup costs of its oil spill in the Gulf of Mexico, has put many of its global assets for sale, including an investment in the Nam Con Son basin off the southern coast of Vietnam. The Vietnam Government has approved a consortium of state-owned Indian energy firms and PetroVietnam to buy out BP's stake. Significantly, this large-scale natural gas project is located in an area of the Nam Con Son basin where BP announced in March 2009 that it would cease exploration in response to pressure from China.[54] As against such backdrop, in October 2010, the Indian Petroleum Minister, Murli Deora agreed to buy BP's 35 per cent stake in the US$ 1.3 billion Nam Con Son gas project in Vietnam, and thereby integrated Indian presence in the oil exploration venture with Vietnam in the South China Sea region. This was not received well by China.

In this background, at the invitation of the Foreign Minister of the Socialist Republic of Vietnam, Pham Binh Minh, the Indian Minister of External Affairs, S.M. Krishna visited Vietnam from 15-17 September 2011, in connection with the 14th India-Vietnam Joint Commission Meeting (JCM) on Trade, Economic, Scientific and Technological Cooperation. During this meeting, both countries expressed their satisfaction with reference to the evolving Strategic Partnership initiatives and agreed to add greater content to bilateral relations in the fields of defence and security, along with other areas. Before this meeting took place, the 6th India-Vietnam Security Dialogue was held in Hanoi on 14 September 2011[55], where both countries expressed satisfaction on the ongoing security cooperation and Vietnam appreciated New Delhi's oil exploration venture. However, this close understanding in oil exploration between New Delhi and Hanoi was not viewed well by China, and on 15 September 2011, Chinese officials firmly objected to the agreement signed between India's state-owned OVL and PetroVietnam for conducting oil and gas exploration in the South China Sea, on the ground that India's venture with Vietnam would naturally delicate its long-term claim that on the whole South China Sea China has 'indisputable sovereignty'. For this, China sent a demarche to India and cautioned against launching exploratory projects in that region.

However, the Chinese objection was flatly rejected by India on the basis that the 'energy ties with Vietnam are as per international regulations'. Before Indian Foreign Minister, S.M. Krishna embarked on a three-day visit to Hanoi, in connection with the scheduled 14th India-Vietnam Joint Commission Meeting on Trade, Economic, Scientific and Technological Cooperation from 15-16 September

2011, Vishnu Prakash, the spokesman of the Ministry of External Affairs, in an interview, while responding to queries raised by the reporters, firmly reiterated New Delhi's position on this issue and said, 'Our cooperation with Vietnam or any other country is always as per international laws, norms and conventions. Trade is an important aspect of India's relations with Vietnam and the field of energy, hydrocarbons and renewable energy is one such important area. We want to see this relationship grow and expand, and China's objection to OVL's explorations in South China Sea has no legal basis as the blocks belonged to Vietnam'.[56] Also, while clearly pointing out that India has an investment of US$ 400 million in Vietnamese hydrocarbon sector, with OVL having investment of US$ 225 million in oil exploration projects in South China Sea, some of which has been objected by China. He said: 'India supports freedom of navigation in the South China Sea and hopes that all parties to the dispute will abide by the 2002 Declaration of Conduct in the South China Sea'. On 16 September 2011, Indian Foreign Minister, S.M. Krishna asserted, 'OVL will go ahead with oil and gas exploration in the disputed region of the two offshore blocks which Vietnam claims as its own', and which was fully endorsed officially. In fact, New Delhi brushed off China's objections to ONGC's oil exploration projects in two Vietnamese blocks in the South China Sea[57], and thereby dismissed Beijing's warning. These repeated Indian retorts have not been propitiously looked upon by the Chinese Government. As a rejoinder to Indian stand, a Chinese Daily, on 18 September 2011, wrote 'India and Vietnam insist on jointly tapping oil resources in the disputed waters of the South China Sea, may risk setting off a new round of tension in the troubled waters. India and Vietnam should understand that China will not back off when it comes to issues concerning its territorial integrity. Beijing is determined to defend its indisputable sovereignty in the South China Sea. Both countries should understand the sensitive and complicated nature of the South China Sea issue, must refrain from making reckless moves that could escalate tensions in the disputed waters. Their planned oil exploration in the waters is not simply an economic issue but one of security and political importance. Any misstep or misjudgement by them could hurt their relations with China. So, jumping on the bandwagon to provoke China on the maritime disputes is not a sensible move on New Delhi's part'.[58] Consequently, S.M. Krishna assured his Vietnamese counterpart, Pham Binh Minh, during his meeting on 16 September 2011, that OVL will go ahead with oil and gas exploration in the disputed region of the two offshore blocks which Vietnam claims as its own, thereby neglecting China's objections[59], and dismissing Beijing's chastise. Following this visit, the President of Vietnam, Truong Tan Sang, paid his first official visit to India from 11-13 October 2011. At the time of this visit, among other agreements, an Agreement on Cooperation between PetroVietnam and OVL was signed.[60] Following this agreement, the Indian Prime Minister, along with the visiting Vietnamese President, in a joint statement stated: 'India and Vietnam are maritime neighbours. We face common security challenges from terrorism, piracy and natural disasters. We believe that it is important to ensure the safety and security of the vital sea lanes of communication. We have agreed to continue and strengthen our exchanges in these fields.'[61] This remark 'obliquely alluded to Chinese objections to India's oil exploration deals with Vietnam in its territorial waters in South China Sea, which Beijing claims in full. India has defended the oil exploration deal, saying its cooperation with Vietnam was in accordance with international laws and has underlined the need for freedom of navigation in South China Sea. India's assertion has been welcomed by Hanoi, which has been wary of Chinese attempts to dominate the region.'[62] However, this agreement instantly provoked Chinese leadership. The Global Times, sister newspaper of the People's Daily, in its editorial titled, 'India-Vietnam Oil Exploration Deal must be Stopped' wrote: 'By inking pacts with Vietnam, India probably has deeper considerations in its regionalist strategy than simply getting barrels of oil and gas. India is willing to fish in the troubled waters of the South China, to accumulate bargaining chips on other issues with China. There are strong political motivations behind the exploration projects. China's vocal objections may not be heeded. China must take practical and firm actions to make these projects fall through'. It further mentioned, 'there is strong political motivation behind this exploration projects. China's vocal objections may not be heeded. China must take practical and firm actions to make these projects fall through. China should denounce this agreement as illegal. Once India and Vietnam initiate their exploration, China can send non-military forces to disturb their work, and cause dispute or friction to halt the two countries' exploration. India has its ambitions on the South China Sea. However, its national strength cannot provide solid support for such ambitions yet. Furthermore, this is not India's urgent task in building itself into a great power. Even in respect of its own interests, India is just poking its nose where it does not belong. Indian society is unprepared for a fierce conflict with China on the South China Sea issue.'[63] However, this new agreement between India and Vietnam mainly talked about the enhancement of those activities and greater interactions in the petroleum sector. This is not a declaration of an axis or nexus against any entity.[64]

Summarily then, it can be contended that the above issue basically signifies the urge for Indian exploration of oil and gas in Vietnamese waters, on account of New Delhi's growing economic and strategic clout in the emerging Asian security architecture.

Moreover, the bilateral relations between the United States and the Socialist Republic of Vietnam have evolved since 1995, which was not looked upon favourably by China. Presently, the United States remains the leading source of foreign direct investment (FDI) to Vietnam as well as Vietnam's largest export market, and building strong security ties with the US. China's accelerated economic growth, increasing economic footprint, global search for natural resources, and rapid pace of military modernization, along with evolving tensions in the South China Sea, have enhanced the anti-China sentiment in Vietnam and that led the latter to develop better ties with the US to balance the power equation in the Southeast Asian region, since Vietnam figures prominently in the strategic calculus of the US and China in their approaches to East Asian security. Similarly, the present strategic cooperation between India and the US also made India's Indochina policy (mainly with Vietnam) more cordial in its entirety, on account of the China factor. The majority countries of Southeast Asia including Vietnam want to keep India and other countries engaged in the region to have a comfortable regional balance, and that has been reflected through various means mentioned above. Thus, the strategic relationships between these major Asian players are transiting through the sphere of ambiguity and fretfulness. The prime challenges of India's Look East Vietnam strategy has been presently confined to four major indices. They are, the growing Chinese economic and strategic strength; the evolving power equations between India, China, Vietnam and the US; the power politics in the Southeast and East Asian countries and finally, the willingness of Indian policy-makers to make its Look East Policy more pro-active and Vietnam oriented rather than reactive in its thinking. Strikingly, India, through its promotion of multi-sectoral economic, technical and capacity building assistance towards Vietnam is at present striving to project an image of 'natural alliance' like the earlier years, to play a balancing role in the Asia-Pacific region.

Conclusion

Having explored the emerging strategic partnership between India and Vietnam in the context of the evolving security architecture of the Asia-Pacific region, it is evident that security diplomacy between the two countries is developing its thrust. India's cooperation with Vietnam in economic, political and security spheres are expanding rapidly. It would not only promote the best interests of both countries, but also balance the entire Asia-Pacific region. It is evident that New Delhi on account of the changing global order has modified its Look East Policy from political rhetoric to economic and strategic imperatives. As part of its Look East Policy, India accepts Vietnam's strategic position in the realm of Southeast, East and Asia-Pacific politics. This growing attention towards Vietnam is stimulated by burgeoning bilateral trade, and increasing Chinese naval modernisation and expansion in the South China Sea region. To counter growing Chinese influence, India has started playing a pro-active role in Southeast Asia, to protect the freedom of navigation. With this, India has emerged as one of the major competitors of

China in the region and limited Chinese plans to increase its sphere of influence. Beijing's prying in the Indian Ocean; including port construction in Myanmar, southern Sri Lanka and Pakistan etc. has placed New Delhi in a disadvantaged position in the South Asian region. To contain this strategic posture of China, India is helping Vietnam in Defence, Air Force and Naval matters, and thereby acting as a catalytic pressure point against Beijing. So, New Delhi's defying of Chinese objection and threat and agreeing to continue OVL's oil and natural gas exploration projects in two Vietnamese blocks in the South China Sea, exhibits a new dynamics of its Look East Policy, which is strategically correct and diplomatically pragmatic. Furthermore, this signal of India also mirrors its assertiveness in the politics of the Asia-Pacific region and reveals that regional politics can no longer be monopolized by any single power. India Strategic Partnership with Vietnam has added a new dimension to its Look East Policy, through concrete programmes and projects, which will act as a catalytic factor for the expansion of strategic cooperation and a pressure point against China. Unlike China, Vietnam as a regional power would not be hostile to India or Indian national security interests in the region. The broad-based multifarious cooperation and increasing understanding between India and Vietnam could provide a new mini-security ambit in the evolving dynamics of the Asia-Pacific security architecture and which in due course would help to build up the broader frame to contain evolving tensions. Needless to say, this strategic initiative and reactive Look East Policy of India needs to be sustained without losing track of its core objectives, in the backdrop of the evolving security architecture in the Asia-Pacific region. Finally, it is imperative to integrate these mini-security units into a single chain, to have comprehensive macro security architecture in the Asia-Pacific region, within the framework of which the constituent nodes would take cognizance of the salience of remaining adhered to each other, given the interdependent nature of post-cold war economic and security dynamics. This strategic focus, not akin to military alliances of the Cold War epoch, would be relevant in forging greater cooperative and developmental linkages between and among the constituent units, for ushering in the ultimate peace, progress and stability in the Asia-Pacific region and beyond.

NOTES

1. For details, see 202.151.160.183/qdndsite/en-US/75/72/182/155/./Default.aspx (accessed on 25 September, 2012)
2. The main purpose of Indian Air Force Chief, S.K. Mehra's visit to Vietnam was made strictly confidential. But it was reported that this visit remained quite important from the perspective of the sudden deterioration of Sino-Vietnamese relations on account of Spratly Islands problems in the South China Sea. For details see *Vietnam Information Bulletin,* Vietnam Embassy (New Delhi), Vol. XIX, Nos. 5 and 6, 29 March, 1989, p. 4.
3. The Summary of World Broadcasts (SWB), BBC, Part 3, Far East, Third Series, FE/0916/A3/4, November 8, 1990.
4. SWB, BBC, Part 3, Far East, Third Series, FE/0233/A3/4, 18 August, 1988; See also *The Indian Express,* 17 August 1988.
5. Tridib Chakraborti, "Three Stages in Indo-Vietnam Relations: An Overview", in Santimoy Ray and Tridib Chakraborti (eds), *Vietnam: A Changing Horizon*, Chatterjee Publishers, Calcutta, 1992, p. 44.
6. Vice Admiral P.S. Das, "A Navy for 2020", in General V.P. Malik and Brig. Vinod Anand (eds.), *Defense Planning: Problems and Prospects*, Manas Publications, New Delhi, 2006, p. 123.
7. Tridib Chakraborti, "India and Vietnam: Sprouting Strategic Partnership", *World Focus*, New Delhi, Vol. 32, No. 11-12, November-December 2011, p. 896.
8. Tridib Chakraborti, Strategic Convergence between India and Vietnam in the Twenty-first Century: 'Look East' as a Parameter, *Indian Foreign Affairs Journal,* New Delhi, Vol. 3, No. 4, October-December 2008, p. 43.
9. Tridib Chakraborti, *India and Vietnam: Sprouting Strategic Partnership*, World Focus, New Delhi, Vol. 32, No. 11-12, November-December 2011, p. 896.
10. For details see G.V.C. Naidu, "Whither the Look East Policy: India and Southeast Asia", *Strategic Analysis*, Vol. 28, No. 2, April-June 2004.
11. Tridib Chakraborti, "*India and Vietnam: Sprouting Strategic Partnership*", World Focus, New Delhi, Vol. 32, No. 11-12, November-December 2011, pp. 896-897.
12. *Ibid.*, p. 897.
13. *The Hindu*, 8 September 1994; see also *The Pioneer*, New Delhi, 8 September 1994.
14. *The Times of India*, 3 August 1997; see also *The Statesman*, Kolkata, 3 August, 1997.
15. Tridib Chakraborti, Strategic Convergence between India and Vietnam in the Twenty-first Century: 'Look East' as a Parameter, *Indian Foreign Affairs Journal,* New Delhi, Vol. 3, No. 4, October-December 2008, p. 45.

16. Nhan Dan, 7 July 2007
17. Tridib Chakraborti, "*India and Vietnam: Sprouting Strategic Partnership*", World Focus, New Delhi, Vol. 32, No. 11-12, November-December 2011, p. 898.
18. http://www.india-defense.com/reports-3652 (Accessed on 22 September 2012)
19. For details see http://indiadefenseonline.com/2256/india-to-boost-ties-with-vietnam/ (Accessed on 22 September 2012)
20. For details see http://www.defensetalk.com/forums/military-strategy-tactics/india-vietnam-strategic-partnership-9559,(Accessed on 24 September 2012)
21. Robert Johnson, India Is Preparing To Sell BrahMos Supersonic Cruise Missiles to Vietnam, 20 September 2011, for details see http://www.businessinsider.com/india-to-sell-brahmos-missiles-to-vietnam-china-2011-9 (Accessed on 22 September 2012)
22. *Annual Report: 2011-2012*, Ministry of External Affairs, Government of India, New Delhi, 2012, pp. 26-27.
23. Vietnam and India hold Defense Strategy Dialogue, 27 September 2012, for details see http://www.defense.pk/forums/world-affairs/210148-india-vietnam-strategic-defense-dialogue-7th.html (Accessed on 16 September, 2012)
24. Vietnam National Defence, Ministry of National Defence, Socialist Republic of Vietnam, Hanoi, 2009, pp. 18-19, see http://admm.org.vn:6789/TempFiles/04f08223-8f23-4aab-ac6b-c85c1dbfa0e5.pdf (Accessed on 26 September, 2012)
25. *Ibid*, pp. 23-24.
26. David Koh, Vietnam Courting Major Powers, *The Straits Times*, Singapore, 10 November, 2011.
27. The first two Defense Dialogue meetings were held in Hanoi (in 2010) and Beijing (in 2011). For details see http://www.thanhniennews.com/index/pages/20120903-vietnam-china-hold-3rd-defense-dialogue.aspx (Accessed on 22 September, 2012)
28. For details see http://www.saigon-gpdaily.com.vn/National/2011/8/96256 (Accessed on 23 September, 2012)
29. Colonel William Jordan, Lewis M. Stern and Walter Lohman, U.S.–Vietnam Defense Relations: Investing in Strategic Alignment, 18 July 2012, see http://www.heritage.org/research/reports/2012/07/us-vietnam-defense-relations-investing-in-strategic-alignment (Accessed on 26 September 2012)
30. http://www.globaltimes.cn/NEWS/tabid/99/ID/705627/India-being-swept-up-by-missile-delusion.aspx (Accessed on 22 October 2012)
31. The document released by India's navy chief in April 2004, and clearly identified four major roles for the Indian navy in supporting New Delhi's foreign and defence policies. First, the military task emphasizes the growth of

the capacity to project force and the building of trust and inter-operability with foreign navies. Second, the navy's diplomatic task was to improve India's relations with its neighbours and with countries of strategic importance in the Indian Ocean region, including Southeast Asian states such as Singapore, Malaysia, Indonesia, Thailand, Vietnam and Myanmar. Third, the navy's constabulary function was to assist with the coast guard to maintain stability in the Indian Ocean region with the aim of reducing interruption of maritime commerce and energy supplies between the Middle East and East Asia. Finally, the doctrine stressed the navy's humanitarian role, which included search and rescue missions and support during calamities such as floods, tsunamis and earthquakes. See Bilveer Singh, Southeast Asia-India Defence Relations in the Changing Regional Security Landscape, IDSA Monograph Series, No. 4, Institute for Defence Studies and Analyses (IDSA), New Delhi May 2011, p. 17.

32. For detailed speech see Address by Mr. Pranab Mukherjee, Defence Minister of India at the Fifth IISS Asia Security Summit on 3 June 2006, (Shangri-la Dialogue), Singapore, 2-4 June 2006, www.iiss.org/EasySiteWeb/getresource.axd?AssetID=2247&type. (Accessed on 28 September, 2012)
33. *Annual Report: 2000-2001*, Ministry of External Affairs, Government of India, New Delhi, 2001, p. 25.
34. *Annual Report: 2001-2002*, Ministry of External Affairs, Government of India, New Delhi, 2002, pp. 22-23.
35. *Annual Report: 2004-2005*, Ministry of External Affairs, Government of India, New Delhi, 2005, p. 38.
36. *Annual Report: 2005-2006*, Ministry of External Affairs, Government of India, New Delhi, 2006, p. 28.
37. *Annual Report: 2006-2007*, Ministry of External Affairs, Government of India, New Delhi, 2007, p. 29.
38. *Annual Report: 2007-2008*, Ministry of External Affairs, Government of India, New Delhi, 2008, p. 63.
39. Nhan Dan (The Official Organ of the Vietnam Communist Party), 7 July 2007.
40. For details see http://indiaDefenseonline.com/2256/india-to-boost-ties-with-vietnam/ (Accessed on 21 October 2012)
41. http://www.defensenow.com/news/223/vietnamese_naval_chief_visits_india_to_foster_defense_ties.html (Accessed on 25 September 2012)
42. Rajat Pandit, India to help Train Vietnam in Submarine Operations, *The Times of India*, 15 September 2011.
43. Sujan Dutta, China in Mind, Salute & Port Plea to Vietnam, *The Telegraph*, 17 September 2011.
44. news.rediff.com/column/2010/oct/07/co (Accessed on 19 October 2012)

45. Tridib Chakraborti and Mohor Chakraborty, South China Sea: The Refashioned Conflict and the Road Ahead, *World Focus*, New Delhi, Vol. 32, No. 4, April 2011, p. 226.
46. Vijay Sakhuja, India, Vietnam: Time to Expand the Strategic Partnership, 10 September 2011, http://sspconline.org/opnion/India_Vietnam_Timeto Expand_StrategicPartnership_10092011 (Accessed on 25 September 2012)
47. For details, http://www.pib.nic.in/archive/pm_visit_iv/indoiv.html(Accessed on 16 October 2012)
48. Tridib Chakraborti, Strategic Convergence between India and Vietnam in the Twenty-first Century: 'Look East' as a Parameter, *Indian Foreign Affairs Journal,* New Delhi, Vol. 3, No. 4, October-December 2008, p. 47.
49. For details see http://www.ongcvidesh.com/op_vietnam.asp (Accessed 16 October 2012).
50. Tridib Chakraborti, Strategic Convergence between India and Vietnam in the Twenty-first Century: 'Look East' as a Parameter, *Indian Foreign Affairs Journal,* New Delhi, Vol. 3, No. 4, October-December 2008, p. 51.
51. *Annual Report 2006-2007*, Ministry of External Affairs, Government of India, New Delhi, 2007, p. 29.
52. S.D. Muni, The Turbulent South-China Sea Waters: India, Vietnam and China, ISAS Working Paper, No. 140, 11 October 2011, p. 9, Institute of South Asian Studies, National University of Singapore, see www.isas.nus.edu.sg (Accessed on 28 September 2012)
53. For details see Pankaj K. Jha, India–Vietnam Relations: Need for Enhanced Cooperation, *Strategic Analysis,* Vol. 32, Issue 6 , November 2008, pp. 1085-1099.
54. For details see http://thehanoist.wordpress.com/2010/07/29/vietnam-hedges-its-china-risk/(Accessed 13 October 2012).
55. Annual Report: 2011-2012, Ministry of External Affairs, Government of India, New Delhi, 2012, p. 27.
56. www.daijiworld.com/news/news_disp.asp?n_id=115968 (Accessed on 16 September 2012)
57. *The Times of India*, 17 September 2011.
58. http://ftpapp.app.com.pk/en_/index.php?option=com_content& task=view& id=154075&Itemid=2 (Accessed on 16 September 2012)
59. *The Times of India*, 17 September 2011.
60. *Annual Report: 2011-2012*, Ministry of External Affairs, Government of India, New Delhi, 2012, p. 27.
61. Ashok Tuteja, India, Vietnam sign oil exploration pact, *The Tribune*, Chandigarh, 13 October, 2011.

62. For details see http://in.news.yahoo.com/china-factor-india-vietnam-sign-oil-deal-launch-104755426.html) (Accessed on 22 September 2012)
63. People's Daily Online, Opinion-Editorial-India Vietnam oil exploration deal must be stopped, *Global Times*, October 14, 2011, available in http://english.peopledaily.com.cn/90780/7617306.html (Accessed on 20 September 2012)
64. Rajeev Jayaswal, ONGC Videsh signs an agreement with PetroVietnam, *The Economic Times*, 12 October 2011.

11
Evolving Asia-Pacific Security Architecture

Nguyen Nam Duong

Introduction

In 2010 and 2011, the regional security architecture in the Asia-Pacific experienced enormous changes, exerting profound effects on international relations and foreign policies of countries in the region. The ongoing changes in great power relations, amid China's impressive rise and growing assertiveness, are the main impetus precipitating the evolution of a new model of Asia-Pacific regional security architecture. This has led to the emergence of a number of new bilateral and multilateral security arrangements in the region.

The shaping of the new regional security architecture has brought out many challenges for small and medium powers in the region whose economic development are threatened on account of uncertainty associated with peace and stability in the region. The new regional architecture has also posed many questions for ASEAN's central role in multilateral cooperation in the Asia-Pacific region. Facing the profound impact of the new regional architecture in 2011 and beyond, several regional countries are adjusting their policies to ensure national independence, peace and stability in the region. This chapter outlines the contours of the evolving regional security architecture in the Asia-Pacific region, and makes some observations on the role of ASEAN in the emerging new regional architecture.

Diverse Perspectives on Security Architecture of the Asia-Pacific Region

The concept of 'regional architecture' has been commonly used in ASEAN's documents as well as in the policy circle and academia in recent years. Currently, there has not yet been a widely accepted definition of 'regional architecture', but its connotation often refers to an integrated system of organisations, institutions, mechanisms, arrangements, processes, etc. aimed at preserving peace and stability in the region[1]. The architecture often consists of two key components, i.e. bilateral arrangements and multilateral institutions, primarily in the field of politics, security and economics in the region. However, this chapter will focus only on the security aspect of the Asia-Pacific regional architecture, although it will make reference to the economic architecture for analytical purposes. The geographical limits of the Asia-Pacific region connotes the common understanding of the region covering Southeast Asia, Northeast Asia and North America, including some other actors with roles and interest in the region such as India, Russia and Australia.

The concept of 'regional architecture' has a close connection with 'regional order'. 'Regional order' is a concept used to describe the general patterns of relations among entities in a certain geographical area. The concept is also related to power distribution in the regional system and the movement of power relations; whereas, the concept of 'regional architecture' only refers to bilateral and multilateral institutions for cooperation among entities in that given geographic area. It is fair to suggest that regional architecture is just the manifestation of regional order. In international relations theory, neo-liberal institutionalism appreciates the importance of cooperative institutions in international relations, and promulgates that cooperative institutions can help change state behaviour in a direction that minimises the negative impacts of international 'anarchist environment'[2].

The regional security architecture in the Asia-Pacific region dates back from the Cold War period with two original pillars: the US-Sino-USSR strategic triangle and the US-led 'hub-and-spokes' bilateral alliances with Japan, South Korea, the Philippines, Thailand

and Australia, which were set up to contain communism in the region. In addition, the establishment of ASEAN in 1967 was also an important component of the regional architecture. After the end of the Cold War, the regional security architecture in the Asia-Pacific made remarkable progress in the 1990s and in the early 21st century with the evolution of US-led bilateral alliances, along with the emergence and development of multilateral institutions such as the ARF in 1994, ASEAN+3 in 1997, EAS in 2005, ADMM+ in 2010, and others. Thus, in nearly two decades, the regional architecture has made relatively rapid strides, in the context of multi-polarisation and harmonious great power relations in the region[3].

In the last two or three years, the Asia-Pacific regional architecture has been affected by many factors which brought about its impressive development. The dramatic rise of China and its assertive behaviour in regional affairs have been the main drivers boosting the evolution of the regional architecture. The correlation of forces and relations among the major countries in the Asia-Pacific region has undergone significant changes, corresponding to the rise of China. Regional hot-spots and conflict areas such as the Korean peninsula, the Diaoyu (Senkaku) islands, the South China Sea issue have escalated since 2009 and became more complex, in which the impact of China's assertiveness has been rather strong.

In the new context, the countries concerned have all adjusted their views and policies in constructing the regional architecture to ensure their national interests, as well as common interests to ensure peace and stability for the development in the region. Therefore, the shape of the regional architecture will be influenced by various perspectives and policies of key stakeholders in the multi-polar and multilayered regional order of the Asia-Pacific region. China and the US are two major powers who have a stake in the region, followed by Japan, India, Russia and ASEAN countries.

China

The rise of China has been one of the main features of the post-Cold War era. The global economic crisis of 2008-09 brought about a golden opportunity for China to rise vigorously, making the global balance of power shift towards China. In 2010, China replaced Japan as the second largest economy in the world, the position held by Japan since the 1960s. Concerning military capability, with its rapid pace of defence modernisation throughout the decades, China has considerably narrowed the military gap with the US. China's soft power has also increased and its model of economic development and cultural values have been accepted and shared by many countries, especially after the global economic crisis.

The unchanged overall strategic objective of China is to become the most prosperous and powerful state in the world, realising its 'hundred-year' dream of being 'the number-one world power'[4]. In recent years, China appears not to be bound by the 'rules' in the contemporary international system established decades ago by the West. China has been striving for reforms of international financial and economic institutions such as the International Monetary Fund (IMF), World Bank (WB) and World Trade Organisation (WTO) and interpreting international conventions such as the United Nations Convention on the Laws of the Sea (UNCLOS) in a way beneficial to China.

China has been pursuing a closed and Chinese-led framework of East Asian integration through the promotion of free trade areas in East Asia, under the initiative of 'one axis, two wings'. Through the Chiang Mai Initiative, China strengthened its political and security cooperation with ASEAN countries on the principle of 'national sovereignty', in contrast to US bilateral 'hub and spokes' alliances. China's vision of the regional architecture in the Asia-Pacific region includes 'two concentric circles', in which ASEAN +3 should be central while the US and other countries should be at the outer circle. In addition, China attaches great importance to the SCO, in which China plays a leading role.

The US

Overarching goal of the US is to perpetuate its current position as the most powerful country in the world and prevent any emerging power or forces from challenging its dominant role. At the same time it wants to build a world order based on its own value system. At present, no country in the world or in the Asia-Pacific region, except China, has the potential to challenge the US's dominant position. In the medium term, China could overtake the US in terms of economic size. It seems that China would neither become a democratic country as the US expects, nor would it become a 'responsible stakeholder' in regional as well as global affairs. At the same time, the Obama administration is now facing the fact that the US power has been in relative decline after the economic crisis; and economic interdependence between the US and China has become much deeper.

In May 2010, National Security Strategy of the US clearly stated that the alliances with Japan, South Korea, Australia, the Philippines and Thailand constitute the foundation for prosperity in the Asia-Pacific region[5]. Besides, this strategy also emphasises the importance of US bilateral relations with Russia and India in promoting trade, combating extremism and countering proliferation. The Quadrennial Defense Review of the United States of February 2010 stated that the US should develop new strategic relations with newly emerging countries such as Indonesia, Malaysia, etc[6].

Besides, the US has sought to promote multilateralism through regional cooperation mechanisms like APEC, TPP, ARF and EAS, as key orientation in its strategy of re-engaging with the Asia-Pacific region. Although the US is not the founder of these mechanisms, its policy has recently shifted towards strongly supporting and promoting the role of multilateral institutions in the region. The US seeks to contain China with these multilateral institutions, and also intends to universalise its values such as democracy, human rights, and the rule of law, which it adheres.

Japan, India and Russia

Japan considers the US-Japan alliance as the backbone of the regional architecture in the Asia-Pacific region. The alliance has been strengthened after the face-off between Japan and China in the Diaoyu/Senkaku islands in late 2010, and the triple disasters which engulfed Japan in March 2011. The rapid growth of China both economically and militarily, has made Japan insecure even inside the US 'security umbrella'. Japan fears that China's control of Southeast Asia will endanger Japan's trade and energy arterials. Therefore, Japan has been strengthening its ties with India, Australia and ASEAN to counter growing Chinese influence. However, Japan's multilateral cooperation with ASEAN always lags behind China. As Japan is concerned about Chinese hegemony in East Asia, it has speeded up its efforts to build multilateral mechanisms involving the US and other countries in regional organisations such as EAS and APEC. Thus, Japan has been playing a connecting role between the two sides of the Pacific in the regional architecture, and is seen as a bridge for the US participation in the multilateral cooperation in East Asia.

India's economic and political rise has been no less impressive than that of China's. Although India is a South Asian country, it has actively implemented the Look East Policy, viewing itself as an inseparable part of the Asia-Pacific regional architecture, and views the region as its 'extended neighbourhood'. To cope with the pressure from China over territorial and boundary issues, India has established strategic partnership with the US and other countries such as Japan and Australia, forming an unofficial 'coalition of Asian democracies'. Besides, India attaches great importance to ASEAN-centred multilateral cooperative mechanisms, especially EAS of which India is one of the founding members. However, the economic coherence between India and other Asia-Pacific countries is still limited. So far, India has not been accepted as a member of APEC.

Russia has always emphasised that it is a Pacific power, but its involvement and influence in the region has been modest in comparison with other powers. In recent years, Russia has started building ties with ASEAN and was accepted to join the EAS in 2010. However, Russia is still an indispensable power in the Asia-Pacific region, serving as a buffer between China and the US.

ASEAN

ASEAN aims to build architecture for the Asia-Pacific region based on the 'ASEAN way', the basic principles of the grouping, in order to maintain peace and stability for the development of the region. ASEAN supports a multi-layered architecture, which is based on the existing and complementary processes of regional cooperation. In that regional architecture, ASEAN seeks to play the central role and serve as the driving force[7]. ASEAN does not support a single overarching institution for the Asia-Pacific region. In order to accomplish the goal of building the ASEAN Community, ASEAN also supports harmonious relationship among the major powers and encourages them to actively contribute to regional peace and stability.

In general, all the countries of the Asia-Pacific region are in need of building the security architecture to maintain regional peace and stability for development, and to prevent the risk of large-scale regional armed conflicts, which is the common denominator for all regional countries. However, due to differing interests, each country has adopted a different perspective and vision of the shape of the evolving regional architecture. Even the countries' understanding of the concepts of 'peace' and 'stability' are different. Therefore, the emerging regional architecture in the Asia-Pacific region should be the result of cooperation and compromises among regional countries, based on the existing correlation of forces and the developments in the regional security situation.

Characteristics of Evolving Asia-Pacific Security Architecture

In recent years the Asia-Pacific regional architecture has undergone remarkable transformation. While the old shape of the regional architecture, which has existed since the beginning of the 21st century, has not been broken, crucial changes in the regional architecture have taken place. Although, up to now, the new shape of the regional architecture is still not very clear, some key features of the evolving regional architecture can be sketched out as follows:

a) The Relationship between China and the US

The two dominant powers of the Asia-Pacific region, the US and

China have become the defining factor of the regional order and architecture. Although the multi-polar and multi-layered order of the region includes many other major countries such as Japan, India and Russia, their external relations are heavily influenced by the Sino-US axis. After the 'honeymoon' period in the context of the global campaign against international terrorism got over, Sino-US relations gradually cooled during the second tenure of President Bush and have deteriorated markedly since President Obama took office in 2009. The dominant characteristic of US-China relationship today is between a sole superpower declining in strength and a rising power having the potential to challenge the position of the former. However, the level of economic interdependence between the two powers have never been higher, and they need to work together to address regional and international issues. In this context, the US tries to maintain the status-quo through various measures to constrain China in the long run, while China seeks to revise the current international system dominated by the US and Western countries through peaceful means. However, China's recent behaviour in the surrounding area has revealed that it has different standards for 'peace'.

Although the strategic competition between China and the US has become more intensified, the cooperation between the two countries has not broken. China and the US have managed to build a relatively stable framework for bilateral cooperation, as manifested in the annual strategic and economic dialogues between the two countries which began in 2009. The annual dialogues signify that the two sides would not let their cooperation collapse even when their relations have deteriorated. The two countries still cooperate in global and regional institutions, especially the UNSC, to address international issues that neither of them can undertake alone. Therefore, multilateral institutions in the Asia-Pacific region still have the opportunity to develop with the involvement and support of both the powers. Competition and cooperation between the two powers in multilateral institutions will be decisive to chart the evolution of these institutions.

Since both China and the US are keen to maintain the big picture of peace, stability and regional prosperity, the Asia-Pacific regional architecture may not experience dramatic mutation but would evolve incrementally, in parallel with the fluctuation in their bilateral relations. The current international and regional systems would not be fundamentally broken, as both China and the US find them acceptable temporarily. (The current US preference is to maintain the global status-quo for economic recovery, while China's priority goal is to focus on modernisation). However, due to sustained struggle and cooperation between China and the US in the international and regional systems, the security architecture in the Asia-Pacific region would continue to evolve in a manner that is dependent on the intensity and nature of cooperation and compromises between the two powers.

b) New Regional Architecture

Among the components of the new regional architecture, the bilateral security arrangements continue to maintain their relevant positions. The US-Japan alliance affirms its role as a pillar in the regional security arrangements, aiming to respond to security challenges in Northeast Asia, especially to deter and constrain China. The US-Republic of Korea (ROK) alliance has been strengthened after the Cheonan incident and the fiery exchanges in the Korean Peninsula. The US-Philippines alliance has also been revitalised, looking outwards after various incidents in the South China Sea in 2011. The US-Australia alliance has shown sustainability over time after meeting the challenges in Iraq and Afghanistan. US-India relationship has also been upgraded to a strategic partnership level to meet the demands for cooperation between the two countries in the new context. It has been hailed as the relationship that 'defines the twenty first century'[8].

On the other hand, the US-led traditional alliances no longer maintain the 'hub-and-spokes' model as they did earlier. Instead, there has been more coordination among these US-led alliances and among the 'spokes'. The US-Japan-Australia military exercise in July 2011 in the southern part of the South China Sea was a specific example. These alliances tend to accumulate into a network of multilateral defence without the need to establish an Asian North Atlantic Treaty

Organisation (NATO). This is the difference in security architecture between the Asia-Pacific region and Europe. The European regional architecture was founded upon highly institutionalised organisations such as the NATO and the Organisation for Security and Cooperation in Europe (OSCE). The US itself encourages its allies to be more proactive and to share responsibilities with the US in the context of relative decline in the US power. In addition to strengthening their ties with the United States, these countries also promote joint action among themselves, creating multiple cards which can be played against China in the future. The strengthened Japan-India, Japan-Australia and South Korea-Japan relations, etc. are apt examples in that regard. While watching out for a more assertive China, these countries have also made use of any opportunity to improve their relations with China, as they do not feel absolutely secure in the US security umbrella.

c) Multilateral Security Institutions

Currently the multilateral security institutions do not yet have a clear direction of progress in the regional architecture. Basically, the multilateral institutions in the Asia-Pacific region can be categorised into two: the first type is based on the coordinating role of the ASEAN such as ASEAN+3, ARF, EAS, ADMM+, etc. and the second type covers the rest of the institutions such as APEC, the TPP, SCO, etc. In the medium term, all these institutions will continue to co-exist, both competing with and complementing each other and it is unlikely that an institution would evolve into an overarching institution covering the entire region. The overlapping and intertwining manners and the low efficiency of these multilateral institutions will be the inherent characteristic of regional cooperation in the Asia-Pacific region in the times to come[9].

On the other hand, changes in the multilateral diplomatic policies of major countries, especially the US, would cause respective changes in multilateral institutions. The active participation of the US and Russia in the EAS would push cooperation faster than in other institutions. The EAS has received whole-hearted support from

Australia, India, Japan and many ASEAN countries. Since EAS meetings take place at summit-level, EAS has the potential to become a key forum for political-security dialogue and cooperation in the Asia-Pacific region. ARF and ADMM Plus are likely to become 'subordinate' to the EAS in political and security cooperation. On the division of labour, EAS and ARF would focus on political policymaking issues, while the ADMM Plus would focus on specialised issues such as maritime security, disaster relief, defence cooperation, etc.

d) Regional Economic Architecture

Regional economic architecture, which exists in parallel to the political-security architecture, has also seen remarkable changes in the recent times. ASEAN supports FTA between ASEAN and an ASEAN dialogue partner as pillars for the regional economic architecture, with an aim to strengthening the central role of ASEAN[10]. However, these ASEAN+1 FTAs have not yet yielded the desired effects due to the low level of economic integration in these mechanisms. The weakness of the FTAs between ASEAN and its dialogue partners has a negative impact on the central role of ASEAN in the evolving economic architecture in the Asia-Pacific region. Due to its limited economic strength, it is difficult for ASEAN to assert a leading role in promoting economic cooperation in multilateral settings. Looking at the wider East Asian region, the economic cooperation mechanisms such as East Asia Free Trade Area (EAFTA) and Comprehensive Economic Partnership for East Asia (CEPEA) is still a distant dream. The future of economic integration based on the geographic areas of East Asia is also distant.

Meanwhile, the rise of Trans Pacific Partnership (TPP) in recent years, presents a new element to the landscape of multilateral economic cooperation in the Asia-Pacific region. Currently, TPP and APEC are two mechanisms playing the role of economic connection between the two sides of the Pacific. Although TPP was formed on the sideline of the APEC and has been considered as 'the path finder' for APEC, it is less likely that TPP will completely replace APEC in the near future. At least in terms of membership, TPP has not been extended to all APEC economies. However, if TPP negotiations progress smoothly and attract key regional economies such as Japan, South Korea. etc., it is possible for the TPP to become the leading mechanism for economic liberalisation in the Asia-Pacific region. On the other hand, the development of TPP poses the risk of division within ASEAN, as not all ASEAN members participate in TPP negotiations.

Role of ASEAN in the New Regional Architecture

The shape of the Asia-Pacific regional architecture with its basic characteristics as mentioned earlier will bring about both opportunities and challenges for ASEAN. Maintaining the central role of ASEAN in the regional architecture is one of the fundamental goals of ASEAN, apart from building the ASEAN Community. From ASEAN countries' perspective, ASEAN's central role in the regional architecture is prerequisite to ensure independence and sovereignty, and to maintain peace and stability for the development of regional countries, especially for small and medium powers.

In fact, ASEAN plays an intermediary role between regional actors through multilateral institutions chaired by ASEAN such as the ASEAN+3, ASEAN+1, ARF, ADMM+, EAS mechanisms. However, the past two decades have witnessed the limited effectiveness of these mechanisms in managing regional conflicts such as in the Korean peninsula and in the South China Sea. The bewilderment of ASEAN in handling the Thai-Cambodian border conflict is an example of its ineffectiveness. This has raised questions about the centrality of ASEAN. ASEAN is also facing many problems in the process of building ASEAN Political-Security Community (APSC).

To maintain the intermediary role in the evolving regional architecture, ASEAN needs to adapt to the adjustments in major countries' policies towards the Association. In multilateral settings, ASEAN's 'driver's seat' continues to be recognised by major countries, at least nominally, because big countries basically suspect each other. In these institutions, China has voiced its strong support for ASEAN's leading role in the process of constructing the regional architecture.

China praises ASEAN as a pillar in the multi-polar Asia-Pacific security order. On the other hand, in some critical matters such as the South China Sea, China has applied a policy of 'divide and rule', and constantly seeks to reduce the role of ASEAN and its related mechanisms in dealing with conflicts.

In the 're-engagement with Asia' campaign waged by the Obama administration, the US appears to acknowledge the role of ASEAN in multilateral diplomacy in the region and supports the various processes coordinated by ASEAN. On her first trip abroad after inauguration, Secretary of State Hillary Clinton visited Indonesia and the ASEAN Secretariat, and signed the Treaty of Amity and Cooperation (TAC) with ASEAN, which the previous US administrations had refused to do. The fact that the US has actively engaged in multilateral networks in Asia can be compared to the US support to Western Europe's integration after World War II, constructing a Western Europe strong enough to cope with the growing influence of the Soviet Union and socialist countries. In addition, Japan, India and Russia see ASEAN as a bridge linking these countries in the Asia-Pacific regional architecture. These countries have strengthened their relations with ASEAN through respective 'ASEAN plus One mechanism', and together with ASEAN have promoted the role of multilateral mechanisms in realising the common interest of moderating Sino-US relations.

Harmonious relationship with major countries is also a target as well as an important function of ASEAN since its inception. In 2005, ASEAN took the initiative to expand the East Asia cooperation process, engaging India, Australia and New Zealand in the EAS mechanism in order to counter China's influence. With the dramatic rise of China in recent years, ASEAN has continued to expand East Asia cooperation and invited Russia and the US to join the EAS, to ensure a balance in the East Asian regional security architecture. The emergence of the EAS will bring huge challenge for ASEAN in the regional architecture. If EAS is rapidly institutionalised, the major countries will dominate the forum, which would reduce the regulatory and connecting functions of ASEAN.

Conclusion

Overall, in order to maintain ASEAN centrality in the new evolving regional architecture, it is necessary to construct a closely integrated ASEAN in order to form a solid foundation for cooperation with its partners. At the same time, ASEAN needs to enhance its effectiveness in handling regional issues such as the Thai-Cambodian border, so as to avoid a pretext that major countries can use to intervene in regional affairs. ASEAN also needs to promote the efficiency of the existing institutions, define a sound division of labour and establish practical mechanisms for coordination among various institutions to make regional architecture operate effectively and respond decisively to emerging security challenges in the region. To do so, ASEAN need to continue meeting the interests of major countries in the ASEAN-centred institutions, in order to establish equilibrium and harmony in the region.

NOTES

1. US Secretary of State's perspective on 'regional architecture': "Now, architecture is the art and science of designing structures that serve our common purposes, built to last and to withstand stress. And that is what we seek to build: a network of alliances and partnerships, regional organizations and global institutions that is durable and dynamic enough to help us meet today's challenges and adapt to threats that we cannot even conceive of, just as our parents never dreamt of melting glaciers or dirty bombs." Hilary Clinton's speech at the Council on Foreign Relations (US), 8/9/2010, Washington; accessible at http://www.cfr.org/diplomacy/conversation-us-secretary-state-hillary-rodham-clinton/p22896
2. Robert O. Keohane and Lisa L. Martin, The Promise of International Institutions, *International Security*, Vol. 20, No. 1, 1995.
3. U.S Congressional Research Service, East Asian Regional Architecture: New Economic and Security Arrangements and U.S. Policy, Jan. 2008.
4. Liu Mingfu, *The China Dream: The Great Power Thinking and Strategic Positioning of China in the Post-American Age*, New Age Publishing House, Hanoi, 2011.
5. The White House, National Security Strategy, May 2010; accessible at http://www.whitehouse.gov/sites/default/files/rss_viewer/national_security_strategy. pdf
6. US Defense Department, Quadrennial Defense Review, February 2010; accessible at http://www.defense.gov/qdr/images/QDR_as_of_12Feb10_1000.pdf

7. ASEAN Charter, Article 41, accessible at http://www.aseansec.org/publications/ASEAN-Charter.pdf
8. Hillary Rodham Clinton, Remarks on Regional Architecture in Asia: Principles and Priorities, Jan. 2010; accessible at http://www.state.gov/secretary/rm/2010/01/135090.htm
9. Kei Koga, "Competing Institutions in East Asian Regionalism: ASEAN and the Regional Powers", *Issues and Insights,* Vol. 10, No. 23, October 2010.
10. ASEAN Economic Community Blueprint, Nov. 2007, Article 65, accessible at http://www.aseansec.org/5187-10.pdf and Chair's Statement of the 18th ASEAN Summit, May 2011, Article 43; accessible at http://www.asean.org/Statement_18th_ASEAN_ Summit.pdf

REFERENCES

'ASEAN Economic Community Blueprint', November 2007, Article 65, accessible at http://www.aseansec.org/5187-10.pdf and 'Chair's Statement of the 18th ASEAN Summit', May 2011, Article 43; accessible at http://www.asean.org/Statement_18th_ASEAN_Summit.pdf

ASEAN Charter, Article 41, accessible at http://www.aseansec.org/publications/ASEAN-Charter.pdf

Clinton, Hillary Rodham (2010), 'Remarks on Regional Architecture in Asia: Principles and Priorities', January 2010; accessible at http://www.state.gov/secretary/rm/2010/01/135090.htm

Fu, Liu Ming (2011), 'The China Dream: The Great Power Thinking and Strategic Positioning of China in the Post-American Age', New Age Publishing House, Hanoi.

Hilary Clinton's speech at the Council on Foreign Relations (U.S.), 8/9/2010, Washington; accessible at http://www.cfr.org/diplomacy/conversation-us-secretary-state-hillary-rodham-clinton/p22896

Keohane, Robert O. and Lisa L. Martin (1995), 'The Promise of International Institutions', International Security, Vol. 20, No. 1.

Koga, Kei (2010), "Competing Institutions in East Asian Regionalism: ASEAN and the Regional Powers", Issues and Insights, Vol. 10, No. 23, October 2010.

The White House, 'National Security Strategy', May 2010; accessible at http://www.whitehouse.gov/sites/default/files/rss_viewer/national_security_strategy.pdf

U.S. Congressional Research Service (2008), 'East Asian Regional Architecture: New Economic and Security Arrangements and U.S. Policy', January 2008.

US Defense Department, Quadrennial Defense Review, February 2010; accessible at http://www.defense.gov/qdr/images/QDR_as_of_12Feb10_1000.pdf

12
India-Vietnam Strategic Partnership: Political and Security Cooperation

Vijay Sakhuja

Introduction

The transformed Asian landscape features burgeoning economic growth flavoured with a complex strategic environment. In the second decade of the 21st century, Asia is expected to witness continued high rates of economic growth and rapid industrialisation pivoting on high-technology and manufacturing. The much spoken 'Asian Century' is ushering in the dominance of Asian markets that are now emerging as catalysts and hubs of global economic development. However, the Asian strategic environment negates the silver lining presented by the regional economic outlook which needs to adjust to the changes and power shifts among the regional countries including extra-regional powers. The Asian countries are propelled by a high degree of nationalism, there are a number of boundary disputes, increasing defence expenditure of some countries and frequent incidents of aggressive posturing. In essence, in the Asian region, economic growth and strategic competition are intertwined offering a complex security milieu.

In this backdrop, India and Vietnam are developing strategies to make the 'strategic partnership' more robust by harnessing their respective power potential to meet a host of political, economic and strategic challenges confronting the region. India celebrated five significant events in 2012. First, it commemorated six decades of diplomatic ties with Indonesia; celebrated 40 years of the establishment of diplomatic relations between India and Vietnam, and five years of strategic partnership with Vietnam; 20 years of its Look East Policy; 10 years of Summit-level dialogue with ASEAN. Later in the year in the month of December, the India-ASEAN Summit will be held at New Delhi. These events gain salience in the broader context of the beginning of the third decade of India's Look East Policy which has witnessed phenomenal growth over the years in bilateral and multilateral relations with ASEAN countries.

This chapter attempts to highlight the political and security dimensions of India-Vietnam Strategic Partnership. It begins by discussing the salience of Asia's rise to both India and Vietnam. It then presents four templates of cooperation in political, security, defence and high technology fields that can make India and Vietnam strategic partnership successful.

Salience of Asia's Rise to India and Vietnam

It is generally agreed that the rise of Asia is a recent phenomena but it is instructive to recall that some Asian countries had begun to experience substantive growth rates and had risen to eminence soon after the World War II. The war ravaged economies of Japan and South Korea had begun to witness prosperity as early as the 1960s, primarily due to the initiatives of the US which had acted as the helmsman and steered these countries through generous economic aid, investments and technology transfers. Besides, the US also served as the 'anchor of stabilisation' in the region by offering these countries security guarantees through alliance arrangements and forward military presence, that not only served as a stabilising element in the security environment but also as a source for the growth of high-technology military-industrial complex in these countries. The economic and defence miracle of Japan shot the country to prominence primarily due to the peaceful regional security environment.

The evolving democratic and liberal economic order led to

resurgence of Asia in the form of tiger economies with abundance of economic resilience. The current trends in China with emphasis on economic growth and technological transformation have spurred the Asian engine of growth, seasoned with Chinese characteristics. China's state centred development rooted in its communist principles has provided a new form of capitalism, referred to as 'Maoism to Modernity', has impacted the region.

Vietnam's goals of economic self-reliance and greater accent on development started with its 'doi moi' reforms in 1986. The economic and strategic transformation of Vietnam since then is propelled by the templates of new wave of economic growth driven by dynamic workforce, their ability to adopt and assimilate technologies, immense social resilience, and the catalytic motivation to move out of poverty, resulting in high-growth economy. Similar trends have been in occurrence in India that began with economic reforms in 1991 has catapulted Indian economy from 'Hindu rate of growth' to occupy 'commanding heights' in the global system.

It is therefore fair to argue that India and Vietnam are inevitable strategic partners and there is robustness in their political engagements. Both have strived for economic interdependence, and are willing to discuss strategic issues. India's footprint in Vietnam has been through political engagements, trade, and defence cooperation. However, Vietnam's engagement with India is limited to political exchanges and trade, and has not yet reached its full potential in defence and investment sectors.

Notwithstanding that, there are prominent templates of political cooperation, and cooperation in science and technology. Both countries common security concerns have also led to enhancement in defence cooperation, which is fast-growing in the naval and air domains.

Templates of Political Cooperation and Multilateralism

In 2007, India and Vietnam signed the Strategic Partnership that envisages bilateral political and economic engagements, security and defence cooperation, scientific and technological capacity building and enhanced cultural contacts. Further, the two sides also committed themselves to diversify and deepen relationship and work closely in regional and multilateral forums to address the rapidly changing security environment.

Since the signing of the Strategic Partnership, India and Vietnam have deepened their relationship and expanded their political, economic and strategic interactions. In 2010, Vietnam hosted the ASEAN-India Summit and the East Asia Summit. These engagements have paved the way for greater trade opportunities and business investments between the two countries.

Multilateralism is an intrinsic feature of India-Vietnam relations. India's Look East Policy acknowledges Vietnam's position and role in the ASEAN, values relationship other member-countries of ASEAN, and attaches importance to the ASEAN-driven institutions. India's engagement with ASEAN member countries is built under the aegis of ARF, EAS and ADMM plus which serve as a platform for building inclusive security architecture and foster a spirit of consensus on all issues of mutual concerns. Further, India and Vietnam are partners in the six-member MGC, a sub-regional grouping constituted in 2000 which aims to promote sectoral cooperation in the field of transportation, tourism, human resources and culture. The other members of the group include Cambodia, Laos, Myanmar and Thailand. Bangladesh too has expressed interest in joining the MGC.

At another level, multilateralism, interdependence and economic cooperation among Asia-Pacific countries has been the best insurance against conflict. It has also augmented cooperation in a number of other transnational challenges like piracy, terrorism, illegal activities and transnational crime, disaster management and cooperative measures in the maritime commons. Similar cooperation over food, health and development issues has been a vital benchmark of cooperation.

Templates of Security Cooperation

India has vital stakes in transforming Asia-Pacific security environment. New Delhi favours peace and stability in the region with assents on economic growth and human development. It is also concerned about regional tensions that could undermine Asia-Pacific security and stability which is critical for India's economic growth. In this context, India-Vietnam convergence is crucial. There are a number of regional security issues that have attracted the attention of India and Vietnam and these relate to the rise of China, its comprehensive military and strategic modernisation, disputed claims in the South China Sea and varying interpretation of the UNCLOS thus challenging freedom of navigation.

The Chinese assertion of its 'peaceful rise' and its 'charm offensive' has an ambitious and aggressive intent that has serious implications for the Asia-Pacific region. It is well known that China has been in the throes of an impressive military modernisation and has sent discomforting signals among the regional countries. These countries including Vietnam are now propelled into building capability to protect their national interests which are reflected in a strong penchant to acquire modern military hardware such as aircraft, ships, expeditionary platforms and cruise missiles.

The Chinese position with regard to its claims in the South China Sea continues to unnerve the Southeast Asian claimants. Likewise, other regional and extra regional stakeholders are apprehensive of any escalation of military tensions among claimants. Beijing has exhibited assertiveness at sea, objected to offshore exploration activities in the EEZ of claimant States, challenged internationally accepted freedom of navigation in international waters, and on occasions engaged in sabre-rattling. The claimants have thus far attempted to keep military activity in the defensive mode; however, as sovereignty issues gains primacy and energy exploration activities intensify in disputed areas, there is a potential for tensions in the region.

There is little doubt that Asia-Pacific countries have high stakes in keeping the sea-lanes open for their economic vitality which pivots on assured supply of energy and safe and secure trading routes in the region including the Straits of Malacca. Besides, their shipping is faced with a number of threats and challenges posed by non-state actors with transnational capabilities. In recent times, piracy has been an issue that has been high on agenda among the Asia-Pacific leaders who have expressed their commitment to fight piracy.

India is an important stakeholder in the evolving security dynamics in the South China Sea. This is due to the fact that nearly 50 per cent of India's trade with the Asia-Pacific region, west coast of the US and Latin America transits through the South China Sea. Therefore, the safety and security of the sea lanes in the region is of interest to India. New Delhi believes in 'an open and inclusive architecture of global maritime security' and keeping sea lanes in the South China Sea open, which is critical for international shipping. Further, 'in an era of globalisation and interdependence, the balance between the rights of states and the freedoms of the larger global community, is vital for international trade and global security'.

India also has economic stakes in South China Sea through its joint ventures in the energy sector. OVL, the offshore subsidiary of the ONGC has been engaged in offshore energy development projects in partnership with PetroVietnam in Vietnam's EEZ in the South China Sea.

India hopes that the claimants can establish a binding 'Conduct of Conduct' on the South China Sea and develop concrete mechanisms to institutionalise a regional dialogue among the claimants and other stakeholders which will serve in de-escalating tensions in the region.

Templates of Defence Cooperation

In 1994, India and Vietnam signed a MoU on defence cooperation which envisaged cross-servicing arrangements for Soviet made military hardware particularly MiG aircraft. The defence engagement was further expanded in 2000 through a fresh protocol to institutionalise a variety of defence-related activities such as training, naval exercises, visits by military heads, and supply of military hardware including assistance for the production of small arms. In 2007, India and Vietnam signed the strategic partnership that further catalysed bilateral security and defence cooperation. Both sides are in the process of establishing a regular security dialogue between the Ministry of Home Affairs and Ministry of Public Security for capacity building, border management and police modernisation. In essence, India-Vietnam defence cooperation is well-established and has the potential for expansion in a number of areas.

India and Vietnam have the vital tasks of securing the region against asymmetric threats and challenges through the spectrum of benign, constabulary and humanitarian operations. The maritime forces of the two countries need to forge strong partnership so as to establish order in the maritime commons of the Asia-Pacific region. Likewise, proliferation of WMDs and their delivery systems is of concern to India and Vietnam. The two partners have immense operational and intelligence capital that would have to be harnessed for securing the 'Global Commons'.

Naval cooperation between the two partners has made significant headway and Indian naval ships have on a regular basis called at Vietnamese ports on goodwill visits. The two sides have also discussed issues relating to enhancement of maritime security. Besides, Indian naval ship visits have also been useful in showcasing Indian naval shipbuilding capability and Vietnam has shown interest in naval vessels from India. During his visit to India in June 2011, the Vietnam's navy chief visited the defence public sector shipbuilder Mazagon Dock Limited in Mumbai and Hindustan Shipyard Limited in Vishakhapatnam and was briefed about Indian warship building capacities and functioning of the defence shipyard. The imperative to collaborate in naval ship-building would bring to bear on Vietnam's technological advantage in this area. Building capacities in civilian shipping and partnership in Indian defence production and procurement would strengthen Vietnam's technological prowess.

High Technology cooperation is an important priority for India and Vietnam. It is important to harness the scientific and technological capital of India and Vietnam in collaboration to develop more innovative and effective high-end technologies. Harnessing the technological dividend and investing in the development of dual-use technologies would be highly important for both the countries.

Military interoperability is of strategic consequence. India and Vietnam could consolidate their engagements in counter-insurgency, counter-terrorism and expand into areas of joint army, navy and air forces exercises, special operations forces training and exercises, and intelligence cooperation.

India and Vietnam have a history of operating Soviet/Russian aircraft. Significantly, bulk of their military inventory is of Soviet/Russian origin. Thus there is convergence in terms of operational philosophies, techno-maintenance schedules and training practices for modern Russian aircraft and naval platforms. Vietnam has acquired Kilo Class submarines and SU-30MKK fighter jets from Russia, for these India can offer training assistance to the Vietnamese military.

Vietnam has shown interest in the Brahmos missile which is compatible with the Su-30 aircraft and submarines (Kilo/Amur class). The Su-30 can be fitted with up to three missiles, one under the fuselage and the other two can be mounted on wing pylons after strengthening the support points. As far as submarines are concerned, up to eight missiles packaged in containers can be fitted on the Russian Amur class submarines.

Templates of High Technological Cooperation

Currently, Vietnam does not have any nuclear power plant but it has drawn plans to harness nuclear energy for power generation to diversify its energy mix and also to reduce its dependence on hydrocarbon based energy resources. Vietnam plans to build eight nuclear power plants in five provinces by 2030 with a total capacity of 15 Gigawatts, or 10 per cent of all electricity produced in the country. Vietnam's first nuclear power plant is expected to be built between 2015 and 2020 in Ninh Thuan province. Vietnam signed two agreements in 2010 with the US and Russia for acquiring nuclear reactors. The Russian agreement envisages building two power units with a capacity of 1.2 Gigawatts each, and would also provide loan for the nuclear power plant construction. However, Vietnam does not possess trained human resources to manage the nuclear infrastructure, draft national legislation and conceptualise nuclear safety and security arrangements. Post Fukushima nuclear disaster, the Vietnamese government is paying greater attention to the safety of the nuclear power plants that will be built in Vietnam. For this, Vietnam has established a special committee for training of the scientists.

India has rich experience in operating civil nuclear power plants and has the capacity to train Vietnamese technical experts. Besides, India can offer support to the ancillary industry that is critical to support nuclear infrastructure.

Space cooperation would offer new frontier as India and Vietnam engage in transformative technologies and the build-up of space capabilities in satellites and space launches. Joint space exploration and the joint commitment to ensure the peaceful uses of outer space are vital for both countries.

Concluding Remarks

It is true that India Vietnam strategic partnership is making great strides. The 'multifaceted bilateral cooperation' and the 'enduring bond of friendship, which has strong historical roots, is driving the relationship. Significantly, strengthening the strategic partnership is a key priority area for both India and Vietnam. Both countries have enormous stakes in augmenting regional stability which provides for crucial convergence. Even as the Asia-Pacific economic and strategic order transforms, the essence of the bilateral relations should be to contribute to regional stability.

Although India and Vietnam have their respective national challenges and regional threats, their emphasis on the economics would enhance their ability to forge better relations that would have an enduring impact. Finally, it is imperative that the strategic partnership has a transformative impact on the evolution of a consensus between the two countries, to elucidate a common strategic vision that is focused on mitigating ill consequences of the regional transformation and in augmenting greater Asia-Pacific stability.

REFERENCES

Anthony, A.K. (2012) '*Minister of Defence, India, Speech at the 11th IISS Asia Security Summit, The Shangri-La Dialogue*', Singapore, June.

Ikenberry, John (2008), '*The Rise of China and the Future of the West: Can the Liberal System Survive?*', *Foreign Affairs*, January-February 2008.

Lele, Ajey (2011), '*India-Vietnam Space Cooperation: Looking for New Frontiers*', *SSPC*, 14 September 2011.

N.A. (2012), '*Vietnam Seeks U.S. Equipment to Close Military Gaps*', World Political Review, July 6, 2012.

Pitlo III, Lucio Blanco (2012), '*Vietnam's Exploration and Production Contracts: Using Energy Interests to Strengthen Maritime Claims*', *RSIS Commentaries*, No. 106/2012, 21 June 2012.

Sakhuja, Vijay (2011), '*India Vietnam Strategic Partnership: Exploring Vistas for Expanded Cooperation*', Pentagon Press, New Delhi.

Singh, Daljit and Pushpa Thambipillai (ed.), (2012), '*Southeast Asian Affairs 2012*', ISEAS, Singapore.

Thuy, Tran Truong (ed.), (2010), '*The South China Sea: Cooperation for Regional Security and Development*', Diplomatic Academy of Vietnam, Hanoi.

Tran Truong Thuy (ed.), (2011), '*The South China Sea: Towards a Region of Peace, Security and Cooperation*', Diplomatic Academy of Vietnam, Hanoi.

13
Evaluation of Vietnam-India Defence Cooperation

Nguyen Hong Quan

This chapter consists of three parts: bilateral defence cooperation between Vietnam and India; multilateral defence cooperation between Vietnam and India; and measures to strengthen defence cooperation.

Bilateral Cooperation

Since Vietnam and India established strategic partnership in 2007, the bilateral defence cooperation between Vietnam and India has borne many results; which are as follows:

Each year, there are several visits by military and defence officials from both the countries. The most recent are the visit to India by Mr. Phung Quang Thanh, Minister of Defence, in November 2009; and the visit to Vietnam by India's Defence Minister A.K. Antony in October 2010. These visits have enhanced understanding, the traditional friendly relations and linkages between the two countries.

Since 2003, the two countries have alternately organised seven dialogues forums for information sharing and evaluation by strategic communities, on issues of mutual concern.

Since 1993, India has provided training to Vietnamese Army (20-30 trainees each year, the total number to date is about 180), and since 2009, India has deputed English teachers to teach Vietnamese trainees. On the other hand, Vietnam admits 1 Indian officer to Vietnam's Academy of Defence since 2008 and 1-2 Indian officers to Vietnamese language course at Vietnam's Academy of Military Science each year.

The armies and naval forces of the two countries have conducted joint projects on military tactics, education and training. Indian naval ships have visited Vietnam's ports 22 times, and the Indian Navy has presented Vietnamese Navy with equipment and spare parts. The Indian Navy has been offering training in command and control, logistics and engineering, ship repair, military science and technologies, hydrography, foreign languages and computer skills to the Vietnamese Navy. Two Indian naval vessels visited Hai Phong city from 19-23 May 2012 and conducted military exercises in maritime search and rescue together with the Vietnamese Navy. Besides, the two sides have exchanged several delegations for conducting surveys, exchanging experiences in building up forces, educating high-level personnel, training, logistics and engineering, repair and maintenance, organisation of staff and equipment; production, repair and up-gradation of arms and technical equipments. Both the navies are also cooperating in coping with non-traditional security issues like, counterterrorism, environmental pollution, natural disaster relief and prevention. Other areas of cooperation are: sharing information on developing maritime strategies and management; creating digital nautical charts, shipping, underwater sound and magnetic fields information; exchanging information about activities in the East Sea and Southeast Asian region.

India has expressed interest in Vietnam's defence industry. To date, the two sides have signed a number of contracts for transaction of arms and equipments. However, the transactions are still limited in both quantity and value. It is hoped that in the coming years the two nations will further cooperate in this area on the basis of mutual benefit.

Nevertheless, there is still a need to further enhance this linkage to conform to the framework of strategic partnership.

Multilateral Cooperation

At present, India has a number of collaborative ties in defence and security with ASEAN, for example, TAC, ARF, etc. In international forums, Vietnam and India have bolstered cooperation within the United Nations and in multilateral forums on nuclear security. As India is a big nation, Vietnam hopes that India would participate with more vigour in institutions, mechanisms and forums, relating to defence and multilateral security arrangements in the region. Vietnam supports the consolidation of India's role in these institutions and welcomes India's contribution to the *ADMM+*, *ARF*, etc. for the peace, stability and development in the region.

Measures to Strengthen Defence Cooperation

In recent years, defence cooperation between Vietnam and India has flourished. Yet the current level of cooperation has not unleashed the full potential of the two countries. Swift changes in the international and regional situation require Vietnam and India to further promote defence relations on the major realms listed below:

Both countries need to increase exchanges of delegation at all levels. Priority should be given to high-level visits; interaction between young officers, institutes, schools and experience sharing. Vietnam would like to receive visits from young Indian military officers. The two countries also need to enhance cooperation in education and training. Both the countries can promote cooperation in personnel training in English, S&T, and Command and Control. Vietnam would welcome more Indian military trainees to learn Vietnamese.

It is suggested that India provides more scholarship for Vietnamese military trainees to learn English at tertiary level. India may provide one year advanced English course to Vietnamese trainees before offering any major courses. Indian teachers are welcome to take part in teaching English and imparting computer skills at Vietnamese military academies.

Vietnam and India need to continue fostering cooperation between their naval forces on agreed terms. Vietnam appreciates the visits of Indian naval vessels and the joint activities, e.g. sharing experiences in equipment use, joint training in search and rescue missions, humanitarian assistance and disaster relief; which are organised during the visits.

Vietnam can provide Indian Navy access to the ship repair and maintenance facilities in Cam Ranh Bay civil area. Vietnam invites Indian shipbuilding entrepreneurs, both public sector and private sector, to collaborate in building an amphibious base for the Vietnamese Navy and the naval forces of other nations. In order to enhance Vietnam's capability in coastal management and protection, the Indian Navy can explore the possibility of transferring used naval vessels (armed or unarmed) to Vietnam.

Both the countries need to boost cooperation between government bodies and between research institutes and evolve exchange mechanism and partnership between Indian and Vietnamese academies, i.e. the Academy of National Defence, the Military Strategy Institute, the Institute for Foreign Defence Relations.

Vietnam is actively preparing for UN led operations and offer support as military observers, explosive ordnance disposal unit and medical teams to participate in the United Nation Peacekeeping Operations. During the preparation process, Vietnam would like to foster cooperation with India in these fields.

Section IV

Development of a Knowledge Economy: Cooperation in IT, Science and Technology and Related Fields

14

India-Vietnam Relations: Enhanced Cooperation in IT, Science and Technology

K. Raja Reddy

This chapter is structured into two parts. The first part discusses the evolution of relations between India and Vietnam over the years and the second part describes India's emergence as a growing science and information technology country to become knowledge-based economic power. The chapter highlights the rationale for enhancing cooperation between the two countries as both have interest in promoting peace and stability in the region.

Evolution of India–Vietnam Relations

Even before India and Vietnam achieved independence from the colonial rule, Jawaharlal Nehru and Ho Chi Minh got inspiration from each other in responding to the problems of the oppressed multitudes of Asia and Africa. Holding the reins of their respective countries, they became part of Asian history, each in its own way, and their statesmanship moulded the destiny of their respective nations. The mutual admiration of these two leaders coupled with their commitment to the cause of downtrodden nations formed the firm basis for India-Vietnam relations to evolve. Nehru urged the colonial French rulers to respect the aspirations of Vietnamese independence and quit the region. Besides, common Indians expressed their solidarity with the indomitable Vietnamese struggle for independence and unity and this has few parallels in the history of mankind. The Vietnamese struggle for independence became a sentimental affair with Indians and this has played its part in India's foreign policy and India's relations with Vietnam. V.P. Dutt, an Indian foreign policy expert, rightly observed that: 'Sense, sentiment and sensibility all seem to have gone into the making of India's Vietnam policy'.[1]

When Indira Gandhi was at the helm of affairs, India-Vietnam relations reached a new height. In the thick of Vietnamese war against US troop involvement in Vietnam, in September 1971, she emphatically declared: 'I will support the inalienable rights of all peoples, especially those of the Vietnamese people, to national independence and freedom'. To give a new direction to the bilateral relations, India upgraded the diplomatic representation to the level of Embassy on January 7, 1972.[2] The Democratic Republic of Vietnam (DRVN) consulate was likewise upgraded to Embassy in New Delhi to give parity to the relations.[3]

The unification of Vietnam in 1976 was welcomed by India. The first ever change of government from the hands of Congress Party in New Delhi in 1977 did not alter India's attitude towards Vietnam. A.B. Vajpayee, the then External Affairs Minister, stated that: 'It is a matter of some pride that India is the first country outside the Socialist Bloc to which Vietnam, which is as much non-aligned as it is socialist, has turned to us for a close, abiding and mutually advantageous relationship'.[4] Vajpayee's abrupt end of his visit to China and return to New Delhi on the so called Chinese 'punitive action' against Vietnam in February 1979 was the clear demonstration of Indian government's resolve to defend Vietnam. The press and the public in India reacted with vehemence against China that reminded one of the Indian resentment during 1962 war.

The visits of the Prime Minister of Vietnam, Pham Van Dong, to New Delhi in February 1978 and in April 1980 were designed to enhance the relations between the two countries. Both sides agreed to further improve the relations through economic and cultural cooperation. The high level visits between New Delhi and Hanoi and vice versa, signalled the growing warmth between the two countries. According to John W. Garver, there was 'a convergence of

Vietnamese and Indian views as both were concerned with checking the southern advance of Chinese power'.[5] The Indian recognition of Vietnam-backed Cambodian regime was the result of this convergence and there was a broad consensus of opinion in the country on this issue. Mrs. Gandhi also stoutly defended the recognition in praise of Vietnam in the international fora.[6]

The first concrete step to deepen the political relations through economic engagements between India and Vietnam was taken in December 1982, with the establishment of Joint Commission for Economic, Scientific and Technical Cooperation, during the visit of the Vietnamese Foreign Minister Nguyen Co Thach to New Delhi. The plan of action agreed upon included India's assistance to Vietnam in metallurgy, remote sensing, new energy sources, electronics, science and policy management including the training of the Vietnamese personnel.[7]

Indira Gandhi's assassination was a shock to the Vietnamese. The Indian Embassy in Hanoi was flooded with people to express their sorrow for the departed leader. The Vietnamese respect for the departed leader was amply demonstrated by the posthumous conferment of the Vietnam's highest award, 'The Order of the Golden Star', on Mrs. Gandhi. Her Son and then Prime Minister Mr. Rajiv Gandhi visited Vietnam exclusively to receive the award in November 1985.

The unfolding developments at the global level at the time of Rajiv Gandhi assuming premiership compelled India to look for avenues to stand on its own. The concept of knowledge economy helped India to catch the just started Information and Communication Technology (ICT) revolution. Soon India became a major global source of Research and Development in IT and Science & Technology fields. India's growth in IT and Science & Technology became a model for growing economies and developing nations. Economic liberalisation policies of the country provided necessary stimulation for the investors to invest in all kinds of developmental activities in the country.

IT, Science and Technology Collaboration

The Vietnamese leadership launched a reform programme called 'Doi Moi' in December 1986 to revolutionise every facet of Vietnamese life through renovation.[8] This renovation programme coincided with the policies of *perestroika* and *glasnost* of the former Soviet Union and the economic liberalisation policy initiated by Prime Minister Rajiv Gandhi in India. Both India and Vietnam appraised each other of the fast changing developments in their domestic as well as external front. Rajiv Gandhi's observation on India–Vietnam bilateral relations during the visit of Vietnam Communist Party General Secretary Nguyen Van Linh in 1989 is worth mentioning here:

> I would like to express my satisfaction at the manner in which bilateral relations between our two countries have developed. We have worked together on modernising your textile mills and contributed to the establishment of your jute industry. We have cooperated in the field of animal husbandry. Our scientists have done useful work in rice research. A beginning has been made in exploring and prospecting for oil.
>
> Now new horizons beckon. Our Science and Technology Agreement will pave the way to cooperation in biology and biotechnology, electronics, metallurgy and a host of other areas. Our Cultural Agreement provides the framework for the restoration of our ancient cultural ties and the introduction of our people to each other.[9]

On the common objectives between India-Vietnam he said:

> India and Vietnam share common objectives and goals in regard to the replacement of the present world order by one which is more just, equitable and democratic, a world which is not menaced by nuclear weapons nor anchored in violence. We are both non-aligned countries firmly believing in peaceful coexistence, deeply committed to sustained peace and sustainable development.[10]

A decade of renovation programme in Vietnam and the emergence of India as 'software superpower' provided opportunity for both the countries to develop a meaningful cooperation in the fields of Science, Information Technology and human resource development. By the end of 1999, India and Vietnam signed a protocol on cooperation in the development of Information Technology. The protocol was signed on 12 August 1999 by Ravindra Gupta, Secretary, Department of Electronics, Government of India, and Chu Hao, Vice Minister, Ministry of Science, Technology and Environment, Government of Vietnam.[11] According to the protocol:

> The two sides agreed that the Information Technology and Electronics sector is one of the dynamic sectors of global economy and there is great scope of cooperation in this sector between the two countries. Recognising Indian capabilities in Information Technology development, it was agreed that both countries would closely collaborate in policy management areas so that both the countries can benefit from strengths and opportunities in the field of IT and Electronics. It was also agreed that both sides would exchange policy and technology related information on a regular basis and develop a Joint Web Site for the same so that information exchange is possible in real-time and online basis.[12]

The visiting high level delegation sought all out support from India for the development of IT sector in the country. The delegation visited Bangalore and Mumbai from 12-20 August 1999, to examine ways and means to enhance collaboration in IT between the two countries. It was also decided to set up a Working Group which would meet once a year alternatively in the two countries.

The top leadership in Vietnam recognised the benefits of cooperation with India in the fields of Science & Technology and IT. When President Tran Duc Luong visited India on 1 December 1999, he made a particular reference about the cooperation between India and Vietnam in the fields of Science and Technology. He stated:

> Marvellous achievements in science and technology have opened up unlimited opportunities for humankind and at the same time put the developing countries on a danger of lagging far behind the developed ones. The strong economic globalisation, while offering new opportunities for cooperation and development, have placed weak countries and economics in vulnerable and disadvantageous positions amid an unequal and unfair competition. Given the new context in the region and the world, greater importance is attached to the consolidation and strengthening of the well-rounded cooperation between Vietnam and India. I would like to reiterate the determination of the Vietnamese people, together with the Indian people, to unceasingly promote and develop the relations of traditional friendship and long-term cooperation towards a brighter future, and join other countries in striving for peace, stability, cooperation and prosperity in the region and the world at large.[13]

A year later Prime Minister Atal Bihari Vajpayee visited Vietnam in January 2001. Welcoming Prime Minister Vajpayee to Vietnam the Vietnamese Prime Minister Phan Van Khai stated:

> The Vietnamese people are very proud of our great friend, India. With her great stature, India has a very important role to play in the region and the world. That stature and position have been strongly enhanced by India's recent achievements in nation-building and development in the course of efficient reforms. India today has become a scientific and technological power, especially in software technology. With such an advanced technology, India is rapidly advancing into a new age of information technology revolution and the knowledge [based] economy. Building on your growing strength in all fields and high sense of responsibility in international affairs, India will make greater contribution to peace, stability, co-operation and development in the region and the world.[14]

While addressing an India-Vietnam Joint Business Council meeting, Vajpayee said that India's expertise in Information Technology was of great value to Vietnam considering the potential of Vietnam in this field. He said: 'We have already seen the initiation of this partnership in IT. But this is just the beginning. The future is going to be immensely more attractive and fruitful'.[15] About the human capital in the knowledge economy, he explained: 'This covers a number of fields including frontier sciences such as atomic energy, biotechnology and oceanography. We remain committed to giving further inputs to this'. He also said: 'We shall encourage collaboration between Indian and Vietnamese educational institutions to further this goal. We are also ready to significantly increase the opportunity for Vietnamese students to come to India for studies in technology, medicine, management and other areas'.[16]

Vietnam's played an important role in India's integration with ASEAN. The establishment of MGC was a step forward in that regard.

The MGC not only lends strength to India's Look East Policy, but also offers an opportunity to link one billion Indian people with two hundred million people of multicultural, multilingual and panoramic five countries of Southeast Asia i.e. Myanmar, Thailand, Cambodia, Laos and Vietnam. The 'Vientiane Declaration' issued on 10 November 2000 by ASEAN referred to developing closer relations and better understanding among ASEAN countries to enhance friendship, solidarity and cooperation'.[17] The declaration stated the plan of action to conduct strategic studies and joint-marketing, promote tourism, develop transport network such as 'East-West Corridor' and the 'Trans-Asian High way'. They approached Asian Development Bank and the World Bank for funds to meet the huge expenditure to be incurred to push through Asian Highway project linking India with the Mekong region. The concept paper issued in this regard also visualised certain steps to be taken to give the programme a distinct shape. According to the concept paper, the progress of the programme would be reviewed by the Foreign Ministerial Meetings which follow the ASEAN Ministerial meeting usually held in July every year.

It is India's responsibility to see that MGC initiative gets sustained and pushed forward positively. This is an excellent opportunity for India to build its private sector. In the Ministerial Meeting of MGC held in Hanoi on 28 July 2001, the participants adopted a six year 'Hanoi Programme of Action (July 2001 to July 2007)'.[18] The participants expressed earnestness and seriousness in making this project a reality. They also decided to establish a Directory of Universities, research institutes and the Information Technology institutes, to promote benign interaction among the countries of the MGC project. The Hanoi action plan envisaged the promotion of cultural contacts through performing arts, visual arts, traditional dance, etc.The establishment of resource centres in each country to study economic, cultural and strategic implications of this project and to exchange notes with their counterparts in other countries. This was supposed to promote cooperation in the world of Information Technology and facilitate the communication system.

Cooperation in the field of Science and Technology including Information Technology received a big boost with the signing of Joint Declaration on Comprehensive Cooperation Framework between the two countries in May 2003 during the visit of Nong Duc Manh, General Secretary of the Vietnam's Communist Party (VCP) to New Delhi. As a follow up action, 12th Meeting of the Joint Commission, under the Co-Chairmanship of External Affairs Minister of India, Natwar Singh and Nguyen Dy Nien Foreign Minister of Vietnam, was held in Hanoi on 18 October 2004. It discussed all aspects of India-Vietnam interactions particularly in the fields of economic, commercial, science and technology, information technology, health, education and human resource development assistance and cultural fields. During this meeting 'A Plan of Action for 2004-06' was also worked out to speed the implementation of the Agreements already signed.

Prime Minister Nguyen Tan Dung visited India from 4-6 July 2007. This visit was hailed as a landmark visit ushering stronger diverse developments in India-Vietnam relations in all fields including Science and Technology. During the visit, India and Vietnam signed a Joint Declaration entering into a Strategic Partnership. Apart from the Joint Declaration the two sides signed eight other important documents on cooperation in the fields of power, fisheries and aquaculture, agriculture, culture, education and training. According to Prime Minister Dung, 'these documents serve as important legal basis for the two sides to work out major orientations and concrete measures to promote comprehensive cooperation between ministries, branches and localities of the two countries to help in actively carrying out Vietnam-India strategic partnership in all domains'.[19] India and Vietnam have also signed a Memorandum of Understanding (MOU) for supporting augmentation of high performance computing in Vietnam. According to the MOU, the Indian government agreed to set up a state-of-the art and modern upgradable supercomputing facility known as PARAM at the Hanoi University of Science and Technology at the cost of US$ 1 million. The project will be beneficial to Vietnam as it is a Key technology resource for economic growth and environmental understanding. The Indian side would impart training to the Vietnamese side to create a pool of skilled professionals for pursuing research and development in the area of High Performance Computing (HPC) and promote use of HPC systems in other applications. India has already supported several projects in the field of Information Technology. C-DAC also set up the Vietnam-India Advanced Resource Centre in Information and Communication Technology in Hanoi.[20]

India-Vietnam cooperation acquired great depth due to the high level consultations and agreements reached through political will from both the sides. In this context it may be mentioned that on18 August 2010, India-Vietnam programme of cooperation in Science and Technology under the scientific cooperation between Indian and Vietnamese Scientists and Institutes, coordinated by Department of Science and Technology (DST) of India and Ministry of Science and Technology (MOST) of Vietnam, extended full support to approved joint research projects. The financial support was extended in the areas of Biotechnology including Bio-informatics, Material Science, Information Technology including high performance computation, Science and Technology Management, Ocean Development and Oceanographic Research, Meteorology including Climate Research,

Pharmaceuticals and Medical Research, and Non-conventional Energy.

After having signed the Strategic Partnership the next important step in strengthening all round development was the three day visit of Vietnamese President Truong Tan Sang to India from 11-13 October 2011. The joint statement issued in New Delhi on 12 October 2011, emphasised the importance of Science and Technology collaboration in strengthening India-Vietnam relations. The joint statement states 'The two sides noted with satisfaction the establishment of Business Forum. Advanced Resource Centre in Information and Communications Technologies (ARC-ICT)'.[21]

The cooperation between India and Vietnam in the field of Science and Technology and IT has grown to such a level that Vilasrao Deshmukh, Minister of Science and Technology, observed that Science and Technology has emerged as one of the strong pillars of support for bilateral cooperation between India and Vietnam, at a working secession with the Vietnamese delegation led by Deputy Prime Minister Nguyen Thien Nhan on March 28, 2012. Deputy Prime Minister Nhan described that Vietnam has worked out a strategy to become strong IT nation by 2020 and intends to increase cooperation with India in the fields of Nano-technology, Bio-technology and Oceanology. He stated that Vietnam chose India's IT city Bangalore, as a partner in training IT human resources.[22] During his visit, Deputy Prime Minister Nhan held discussions with the Minister for Human Resource Development and Communications and Information Technology, and expressed keenness to collaborate with the Universities and Institutions in India including Delhi University, Jawaharlal Nehru University, Centre for Development of Advanced computing, Indian Institute of Management and Indian Space Research Organisation.

Conclusion

Ever since India and Vietnam enhanced their diplomatic status in 1972, close and friendly relations developed between the two countries, based on shared commitment for growth. The 'doi moi' renovation process in Vietnam and economic liberalisation in India provided stimulus to bilateral cooperation for mutual benefit. With the global world recognising India's strength in Science and Technology and IT field, India and Vietnam have collaborated in the fields of Information Technology, human resource Management and Science and Technology, Space Technology, Biotechnology and Nuclear Technology. This will go a long way in bringing peace and prosperity for the two countries, the region and the wider world.

NOTES

1. V.P. Dutt, *India's Foreign Policy*, (Reprint), New Delhi, 1997, p. 384.
2. *Asian Recorder*, 12-18 February 1972, p. 10619.
3. *Ibid*, 4-10 November 1972, p. 11067.
4. A.B. Vajpayee, *New Dimensions of India's Foreign Policy*, Delhi, 1979, pp. 63-64.
5. John W. Garver, Chinese-Indian Rivalry in Indochina, *Asian Survey*, Vol. 27, No. 11, 1987, p. 1208.
6. Mohammed Ayoob, *India and Southeast Asia*, London, 1989, p. 56.
7. M. Prayaga, Scientific and Technological Cooperation between India and Vietnam, in A. Lakshmana Chetty (ed.), *India's Relations with Southeast Asia: Problems and Prospects*, Tirupati, 1999.
8. Foreign Languages Publishing House (PLPH), Sixth National Congress of the Communist Party of Vietnam: Documents, Hanoi, 1987, p. 128.
9. Ministry of Information and Broadcasting, Government of India, Speech of the Prime Minister, Shri Rajiv Gandhi, at the banquet held in honour of His Excellency Nguyen Van Linh, General Secretary of the Socialist Republic of Vietnam, New Delhi, 25 January, 1989.
10. *Ibid.*
11. India and Vietnam Sign a Protocol on Information Technology and Electronics http://www.indlaw.com/guest/DisplayNews.aspx? 46954168-4BBC-4FCC-895C-E55ACE83A36C, (Accessed on 4 July 2012).
12. *Ibid.*
13. Reply by H.E. President Tran Duc Luong at the Reception Hosted by H.E. President K.R. Narayanan, 1st December 1999, *Ibid*, p. 4.
14. Speech by Prime Minister Phan Van Kahi, Vietnam, January 2001, p. 10.
15. Speech by Indian Prime Minister Atal Behari Vajpayee, Vietnam, January 2001, p. 9.

16. See Amit Baruah, *The Hindu*, 10 January 2001.
17. *Ibid.*
18. http://www.mfaic.gov.kh/region/Greater%20Mekong.Mekong-Ganga%20 cooperation.html.
19. http://intellibriefs.blogspot.in/2007/07/india-will-vietnam-primary-partner-html.
20. India supports for high-tech growth in Vietnam, http://english.vietnamnet.vn/science-technology/19523/india-supports-for-high-tech-growth-in Vietnam.html, (Accessed on 4 July 2012).
21. India-Vietnam Joint Statement, http://netindian.in/news/2011/10/13/00016506/india-vietnam-joint-statement (Accessed on 5 July 2012). See also Ngo Xuan Binh and Va Le Thi Hang Nga, Quan He Vietnam-An Do Trong Boi Canh Moi, Nghien Cuu Dong Nam A, Vol. 141, No. 12, 2011, p. 11.
22. Vietnam, India look towards stronger IT development, http://talkvietnam.com/2012/03/vietnam-india-look-towards-stronger-it-development, (Accessed on 5 July 2012).

15
India's Potential in Science and Technology: Scope for Cooperation

Pham Hoang Ha

India's Strengths in Science and Technology

Over the past few years, owing to the implementation of appropriate and strategic policies on science and technology, many related research areas of India have developed and achieved various breakthroughs. In basic research, India established several research bodies of international standards in key scientific-technological fields like molecular biophysics, molecular biology, neurobiology, water glass, biological medical devices, super conductor, solid state physics, astronomy, astrophysics, advanced materials, organic chemistry, meteorological forecast, etc.

Several of Indian scientific and technological researches have made great achievements. A few instances are information technology, biotechnology, cosmology, supercomputer technology, etc. Most notably, India has developed its nuclear programme, and gained self-sufficiency in reactor technology, and the complete nuclear fuel cycle. India is capable of designing, constructing and operating nuclear reactor, as well as producing suitable fuel and reprocessing of used fuel. In cosmology, India has shown competence in designing, building and operating remote sensing and telecommunications satellite stations as well as the ability to launch 1000-kg remote sensing satellites into polar sun synchronous orbits. In aviation industry, India has succeeded in using composite materials for the production of experimental aircrafts.

Many of Indian technologies have been developed and commercialised. Technologies in fields like petrochemistry, agricultural chemistry, production of industrial catalysts, pharmaceuticals, production of biological medical devices, food processing, leather tanning, leather production, production of engineering equipment and materials, production of electronics and building materials, have been exported to foreign markets. Markedly, in the area of industrial catalyst, India has been able to produce vital petrochemical products such as p-xylene, ethyl benzene and olefins. In pharmaceutical industry, India has succeeded in producing AZT (anti-AIDS medicine), and Etoposide (anti-cancer medicine). At present, India is carrying out its scientific marine research programs, including exploration and exploitation of marine organism resources, research on atmosphere-ocean interaction, management of coastal areas and Antarctica exploration. Below are some of India's technological achievements:

Information technology tops the list of Indian strengths in science and technology. Its several globally well-known corporations like WIPRO, HCL and many companies of NASSCOM have created a name for themselves in the technological world. The total turnover from software export touched US$ 48 billion in 2006 and US$ 60 billion in 2012. Many countries, particularly the US and the EU, have confidence in Indian software. Today, India has more than 700 companies in software production and information technology services. These companies are located mainly in Bangalore, Mumbai, Chennai, New Delhi, Hyderabad and Pune, employing more than 1.6 million staff.

Biotechnology in pharmaceutical field is another area of India's strength in science and technology. With rich biodiversity of about 17,000 plant species, many of which hold great medicinal properties, India has great potential in developing pharmaceutical bio-technology. Medicines made from the extract of these plants have served the demands of both domestic and foreign markets. In 2006, India succeeded in producing a new anti-colon cancer drug named Biocon, whose sale value has crossed US$ 15 billion. The globally famous pharmaceutical companies of India, like Ranbaxy, Wockhardt, etc. have exported products to 125 countries, including Vietnam.

India's strength in science and technology has supported machinery and equipment production, especially the manufacture of equipment for scientific and technological research. As a result of this, India could minimise import, promote the use of domestic products, and develop and protect its domestic firms. India is capable of producing various commodities like automobiles, motorbikes, air conditioners, refrigerators and other essential products, using indigenous technologies. Many well-known corporations like Tata, Reliance, etc. have been able to produce a variety of products for both domestic and foreign markets.

India has shown competence in space technology, telecommunications, and design and launching of satellites. These technologies play a crucial role in space research, environmental protection and disaster forecast. With 35 years of experience in satellite research, India has successfully constructed satellite launch stations and has produced satellites of various sizes, like INSAT-1, INSAT-4 and so on. In 2008, India launched an unmanned spacecraft to the moon for survey, scientific research and Mars exploration. India also participates in space exploration, survey and research together with other countries like China and Korea.

India's research in defence science and technology has gained international recognition. Relying on accumulated indigenous knowledge and experiences gained from cooperation with 63 countries, India is capable of servicing several types of advanced weapons, especially high-tech weapons like fighter aircrafts like Sukhoi-30 MKI and MIG-29, combat tanks like T-90, and providing ultrasonic rockets such as Brahmos, Trishul, Akash, Nag and Agni, to the other countries. Furthermore, India has successfully produced hydro-fuel and liquid oxygen for rocket engines.

India has robustly developed nano-technology and has applied it in many areas of research like, production of nano-materials, production of defence and medical devices, agriculture, information technology, telecommunications, chemicals, automobiles, etc. In recent years, India has succeeded in using nano-materials to produce light weight aircraft. In the coming years, India expects that the application of nanotechnology will present the market with more than 500 new commodities.

There are nearly 25 million Indian diaspora who are present in every corner of the world, mostly in the US and Europe. The population of overseas Indians is about 3 million and 2.46 million in the US and in the UK, respectively. These overseas Indians have contributed both finance and knowledge to the development of science and technology in India. A large number of them work in science and technology sectors like information technology, medical and high-tech domains, and hold important positions in academics and big research institutes. Many of the overseas Indians working in science and technology spheres have returned to India, and are working on major projects relating to information technology, new materials, aviation, aerodynamics and many other strategic fields in the country.

In addition, Indian private sectors also play an important role in the development of science and technology. Well-known companies like Tata, Infosys, Reliance, Wipro, Ranbaxy, Wockhardt, etc. have penetrated the global market in automobile production, information technology, chemicals, steel production, pharmaceuticals (especially gene-based medicine) and many other key areas.

India's great potential in science and technology results from effective coordination between science and technology bodies, functioning under the supervision and direction of the government. A few examples of these bodies are departments functioning directly under the Ministry of Science and Technology (MOST), Department of Science and Technology (DST), Department of Scientific and Industrial Research (DSIR), Department of Biotechnology (DBT), Department of Atomic-Energy (DAE); and other bodies such as Department of Space (DOS), Department of Ocean Development (DOD), etc.

India-Vietnam Cooperation in Science and Technology Sector

Vietnam and India have been cooperating together in science and technology since 1978, after the signing of the Agreement on Bilateral

Cooperation in Science and Technology. Based on the agreement, a Joint Science and Technology Committee was established by Vietnam's Ministry of Science and Technology and India's Ministry of Science and Technology. The two nations have organised 8 sessions of the Joint Science and Technology committee and implemented 13 joint ventures in information technology, agriculture, animal husbandry, industry, remote sensing, environmental protection, etc.

Apart from the joint ventures, India has helped Vietnam in training atomic energy experts and developing human resources in the IT sector. Every year, India provides hundreds of scholarship, both short term and long term, under various schemes, (e.g. ITEC, ICCR, etc.) for Vietnamese students to pursue higher education. Through joint ventures, India contributes to enhancing the skills of Vietnamese young scientists in areas of mutual concern like biotechnology, geography, agriculture, information technology and so on. Furthermore, Indian government is assisting Vietnam in its PARAM project on supercomputer, which is administered by Vietnam's Ministry of Education and Training.

Within the framework of ASEAN-India space cooperation, India convened the meeting between space agencies of ASEAN and India at Bangalore in March 2012. The meeting focused on establishing a project for establishing an Indian satellite centre for monitoring satellites, receiving and processing images in the Ho Chi Minh City.

At the 8th session of the Vietnam-India Joint Science and Technology Committee in December 2010, the two countries agreed to implement five joint research projects in information technology, biotechnology, remote sensing, geography, etc. The projects will comprise of various scientists working in different institutes and universities. The 9th session was held in the 3rd quarter of 2012 in Hanoi, with a goal to implement the new cooperation programme in mutually concerned areas of technologies.

At the 14th session of Vietnam-India Joint Commission organised at Hanoi in September 2011, the two nations agreed to continue holding meetings for the Joint Science and Technology Committee, promoting the implementation of joint programmes in training and research, and increasing investment in mutually concerned areas. India welcomed Vietnam's proposition that India shall assist in the construction of Science and Technology Park in Vietnam. Additionally, to heighten Vietnam-India cooperation in high-tech domains, Vietnam's Ministry of Science and Technology, in coordination with Hoa Lac Industrial Zone, Ho Chi Minh City Industrial Zone and Da Nang Industrial Zone, made a request for investment from India in Vietnam's High Tech Park.

Ways to Enhance Science and Technology Cooperation from 2012 to 2020

Vietnam and India can bolster cooperation in science and technology in fields like biotechnology (in processing medicinal herbs), agriculture, new materials, nanotechnology (especially nano-materials), space technology (research and design of satellites, application in medical and education), remote sensing technology for disaster forecast, environmental protection, information technology (especially software development and export), supercomputer production, atomic energy technology, development of science and technology firms, and in research and development of science and technology products with an aim to commercialise these products. Vietnam's Ministry of Science and Technology has signed a programme for biotechnology cooperation with India's Department of Biotechnology which functions under Ministry of Science and Technology of India. This will open up a new phase in biotechnology development for the two countries.

Science and technology cooperation between Vietnam and India from now to 2020 can be envisaged in two periods from 2012 to 2014, and from 2105 to 2020.

Vietnam will promote discussion with India in developing projects to construct Science and Technology Park. Both countries need to implement five joint ventures whose terms and conditions were discussed and agreed in the 8th session of the Joint Science and Technology Committee held at New Delhi in the fourth quarter of 2010. These ventures are related to biotechnology, information technology and telecommunications technology. The two countries also need to implement projects proposed at the 9th session of the Vietnam-India Joint Science and Technology Committee, held at Hanoi in the third quarter of 2012. These projects encompass oceanography, clean technology for leather production, space technology for designing and producing of small, micro and nano-satellites, etc.

During 2015-20 both countries can take initiatives to develop large-scale projects focusing on key areas like gene analysis and DNA decoding in biotechnology, development of atomic energy technology for peaceful purposes, cooperation in space technology, application of satellite technology in education and medical fields, cooperation in nano-materials in nanotechnology, etc. India and Vietnam can also give priority to cooperate in industrial automation, computerisation of administration and other areas, supercomputer production, bio-computer technology, software research and development, environmental technology, ocean bottom seismometer technology, earthquake and tsunami warning technology.

16

ICT Industry in Vietnam: Opportunities for Cooperation with India

Tran Quy Nam

This chapter has been divided into three parts: Overview of ICT Industry in Vietnam, Vietnam government's policies and plans to develop ICT industry and opportunities for cooperation with India in the ICT sector.

Overview of ICT Industry in Vietnam

Vietnam has a huge potential in the ICT sector. It is ranked 8th in the 50 most attractive countries for software outsourcing. Vietnam is also in the top 10 leading location for offshore services in the Asia-Pacific region. Hanoi and Ho Chi Minh cities are among the top 100 rising cities in the Information Technology Outsourcing (ITO) and Business Process Outsourcing (BPO). Vietnam's Network Readiness Index (NRI) at global level increased to 55 out of 133 countries surveyed in 2011, from 75 out of 134 countries surveyed in 2001. In Asia its NRI increased to 4th in 2011 from 6th in 2001. Vietnam is at the 7th position in the top internet connectivity countries in Asia, according to data as of March 31, 2011.

In the period from 2001 to 2011, the ICT industry in Vietnam grew at the rate of 25-30 per cent per annum increasing its revenue from US$ 1 billion to more than US$ 24 billion in 2011. Vietnam has about 290 universities and colleges offering courses in the ICT sector and more than 220 vocational schools having IT professional program. Enrolment in the ICT courses doubled to over 64,500 persons in 2011 from 2006 figures.

IT industry in Vietnam grew at the rate of 20-25 per cent per year increasing its revenue contribution from US$ 0.5 billion in 2001 to US$ 13.66 billion. Out of the total IT sector, IT hardware industry grew at the rate of about 20 per cent annually generating US$ 11.32 billion revenue in 2011. Vietnam's IT hardware products worth US$ 10.89 billion in 2011 were exported to more than 35 countries. IT hardware industry in Vietnam employed about 167,000 professionals in 2011. The turnover in the IT hardware sector is about US$ 67,555 per labour annually, with an average salary of US$ 2,279 per labour annually.

IT software industry grew at the rate of 10-40 per cent per year, generating revenue of about US$ 1.172 billion in 2011, an amount four times higher than the revenue generated in 2005. The turnover for software industry is about US$ 14,835 per labour annually, with an average salary of US$ 5,034 per labour annually, employing about 79,000 professionals. There are about 1000 software firms operating in Vietnam, out of which about 30 firms have Capability Maturity Model Integration (CMMI) level of 5, 4 or 3. CMMI is used as a framework for appraising the process maturity of the organisation. It provides guidance for developing or improving processes that meet the business goals of an organisation.

Digital content industry is another booming ICT industry in Vietnam which is growing at the rate of 25-50 per cent annually. Digital content industry generated about US$ 1.165 billion of revenue in 2011, an amount nine times higher than the 2005 figures. The turnover for digital content industry is about US$ 19,352 per labour annually, and the average salary paid to a labour in this sector is about US$ 5,267 annually. There are about 500 firms operating in this industry, employing about 60,000 workers.

IT services is another significant ICT industry developing in Vietnam, with potential in ITO, BPO, integrated services, data centre, call centre, etc.

Financial resources in ICT industry comes from various sources like the government's budget, various enterprises and stock markets, capital funds such as IDGVV, VinaCapital, Mekong Capital, IFC (WB), MEF, etc. Foreign Direct Investment in ICT industry comes from countries like USA (Intel, IBM, Motorola), Japan (Canon, Fujitsu), Korea (LG, Samsung), Taiwan (Foxconn, Compal), etc.

Intel started operations in Vietnam in 2006 with investment of US$ 1 billion in chipset production manufacture in Ho Chi Minh City. IBM has an IT service centre employing about 2000 workers. Samsung has started a mobile phone factory, in which it has completed first phase by investing about US$ 330 million. It plans to invest US$ 670 million to US$ 1 billion more in the factory. Foxconn-Honhai has invested about US$ 5 billion in electronic manufacture in North Vietnam. Canon has plans to invest US$ 500 million to manufacture printer and related products. Taiwanese company Compal has plans to invest US$ 500 million to manufacture laptop in Vietnam. Besides, several other software and IT services companies like Havey Nash, GHP, Hitachi, NEC, Motorola, etc. have plans to invest in the country.

There are software and IT enterprises operating in Vietnam like FPT System integration, CMC, NCS, Vietsoftware, HPT, MISA, Tinh Van, Sao Bac Dau, etc. Companies like FPT Software, CSC, PSV, TMA, Pyramid Vietnam, Global Cybersoft, etc. are working in the domain of software outsourcing. Companies like VTC, VNG, Socbay, VASC, DIGI-Texx, etc. are providing digital contents. There are online games companies like VNG, VTC-Intercom, FPT online, etc. Hardware computer productions are done by companies like CMS, FPT-Elead, VTB, Hanel, etc. Training services for IT are provided by Hanoi DTT, Hanoi eDT, Aptech Vietnam, NIIT Vietnam, etc. Vietnam also has e-newspapers like VNExpress, Vietnamnet, Media, etc. Telecom services are provided by companies like VNPT, Viettel, FPTtel, Hntel, VTCtel, Gtel, etc.

Vietnam Government's Policies and Plans to Develop ICT Industry

Annual ICT revenue contribution to GDP is expected to double by 2020. In 2020, ICT share's in GDP would touch 8-10 per cent annually. Government hopes to increase nation-wide broadband infrastructure, include ICT usage in all aspects of life, which is supposed to contribute in the sustainable development, and enhancing the transparency of the government agencies. IT industry, especially software and digital content industry are likely to become key drivers of the economy, by achieving the highest growth rate among the techno-economic sectors.

In this regard, to promote the development of IT Industry, Vietnam has approved a number of master plans to be developed over a period of time. The 'Strategy on Vietnam Information and Communication Technology Development to 2010 and Orientations Towards 2020' was approved in 2005 with Prime Minister's Decision No. 246/2005/QD-TTg. The national strategy for 'Transforming Vietnam into an Advanced ICT Country' in 2020 was adopted by Prime Minister's Decision No. 1755/QD-TTg on September 22, 2010. 'Master plan to develop Software Industry to the year 2010' was approved by Decision No. 51/2007/QĐ-TTg. 'Master Plan to Develop Digital Content Industry to the Year 2010' was approved by Decision No. 56/2007/QĐ-TTg. 'Master plan to develop Hardware Electronic Industry to the Year 2010' was approved by Decision No. 75/2007/QĐ-TTg. 'Master plan for IT application in government's agencies for 2015' was approved by Decision No. 1605/QĐ-TTg in 2010. 'Master Plan to Promote E-commerce in Vietnam' was approved by Decision No. 1073/QĐ-TTg, on12 July 2010.

There is a need of about one million IT workers in Vietnam. Government of Vietnam intends to develop internationally recognised ICT human resources in the country. It hopes that by 2020, 80 per cent of ICT graduates of Vietnam would join international ICT labour market.

To improve the legal environment for ICT sector, Vietnamese government is trying to make a clear and fair regulation and promulgating policies in this sector. To develop human resources, the government is trying to improve the quality of training and create a pool of talent on ICT in Vietnam. To enhance the abilities of enterprises, the government is encouraging software companies to apply CMMI, ISO 27001 standards. It is helping IT industries in improving technology through collaborative transfers, helping companies to enter new markets, enhancing their competitiveness, facilitating investment and in creating a fair environment for all enterprises, both domestic and foreign enterprises, to operate in the country. The government is investing in building IT industry parks, promoting operation of venture capital funds, and in implementing policies to promote the use of OSS products in e-government projects. It is also trying to develop the broadband telecommunications and internet infrastructure and research and development in the IT sector in some products in which Vietnam has strong advantage. It is focusing on developing software outsourcing and services, implementing Intellectual Property Rights, investor's legal rights, etc.

ICT Legal Frameworks Improvement

ICT related laws	Date of coming into effect
Electronic Transaction Law & Degrees, Circulars detailed the law	1-7-2006
Intellectual Property Law & Degrees, Circulars detailed the law	1-7-2006
Information Technology Law & Degrees, Circulars detailed the law	1-1-2007
Telecommunications Law & Degrees, Circulars detailed the law	1-7-2010
Radio Frequency Law & Degrees, Circulars detailed the law	1-7-2010

The Government of Vietnam is providing four-year corporate tax exemption from the first year for companies having taxable income. It is also providing preferential personal income tax for the people working in the software industry. Vietnam has made Value Added Tax (VAT) exemption for software products and services, zero per cent import tax for materials directly used in the software production and for software products, subsidised internet access fee for enterprises operating in the Software Parks, given investment support from the state's development support fund, and exempted or relinquished the cost of using and renting land as well as land tax. It is supporting IT firms with US$ 25,000 per firm to build CMMI or ISO 27001 standards. Vietnamese policy makers are ready to abolish tax on export products within ASEAN according to Common Effective Preferential Treatment (CEPT) starting from 2015. Based on that, tax rate which has been at 0-5 per cent since 2006, will be decreased to zero per cent i.e. abolish tax under CEPT rule. Currently, 97 per cent of all products have the tax rate of 0-5 per cent, among them tax rate is 5 per cent, on more than 50 per cent of the products. Along with IT products, tax on electronic products will be removed by 2012. There's an updated Harmonized Commodities Description and Coding System (HS table) and products included under this table are eligible to apply the lowest tax rate among other products.

Opportunities for Cooperation with India in the ICT Sector

Vietnam is a dynamic and attractive market that supports quickest ICT growth in the world. ICT businesses in Vietnam receive strong support from the government in forms of training, research and development, land leasing, infrastructure development and tax incentives (hi-tech parks and industrial zones). As the global economy is recovering from the financial crisis, Vietnam is likely to become an attractive destination for investors and multi-national companies.

Vietnam has a number of strengths which is important for developing ICT businesses. Vietnam is a high-demand market, which is continuously growing. It has a young population, with about 60 per cent people in the productive age of 17 to 60 years, with good educational backgrounds. It has a vast pool of talent in the ICT sector which is rapidly growing. IT labour force of Vietnam is creative, hardworking and quickly adaptable to new technologies. The operating costs and salaries in Vietnam are low, about one-third of India, and about one-half of China and Philippines. As Vietnamese culture favours stability, attrition rate in Vietnam is very low at only about 5-7 per cent.

With the signing of the Strategic Partnership and familiarity and close relationship between India and Vietnam, there is good scope for cooperation between the two countries in the ICT field.

Vietnam can cooperate and facilitate for Indian enterprises to invest in IT sector in Vietnam. Vietnam and India can exchange experiences, knowledge and professionals in the ICT sector. Both the countries can share policies and strategies to develop IT industry in their respective countries. Both countries can even cooperate in academic and professional skills training for human resource development and for network security and information security. They can also partner in ITO and BPO development, especially in new market like Japan. They can cooperate in promoting open source software, in high performance computing and developing and implementing 'Cheap PC' program. Both countries can cooperate in organising an Asian and India show and conference on ICT.

SECTION V

Tracing Civilisational Links and Potential for Tourism

17

India and Vietnam: Cultural Contacts Through Buddhism

Do Thu Ha

This chapter attempts to understand relationship between Buddhism and culture in Vietnam. The chapter has been divided into two parts. First, it describes the four main characteristics of Vietnamese Buddhism: amalgamation, creativity, adaptation and harmonisation, and analyses the social milieu in which they evolved. Second part deals with the contribution of Buddhism to Vietnamese cultural aspects like language, system of thoughts, literature, arts, morality, etc. In early times there was a place in Vietnam known as Giao Chau, which can be identified with modern Bac Ninh province.

Vietnamese Buddhism has a long history of more than 2,000 years. Its origin dates back to the 3rd century B.C., when numerous Buddhist missions were sent abroad by Emperor Asoka to disseminate Lord Buddha's teachings in distant countries of South East Asia including Malaysia, Burma, Thailand, Laos, Cambodia and North Vietnam.

Vietnamese Buddhism can be roughly divided into 4 periods: (a) Early Phase: From ancient times to 10th century A.D. (b) Golden Age: From 11th century to 14th century A.D. (c) Decline in 15th century and restoration in later centuries (d) Contemporary Buddhism and its role.

Characteristics of Vietnamese Buddhism

How did the Buddhism come to Vietnam? Many people believe that Buddhism came to Vietnam from China. The reason for this was, China was a big neighbour and Vietnam was influenced strongly by Chinese politics and culture for many centuries. However, this is not true. Buddhism came to Vietnam directly from India. In those times, when people made a trip from India to China or vice versa, it was necessary for them to cross Vietnam. Vietnam, therefore, was a good place to halt for traders and also for Buddhist monks. In the 3rd century B.C., King Asoka organised the Third Buddhist Council to compile the Dharma at Pataliputra in India. After the Council, he sent nine Buddhist monk-delegations overseas to teach Dharma from Afghanistan to the Mediterranean region. One of these delegations led by Sona and Uttara went to Burma then Indochina, including Vietnam. In Haiphong, 60 miles northeast of Hanoi, there is a memorial tower to commemorate King Asoka that was built by local Vietnamese Buddhists to express their gratitude to Asoka. From this evidence, one may conclude that Buddhism came to Vietnam as early as 3rd century B.C., much before it reached China.

In the 2nd century A.D. (A.D. 168-189), Buddhism became popular in Vietnam and flourished with the contribution of three great Buddhist monks who came from India: Marajivaka, K'ang Seng Houei, Tchi Kiang Liang and a local scholar, Mecu-Fo (Mau-Bac or Mau-Tu in Vietnamese). Mecu-Fo played a very important role in developing Buddhism in Vietnam. Mecu-Fo was born sometime around 165-170 A.D. in Ts'ang-Wu. Many Chinese historians claim that Mecu-Fo was a Chinese, but in fact he was a Vietnamese or might have been born and raised in a great Chinese-Vietnamese family. To support this argument, one needs to know that Ts'ang-Wu, which now consists of Kwang-Tung and Kwang-Si provinces, was originally a part of Vietnam. This area was invaded and annexed to China under Han Dynasty in 111 B.C. Mecu-Fo was a talented scholar who understood the philosophies of both great Chinese philosophers Lao Tseu and Confucius well. In any debate, he could easily make the comparison between Chinese philosophical traditions and Buddhism and gained the respect of Chinese scholars at that time. His famous book, 'Reason and Doubt' was considered the first written book about Buddhism not only in Vietnam but also in East Asia. He was a mandarin, who took advantage of his position to teach people about Buddhism. Because of this, Vietnamese Buddhists always consider him as the first lay man. He helped in building a Buddhist stronghold in Southeast Asia, particularly, in Luy Lau, the capital of Vietnam at that time.

The historicity of Buddhism began much earlier in Vietnam is also evident from the fact that the Order of Giao Chau monks was founded before Buddhism spread to other places. From the evidence of historical records under the Latter Eastern Han Dynasty, one may conclude that Luy Lau was the first to adopt the new faith from Indian monks who gradually found their way to the North, i.e. South China and the Yangtse River Valley, and then to Lo Yang, the capital of China, where the two other Buddhist centres were successively founded. According to the documents recorded in Thien Uyen Tap Anh, an Anthology of the most talented figures in Ch'an Park, the most ancient Buddhist literary collection in Vietnam, Master K'ang Seng Hui, a monk of Sogdiana origin was the first Buddhist Master at Luy Lau Centre. He was born in Giao Chau, where he was received into the Order of Monks afterwards. He became the most famous monk scholar who translated a large number of Buddhist Canonical books into Chinese (Sino characters) and later visited Nanking, where he built the first pagoda and preached the Dhamma.

Besides Master K'ang Seng Hui, there were many famous Indian monk scholars such as Mahajivaka, Kalaruci (Tche Kiang Liang) and a Chinese scholar Mao Po (Mui Tsu), who immigrated to Giao Chau and studied Buddhism under Indian monks there. At that time, there were about 20 pagodas and 500 monks at Luy Lau centre. They translated at least 15 Buddhist Text Books. 'The Buddha's Sutta in 42 Sections' which appeared at Giao Chau in the 2nd century A.D. is believed to be the first selection of Suttas translated into Chinese at Luy Lau.

Therefore, one of the characteristics of Vietnamese Buddhism in ancient times was that it had been introduced by Indian missionaries into Giao Chau long before it spread to China. The literary evidence in the above translation proves that from the very beginning, Vietnamese Buddhism adopted the fundamentals of Orthodox Buddhism from Indian monks and in later centuries with the development of Buddhism in China, it received another trend of Buddhist thought, the Mahayana doctrine, especially Chinese Ch'an Buddhism.

Another salient feature of Vietnamese Buddhism is that it has been closely connected with national life. Buddhist monks have made active contribution to the construction and protection of their country. The best learned class of society; Vietnamese monks practised their religion side by side with common people and were on friendly terms with members of other religions such as Taoism and Confucianism. A large number of Ch'an Masters were great Confucian scholars who, besides their religious duty, played an important part in social life. They might have made use of favourable conditions of Chinese Buddhism under the Sui (in the 6th century A.D.) and the T'ang dynasties (in the 7th and 8th centuries) in order to develop Vietnamese Buddhism and further a national movement for liberation from Chinese yoke.

The first period of Vietnam's independence began with King Ly-Nam-De, who highly honoured Buddhism and used to consult Buddhist monks and follow their advice on religious and worldly affairs in protecting the young nation against foreign invasions. The glorious victory at Bach Dang River in 930 A.D. opened a new page in Vietnamese history. For almost 10 centuries, Vietnam was dominated by Chinese. Under the Chinese rule, Vietnamese people suffered a lot. There were many attempts to revolt to liberate the country from the Chinese rule including by two famous Trung sisters in the early years of First century. The Buddhist temples or the Buddhist communities played a key role in those movements. It became the common place to gather and mobilise people. That's why Vietnamese Buddhists consider Buddhism as people's religion. Finally, in 939 A.D. Ngo Quyen, a Vietnamese General, led the Vietnamese people to fight and win the battle against the Chinese army on the Bach Dang river. Vietnam then became an independent state. Still after independence, to build Vietnam into a strong, healthy country, it took almost one century. The Chinese employed the 'Sinicisation' process to uproot Vietnamese traditions and in the long run to annex Vietnam as one of their provinces. However, they did not succeed in their designs, because of Buddhism. Vietnamese people had absorbed the Buddha teaching for many centuries. Buddhism was like a glue to tighten people together to live in peace and happiness. Vietnamese people strongly believed in Buddha teachings, especially in the universal Law of Cause and Effect, and believed that the evil power someday would be eroded.

After the overthrow of Chinese rule, under Dinh Dynasty, Vietnamese Buddhist monks worked closely with the government to help in building the kingdom. In return, the emperor, Dinh Tien Hoang, a Buddhist, helped in organising the Sangha. He also named Khuong Viet, the highest ranking monk as his national security adviser and named Phapthuan as Secretary of State. This was the first time in Vietnamese history when the emperor declared Buddhism as a national religion.

Vietnamese people as well as Vietnamese Buddhists enjoyed the golden time under Ly-Tran dynasty, which ruled for about four centuries, from A.D. 1010 to A.D. 1400. In this period, the country's intellectual class mainly consisted of Buddhist monks. Under the Chinese policy of exterminating Vietnamese culture during their rule spread over 10 centuries, China had put a ban on establishing local education system in Vietnam. Buddhist temples, therefore, were the only places where people could get education. As a result, Buddhist sangha produced many talented scholars as well as public administrators who formed the backbone of country's intellectual class at that time.

Though Buddhism played an important role in shaping the country, it never sought to influence the government. It also did not discriminate against other religions to gain supremacy. Buddhism, Confucianism and Taoism all coexisted in harmony under the Ly-Tran dynasties. Many kings and royal family members from these dynasties were big names in Vietnamese history as well as Buddhist history. The acculturation process of Vietnamese Buddhism formed the depth of traditional culture in Vietnam. For example, during the

Tran dynasty, A.D. 1225-1400, Vietnam brought Champa kingdom under their rule. At this time another school of Buddhism, the Truc Lam, developed in Vietnam. It fused Confucianism, Taoism and Buddhism in a spirit of national unity against foreign domination, especially against incursions by the Mongols. Truc Lam combined the otherworldly aspirations of Taoism and Buddhism with the practical humanism of Confucianism. In those times, however, the political elite increasingly supported Confucianism at the expense of Buddhism. A resurgence of Buddhism occurred in Vietnam in the 17th century, stimulated by the arrival of Chinese monks of the Linji (in Vietnamese, Lam-Te; in Japanese, Rinzai) tradition. The Lam-Te became the foundation of most of Vietnam's present-day monastic institutions.

That's why, another interesting feature of Buddhism during Ly-Tran dynasty was its trend of blending Buddhism with Taoism and Confucianism. This growing tendency of combining the three religions together in a harmonious way resulted in producing experts in the three branches of learning. Many of them were Ch'an Masters, kings and court mandarins who played a very active role as leaders in several struggles against the Sung's army and later the Mongols' invasions. In peace as well as in war times, Buddhists made great effort to bring welfare and happiness to the people. In the period of unprecedented prosperity of Vietnamese Buddhism, both Taoism and Confucianism were also well-developed and very popular with all social classes.

The first few centuries of the first millennium were marked by the expansion of Indian culture and religion into Southeast Asia. Archaeological evidence from Champa, in what is now central Vietnam, yields figures of buddhas and bodhisattvas and Sanskrit inscriptions dating from the 2nd or 3rd century CE. Inscriptions address Hindu gods predominantly, especially Siva, but there are also praises to the Buddha. Later archaeological finds from Dong Duong in central Vietnam indicate the presence of Buddhist temples and statues. Most of these evidences are suggestive of the presence of Mahayana Buddhism in Vietnam. However, a Hinayana presence is mentioned by the 17th-century Chinese traveller Yi Jing. In the 2nd and 3rd centuries CE, the Giao Chi province was visited by such prominent figures as the Sogdian monk Kang Seng Hui and the Indian monks Kalaruci and Mahajivaka. These monks propagated the dharma, founded relic mounds (stupas) and temples, and translated Buddhist scriptures from Sanskrit into Chinese.

Chinese Buddhist influence in Vietnam, however, was eventually far more substantial and enduring than Indian Buddhist influence. Vietnam was ruled by China for more than a millennium (111 BCE–939 CE), and Chinese political domination and culture exerted a more direct and profound impression on Vietnam than on any other Southeast Asian culture. The first recorded instance of a Chinese missionary in Vietnam is Mou Po, who propagated Buddhism in northern Vietnam in the 2nd century CE. However, Mahayana Buddhism from China really became dominant and widespread beginning in the 5th century CE. Buddhism in Vietnam, as in China, existed throughout its long history alongside, and sometimes in competition with, Confucianism, Taoism and ancestor worship. In this way, the national system with families as centre led to the development of Buddhism in Vietnam. That's why, many Buddhist sects and early Sanghas originated in Vietnam.

This characteristic probably began with King Ly Cong Uan. Ly Cong Uan was raised a Buddhist monk by Zen Master Van Hanh in a Buddhist temple since he was 3 years old. Van Hanh was not only his religious master, but also his mentor. Therefore, when he became an emperor, he asked the Venerable Van Hanh to become his national advisor. Under his rein, about 300 Buddhist temples were built, and the Sangha was organised which had about 1,000 excellent monks. Like king Ashoka of India, the emperor applied Buddha teachings into every aspect to govern the country. Full of compassion, after becoming the Emperor the first thing Ly did was to give the order to burn all kinds of fishing nets, to set free all kind of birds, and to free all the prison inmates from the previous dynasty. For people who felt mistreated by the local government, he allowed them to come to the capital to see him directly.

The next emperor of Ly dynasty was also very kind and influenced by Buddhism. He forbade the killings of animals, especially, cows and buffaloes during his reign. He once woke up at midnight in a very cold winter. He saw his lovely daughter was trembling in the cold, and felt very sorrow, not for his daughter but for his all people. He said, 'Oh! My daughter who has all kind of fine winter clothing was still tremble like that. How do my people live who don't have enough clothing?'

After Ly dynasty, Tran dynasty ruled in Vietnam. Like the Ly dynasty, all emperors of Tran Dynasty were Buddhists who well understood the teachings of Buddha. The first emperor, Tran Thai Tong (1225-1258) was a dedicated Buddhist monk. One night, like Buddha, he abdicated the throne, escaped from his family and went into hiding in the mountain to practice Buddhism.

Contribution of Buddhism to Vietnamese Language and Literature

In this section contribution of Buddhism to Vietnamese Language and literature would be dealt in two parts: in the north and in the south. The section on the north would be further divided into Buddhism contribution on Viet groups of language and literature, and its impact on the other ethnic groups.

In the North

Viet Group

According to the History of Vietnamese Buddhism, Luy Lau, during the early Christian era, was one of the three ancient towns of Giao Chau (Luy Lau, Long Bien, Co Loa) which was one of the three greatest Buddhist centres in the Chinese Han Empire. It was also a big political and economic centre. Therefore it became an ideal place for cultural and linguistic contacts. The language of Giao Chau (i.e. ancient Vietnamese) together with Chinese and Sanskrit were used equally in trading and religious activities, and it was not uncommon to see missionaries and even some local people who were trilingual.

In later years, however, Luy Lau suffered much from the social and political instability resulting from the domination of the Chinese.

Not only did the conquerors impose Confucianism on Vietnamese society but they also set up an educational system to train local officials for their administrative needs. All these led to the predominance of Confucianism, Taoism and the Chinese language in Vietnam.

During Chinese rule what happened to Buddhism and Sanskrit, which were the religion and language of the people? Historical evidence shows that not only did Buddhism and, together with it, Sanskrit refused to die out, but it was further strengthened by Buddhism coming from China, following the heels of the conquerors into Vietnam. Buddhism was so much strengthened that it became even more deeply rooted in the Vietnamese society.

Effect of Chinese Rule on Vietnamese Language

In Vietnam's folk literature, there is a legend about Saint Giong. He is a typical representative of the national heroes of Vietnam who, at the dawn of Vietnamese history, helped defend their country from foreign invasion. Legends, by tradition, are usually products of people's imagination, but they are never without a historical basis. What is special about relationship between legends and history in Vietnam is that sometimes the boundary between the two is not very clearly defined. Vietnamese society in general accepts legendary heroes as real heroes and worships them and their legendary exploits in temples. The Bo Dau Temple, which was built a long time ago to honour Saint Giong, can still be seen nowadays at Thong Nhat Village, in Thuong Tin District of Ha Tay Province.

In the recently published results on Bo Dau temple, Cung Khac Luoc and Luong Van Ke (Vietnamese scholars in textology) write, 'We have discovered dozens of parallel sentences, nearly a hundred woodblocks for printing Buddhist scriptures and Buddhist-study certificates, together with documents written in Sanskrit, Chinese and Nom; and many other woodblocks with carved symbols of the Three Religions…'. The discovery by Cung Khac Luoc and Luong Van Ke is of great scientific and historical value. Two things that become amply clear as a result of this research are: first, among the documents found at Bo Dau temple, there are documents written in

Sanskrit. Second Saint Giong, was a real historical figure of unquestionable lineage, as is made clear in his genealogical record worshipped at the temple. There is no doubt, therefore, as to the very early existence of ancient Indian scripts in Vietnamese culture.

It was through Hinduism and Buddhism that Indian language and script made its way into Vietnam. In 'The History of Vietnamese Buddhism' Tran Dinh Huou writes, 'Originating in India, Buddhism came from the south by sea and from the west by land into Vietnam'. In the first few centuries of the Christian era, Luy Lau (Lien Lau) was a great Buddhist centre, a province in Giao Chau. Luy Lau was located in the heart of the Red River Delta, and very early in its history it was frequented by merchants from India and Central Asia. These merchants were followed by Buddhist monks who came to practice and disseminate Buddhism in Vietnam. The monks from India, Sri Lanka and Central Asia on the way to carry out missionary duty in China called at Luy Lau where they familiarised themselves with the Chinese language and script. There, with the help of Vietnamese monks, they translated Buddhist scriptures into Chinese before heading towards mainland China.

In 'The History of Vietnamese Buddhism', there is a mention of a Chinese scholar Khang Seng Huoi/Khuong Tang Hoi, A.D. 220-247, who was of Central Asian origin, but was born and ordained in Giao Chau. He later became an excellent Zen master who gained fame for his profound knowledge of Chinese and Sanskrit literature, and for his erudite Buddhist writings and annotations of Buddhist Scriptures. He later travelled to China to preach Buddhism.

There was great influence of Sanskrit on the Vietnamese language. As has been pointed out above, from its original birth place, Buddhism found its way into Vietnam both directly from India and indirectly from China. Buddhist terminologies that came directly from India were in Sanskrit, whereas those from China were in Chinese or, in Sinicised Sanskrit. In present-day Vietnamese Buddhism terminology, words of Sanskrit and of Sinicised Sanskrit origins can easily be distinguished. Words such as 'But' (Buddha) 'niet ban' (nirvana) and 'da xoa' (yaksa) are among those that had come to Vietnam directly from India much earlier, therefore, these words are more Vietnamised.

How can one be sure that these words had come at a much early times? As a rule, the longer time a loan word is used, the greater change in meaning it undergoes. As far as word form is concerned, then the Vietnamese monosyllabic 'But' is a transformation of 'Buddha'. However to the common people now the word 'But' does not refer to the founder of Buddhism but instead it refers to a merciful deity who is always ready to offer a helping hand to the good people in distress. (The 'But' in the story about Tam and Cam is an example). Originally, the Sanskrit 'Yaksa' had a favourable meaning and was identified with 'a superman or a demi-god', but in the Vietnamese language, it has now come to be associated with a demon that is 'invisible and bent on causing harm to humans' (Huynh Tinh Cua). Also, in the eyes of the common people, 'niet ban' or 'nat ban' refers to that 'land of after-life happiness' reserved for those whose every action in this life is moulded by kindness and benevolence. Buddhologists apart, a few people now know that etymologically this word refers to the state in which one has freed himself from the endless series of births, deaths and rebirths. Besides those words of Sanskrit origin, there exist in the Vietnamese language a great number of words of 'sinicised Sanskrit' origin, otherwise referred to as 'Sanskrit-Sino–Vietnamese' words. Originally these words were Sanskrit but they had been transliterated into Chinese before they came to Vietnam, where they were again transliterated into Vietnamese.

Many Buddhist followers and Buddhist monks use words of 'sinicised sanskrit' group without knowing about their etymology. Here are a few examples: Ty sa mon < Vais'ranana/vaisravana (The God of Wealth, Guardian of The Buddha's teachings); Da la ni < dharani (to maintain and protect virtues and to guard against evils); tam ma dia < Samadhi (deep contemplation); Thien Na < Dhyana (meditation upon a single object); Bat Nha < prajna (knowledge). These Sanskrit-Sino-Vietnamese words were not only used in daily speech but also in writing. Some time ago, historians and archaeologists discovered near Hoang Long River at Hoa Lu (now in Ninh Binh Province) about 20 stone pillars on which Buddhist prayers were inscribed. What attracts attention most in these pillars is the fact that all the stone pillars are inscribed with the esoteric formula known as 'Phat Dinh Ton Thang da la ni' (Usnisavijadharani) in sinicised Sanskrit'. And on the stone pillar in front of Nhat Tru Pagoda at Hoa Lu (erected in 995), the following Buddhist hymn (S. Gatha) can still be seen:

> 'Cac thien than thuong nghe am thanh tieng Phan
> Nghe tung niem Phat dinh da la ni,
> Thi duoc day du tray gaol'
>
> *Translation*:
>
> 'Those spirits that daily listen to prayers
> And to the esoteric formula usnisavijadhaorani in Pali
> Can maintain their spiritual equilibrium
> And keep their faith in the Buddha from wavering'.

Effect of Chinese Rule on Vietnamese Literature

Back to the golden age of Buddhism in Vietnam, Ly and Tran dynasties, there were many eminent Zen masters. Traditionally, before passing away, a Zen master left a poem for their students. It may be in the forms of instructional verse or an expression of the spiritual understanding, experience and attitudes towards life. The writing of Buddhist poetry, or Zen poetry, became a familiar practice among Vietnamese Zen masters which has continued up to modern times. These poems have become very popular and have been learnt by hearts by many generations of Vietnamese Buddhists.

Even though Buddhism in Vietnam was influenced strongly by Mahayana tradition, Zen in Vietnam has different characteristic. It shows that Buddhism had adapted to the cultural atmosphere of the new country in which it was propagated. It also reflects the attitude of Vietnamese people towards life, always optimistic and positive.

King Tran Nhan Tong was the founder and patriarch of Truc Lam Zen School. His famous poem, Cu Tran Lac Dao, 'Living in this world, enjoying with the Tao' is a good example to show the spirit of Vietnamese Zen. It teaches to live in a simple, easy going way. One already has a good fortune, so what one needs is to return to oneself and work with one's mind. Whenever one views things with empty mind, one will walk into the open door of enlightenment.

> 'Satisfied with your present condition and life, enjoy Tao;
> Eat when hungry, rest when fatigued;
> You already have a great fortune, don't need to seek elsewhere;
> View things with empty mind, that's Zen.'

Truc Lam Zen of Vietnam was considered the mature Vietnamese Buddhist thoughts, which was cultivated for almost three centuries from Ly to Tran dynasty. Among the great Buddhist monks from Ly dynasty who left the long-lasting impact on the succeeding Vietnamese generations were Van Hanh and Man Giac. Let's examine one of the poem written by Zen master Van Hanh:

> 'The life span of body is like a lightning, it exists then disappears in a short moment
> It's like all plants and trees, fresh in the spring but fades in the autumn
> Trust in your destiny, unafraid of raising or falling, up or down
> They are like a drop of morning dew on the blade of grass'

This poem carries a very simple idea and reflects one of the principal virtues of Bodhisattvas. The Buddhist spirit to live without fear, in the face of impermanence of the phenomenal world. Van Hanh, one of the most eminent monks of Vietnamese Buddhism, before passing away, taught his disciples the last lesson: Don't be afraid of the constantly changing phenomenal world. He says life is like a drop of morning dew? In the morning, it is bright under the sunrise like a diamond. But in the next moment it vapourises in the air or disappears on the ground, to a complete transformation. One's life is just like that.

Zen master Man Giac, a respected and popular monk whose disciples included the Emperor and the Empress, wrote:

'When spring goes, the hundred flowers wither
when spring comes, the hundred flowers blossom
Things go on, lives passes before our eyes
The childhood fades then old age comes someday
Don't think that as spring ends, all flowers go away
A plum flower blossomed in my garden last night'

Like Van Hanh, in this poem Man Giac refers to the flow of natural events as emblematic of ultimate reality. If one realises the impermanence of the phenomenal world, one will not experience any fear from the changing or unstable world.

The 'Linh Nam Trich Quai' ('Strange Legends of Linh Nam, legendary Vietnam'), compiled by Tran The Phap, relates the story of Chou Noang Tou, a legendary character. In the time of Huong Voong (some hundred years before the Christian Era), Chou Noang Tou was a famous merchant. One day, he met an Indian monk named Kalacharya and become the latter's disciple. Kalacharya with his spiritual faculties and magical powers helped Chou Noang Tou develop his mind and understand Buddhist teachings. Another story of Indian monk is also narrated in the book 'Kien Van Tieu luc' ('Booklet on Literature'), compiled by Le Quy Don, 1726-1783, a prominent Vietnamese historian. A girl named Man Nuong met Master Kalacarya at a pagoda. He gave her a mystical stick. She used that stick to save the regional inhabitants from a severe drought by driving it into the ground to make water gush out.

The above two legends affirm that Buddhism came to Vietnam very long ago and quickly ingrained itself in the religious beliefs of Vietnamese people. Indeed, very early in the history of Vietnamese Buddhism, its practice was greatly affected by Indian tradition as India's civilisation had a considerable influence on Giao Chau. Stories in the Jataka Nikaya related by K'ang Seng Hui (3rd century) makes a very interesting introduction of India morals and culture into the Vietnamese people's lives. (One can see Satparamita Samipata Sutra, Nanjo 143 and Samyukta Avadana Sutra, Nanjo 1359, both selected and translated by K'ang Seng Hui).

In his work 'Ki He Lun' ('Commentary on Reason and Doubt'), Mon Po (2nd century A.D.) noted that: 'Buddhist monks wear their red robes and do not follow the Confucian formality'. The 'Thien Uyen Tap Anh' tells us about the death of Patriarch Vinitaruci. Master Phap Hien organised a ceremony to cremate the body of Vinitaruci. Cremation was not a custom of Chinese, Japanese and Vietnamese peoples in those days. The fact that nowadays many Vietnamese people carry their deceased family members to a crematorium is certainly a fact that has taken its roots from India.

Lots of small clay stupas discovered in the Red River Delta which date from the first few centuries of the Christian Era might be imitations of the ones depicted in the many stories related in Buddhist sutras. They also call up memories of the stupas that Indian Emperor Asoka (3rd century B.C.) had constructed to offer his praises to the Buddha and for the purpose of propagating Buddhism.

A Chinese Buddhist book, 'Tsu Kao Seng Ch'uan' ('Other Stories of the Great Masters'), writes about a Vietnamese Buddhist monk named Hue Thang (5th century B.C.): 'Thich Hue Thang, a Giao Chau native, lived in a pagoda on Mount Tien Chau. He used to travel everywhere, to rivers and mountains light heartedly and read the whole Lotus Sutra each day. He followed a foreign monk named Dharmadeva to practise meditation. He often entered into meditation, then came out from meditation only on the following day'. Dharmadeva the foreign monk mentioned earlier was a famous Indian monk who came to and lived in Giao Chau in the 5th century B.C. So, Dharmadeva might be the first Ch'an Master who taught meditation to Vietnamese monks before Patriarch Bodhiharma established the Ch'an Sect in China. In 580 A.D., a patriarch Vinitaruci, as mentioned earlier, came to Vietnam from China, lived in Phap Van pagoda, taught Buddhist meditation, translated Buddhist Sutras, established stupas and became the first Patriarch of a very important Ch'an (Zen) Sect bearing his name.

Regrettably, there is hardly any knowledge about the Vietnamese monks going to India for their Buddhist studies in the early centuries after the introduction of Buddhism. However, in the 7th–8th centuries A.D., six Vietnamese monks went to India to study

Buddhism and make pilgrimages to Buddhist holy places. They were Van Ky, Giai Thoat Thien (alias Moksadeva), Khuy Xung (Citradeva), Hue Dien, Tri Hanh (Drajnoadeva) and Dai Thang Dang (Mahayanapradika). After returning home, Van Ky, Giai Thoat Thien and Dai Thang Dang taught Buddhism, translated sutras and compiled Buddhist books contributing to the cause of Buddhist study in Vietnam. Khuy Xung, Tri Hanh and Dai Thang Dang died in India. In his book 'Ta T'ang Chiou Fa Kao Seng Ch'uan' ('Stories of the Great Masters in the T'ang Dynasty going to search the Dharma'), I Tsing, (682-727) a Chinese scholar who visited India, said that, he had met Van Ky and Dai Thang Dang in India. Dai Thang Dang (Mahayana pradipa) received Buddhist precepts at Dvararati. Afterwards, he went to Ch'ang An, China, where he met Great Master Tsuan Ch'ang and became the latter's disciple. Much later, he returned to Vietnam, then left Vietnam for East India where he met I Tsing and along with I Tsing, paid a visit to Nalanda University, Varanasi, Vaisali and Kusinagara.

Other Ethnic Groups

In the North of Vietnam (which belonged to the ancient Viets) there are still a lot of ancient documents left behind by the highland groups that inhabited the mountainous regions, away from the ancient cities of the Viets. These groups spoke a variety of dialects belonging to the Thai family. The scripts they used are similar in typology to the ancient Indian script and, according to Mr. Tran Chi Doi (Vietnamese scholar in Linguistics), can be divided into four groups:

- The script used by the Black Thai and the White Thai who inhabited Son La province (Muong La, Moc Chau, Phu Yen) and Lai Chau province (Muong Lay, Muong Xo and Muong Theng) (geographical names in Thai languages).
- The Thai script used by the Thai Thanh (also called Man Thanh or Tay Deng or The Red Thai) who inhabited the region to the west of Nghe An and Thanh Hoa provinces. This script is also known as the Thanh script.

- The Thai script used by the Tay Muong who inhabited Tuong Duong in Nghe An province. This script is commonly referred to as the Lai Pao or Liep Man script.
- The Thai script used by the Tay Do who inhabited the region now known as Quy Chau–Nghe An. This script is also known by the name of Quy Chau script.

An examination of the individual letters used in these scripts reveals the relationship between them and their original scripts (The Laotian script for instance). But some important differences observed in the Quy Chau and Lai Pao scripts may well lead one to the supposition that 'the ancient Thai scripts in Vietnam were less an inheritance than an invention by those who used them'. There are more than a few letters in these scripts that can not readily be traced back to any other scripts. Also, the arrangement of the letters and words in these scripts differs in principle from the arrangement commonly observed in all scripts originating from ancient Indian. In the Quy Chau script for example, the words were not written horizontally (i.e. from left to right) but perpendicularly, much in the same manner as the Chinese language is written now. The Lai Pao script reveals a difference of another kind: instead of being placed before consonants, some vowels (such as 'ay', 'e', 'o',' 'o') were placed after (Tran Chi Doi) consonants.

Why there were such differences in scripts? When did these differences first appear? Though more research must be done before any definite answers can be reached, these questions do drive home the point that, in the north of Vietnam, the influence of the ancient Indian language and script on the Vietnamese language group was by no means superficial and that the division of Indo-china into two spheres of influence referred to in Coedes' book was more administrative than cultural and linguistic.

In the South

The victory of the Vietnamese people over the Chinese Han Empire on the Bach Dang River in 938 A.D. was a turning-point in

Vietnamese history. It marked the end of a long period of foreign domination and the beginning of a new era of independence and development. However at the same time when this ancient kingdom of Dai Viet (Great Viet) was embarking on the task of national reconstruction, it had to prepare itself for resistance against any further invasion from the North and also for its own expansion into the Hinduized state of Champa that lay to the south of Dai Viet. The result was the gradual integration of the Indian-influenced state and the Chinese-influenced state into a larger kingdom in Indochina.

Nowadays, as one travels southwards, one sees more frequently the signs of Indian influence, especially at such historic sites as Nam Cat Tien and Den Vua in Long An Province. However despite the fact that historians, archaeologists and experts on architecture have tried their best, they still have a long way to go before they can give a fuller and more accurate description of the extent of Indian influence on South Vietnam and its peoples. However, the Indian influence on the languages and scripts in the South Vietnam language group is obvious. Let us examine first the Indian influence on the spoken languages now still in use in South Vietnam.

All the ethnic groups that have inhabited South Vietnam since ancient times have joined the Vietnamese community since the Ly dynasty (1009-1225 A.D.). Some ethnic groups are from plains but others had their homes in the coastal regions or high up in the mountains. With the exception of the Chams and the Khmers who inhabit the Mekong Delta, the other ethnic groups did not have a writing system of their own until the beginning of the 20th century. In a language which has a writing system of its own, both its spoken and written forms can provide us with information about the influence of language contact. However, in a language that has no writing system of its own, the only source of this kind of information is its spoken form. This is the case with Austroasiastic and Austronesian languages, spoken by the ethnic groups now inhabiting the mountains and the highlands to the west of South Vietnam.

Some comparative list of Romanised Sanskrit words (taken from the Sanskrit-Russian Vietnamese Dictionary) and their derivatives in the languages spoken by the various ethnic groups in South Vietnam:

Sanskrit Words (Romanised)/Ethnic Group Words and their Meanings in English

bhumi	= land, country
Bhlumi (Ch.)	= land, country, village
Phum (Kh.)	= residential land, garden; the smallest administrative unit
çabda	= speech, voice, word, sound
Ssop ~ xap (Ch.)	= speech
Xom day (Kh.)	= words
Asap (Ed., Ja.)	= speech
Asap (Ra.)	= speech
Sap (Ko)	= speech
çvasana	= spirit, wind, hiss, breathing, respiration
Ssuan (Ch.)	= spirit
Raivai (Ka.)	= soul
Suan (Ko.)	= spirit
guru	= a wise man, master, worthy
Gru ~ kru (Ch.)	= master
Gru (Mn.)	= craftsman, handy man
Mgru (Ra.)	= to learn
kru (Ra.)	= witch doctor
pugru (Ko.)	= master
Devata	= Gob debata (Ch.) = God
Jala	= net, netting
jal (Ch., Ed., Mn., Ra.)	= fishing net
juo (Ka.)	= fishing net
jal (Ko.)	= fishing net

Jaiyak	= victory
chai (Ch.)	= to win,
chaidak (Ch.)	= victory
jai (Ra.)	= to win
Karpasa	= cotton wool
kapah (Ch.)	= cotton wool
kopaih (Bah.)	= cotton wool
Krapas (Kh.)	= cotton wool
Marica	= chilli pepper
Amrek ~ mrek (Ch.)	= chilli pepper
A mareq (Ra.)	= chilli pepper
Proiq (Ka.)	= chilli pepper
Prik (Pa.)	= chilli pepper
Mre (Ko.)	= chilli pepper
Manusya	= man, person
Munuih (Ch., Ed.)	= man, person
Monuih (Ja., Ra., Chr.)	= man, person
Manuih (Ka.)	= man, person
Vonus (Ko.)	= man, person
nagaraja	= snake king
Karai ~ kirai (Ch.)	= dragon
grai (Ja.)	= dragon
rai (Ed.)	= dragon
nagara	= city, country nugar ~ nukan (Ch.) = region, homeland, country
logar (Ra.)	= hamlet
logar (Ko.)	= country
ratha	= vehicle Radeh ~ rideh (Ch.) = vehicle
Rodeh (Ra.)	= vehicle
Ndeh (Ma.)	= vehicle

rodeh (Ko.)	= vehicle
rupa	= appearance, body
rup (Ch.)	= body
rup (Pa., Ed., Ja.)	= body
rup (Ko.)	= body
yaksa	= demigod, superhuman
Being raksa ~ rak (Ch.)	= demon

Though this list is incomplete, it throws light on the influence of Indian language on the languages of the Vietnamese ethnic groups. All the ethnic group words that appear on this list have been transcribed into present day Vietnamese. The abbreviations given in parentheses refer to the various Vietnamese ethnic groups: Ch. = Cham, Br. = Bru, Ed. = Ede, Ja. = Jarai, Ka. = Katu, Kh. = Khmer, Mn. = Mnong, pa. = Pacoh, Ra. = Raglai, Ma. = Ma, Ko. = Koho. All these ethnic groups use languages belonging to the Austronesian and Austroasian families. The list shows that the Sanskrit words that have found their way into the language group of South Vietnam belong to the spheres of spiritual and material activities. The borrowed Sanskrit words, once integrated into the Vietnamese language group, usually take on new meanings. But even these new meanings are not too far removed from the original meanings of the Sanskrit words. Also, the borrowed words usually undergo some phonic changes in accordance with the phonological rules of the borrowing language.

Since the list given earlier is incomplete, it only gives us a general idea of the problem involved. A more serious and specific research project is needed for a more detailed observation and better understanding of the influence of the ancient Indian language on the Vietnamese language group.

In the lowland and coastal regions, the Indian influence is observed not only in the spoken language but also in geographical names and in the writing systems of various ethnic groups. All the geographical names common at the times of the ancient Champa kingdom have been either replaced by Sino-Vietnamese names or transliterated into modern Vietnamese. However, with the help of ancient documents and by comparison between the new and the ancient Sanskrit names, one can easily detect the relationship between them. Here are a few examples:

Sanskrit-based names	*Present names*
Sri Bamui	Dong Hoi
Amaravati	Tra Kieu (Quang Nam province)
Indrapura	Dong Duong (Quang Nam province)
Vijaya	Do Ban, Thi Nai (in Binh Dinh province)
Kauthara	Nha Trang
Panduranga	Phan Rang
Bal Chanar	Ca Na (in Binh Thuan province)

However, the Indian influence is most obvious in the writing systems of the Chams and the Khmers who now inhabit the Mekong River Delta. In the region which was ancient Champa, scientists have discovered hundreds of stelae erected over a period of ten centuries, from the 4th century to the 14th century. These stelae allow us to examine not only the written form of the ancient Cham language but also how that written form was influenced by the ancient Indian Script. Scientists have discovered that during those ten centuries, the Cham script was revised and improved until at last it proliferated into a couple of variants. However, these variants, as well as the other Southeast Asian scripts that are typologically similar to the Indian script, can easily be traced back to the Brahmi script of South India. One of those variants is the akhar thrah script, which is now being used by the Chams in Ninh Thuan and Binh Thuan province.

The Khmer script in the Mekong River Delta, like its cousin in Cambodia, originated from the Brahmi script. At first this Brahmi script was used to phonetically transcribe the language spoken by the Khmers in the Mekong Delta. Later, it was improved, with some signs modified and new signs added, until at last it became the Khmer script as seen nowadays.

Beside the Cham and Khmer scripts which originated from the Brahmi script, the words inscribed on the artefacts found at the excavation site of Chua Vua in Long An province have also been ascertained as belonging to the ancient Indian script. And who knows, in the future, Vietnamese archaeologists, with their enthusiasm, will discover further evidence of similar Indian influence at such new excavation sites as Nam Cat Tien (in Lam Dong province).

Conclusion

Reviewing the influences of Buddhism on the Vietnamese language and culture, one can affirm that Buddhism has come to Vietnam directly from India and left a deep imprint on its social life. After a long process of acculturation, Buddhism in Vietnam changed itself to the local conditions, still, the essential values remained intact. Suzuki, a Japanese researcher for Buddhism said that the 'culture of Asian countries comes from the pagodas'. In the words of H.G. Wells, an English historian 'Buddhism has made a much greater contribution to the progress of civilisation of mankind than any other influence in human history'. Taking these into account and above discussions, it can be surmised that the Buddhism in Vietnam has been able to co-exist in peace with other religions for over 2,000 years. Generations of Vietnamese monks, nuns and lay followers, have contributed in making Buddhism a unique religion in Vietnam in tune with local customs and traditions. This in turn, had a great influence on Vietnamese literature, art, music and architecture.

REFERENCES

Coedes, C. (1948), '*Les etats hindouies d'Indochine et d'Indonesie*', Paris.

Coedes, C. (1949), '*Les Langues, in Les langues de l'Indochine*, Paris.

Dahomid and Dorohiem (1965), *Dan toc Cham Luoc su-Survey of Cham people*, Saigon.

Gerini (1902), '*Plan d'un ouvrage sur la geographie ancieme de L'Indochine*' (Compte rendu analytique des séances, 1et Congres international des etudes d'Extreame Orient).

Katti, M.N. (1994), '*Script, Indian, Northern in the Encyclopedia of Language and Linguistics*', Vol. 7, Pergamon Press, pp. 3697-3707.

Kotserghina V.A. (1987), '*Sanskrit–russkiy Slovar*', 2nd edition, Moskva.

Luoc, Cung Khac and Luong Van Ke, '*Phat hien moi ve truyen thuyet Thanh Giong: Phu Dong Thien Vuong cuu me-A New Finding of the Spirit Giong Legend: PDTV Saves his Mother*', Nhan Dan Newspaper, 26 April 1998.

Majumdar, R.C. (1985), '*Champa: History and Culture of an Indian Colonial Kingdom in the Far East 2nd–16th century A.D.*', (reprinted) Delhi.

Nguyen Tai Thu, '*Lich su Phat Giao Viet Nam*', '*The History of Vietnamese Buddhism*', Hanoi, 1988.

Nguyen, Lang, '*Viet Nam Phat Giao Su Luan*', 'A Critical History of Buddhism in Vietnam', Vol. II.

R. Tran Chi Doi (1998), 'Mot vai nhan xet ve cac kieu chu Thai co o Viet Nam-Thai-script in Vietnam', Read at the International Congress for Vietnamese Studies in Hanoi.

Smyth, D.A. (1994), '*Southeast Asian Scripts in the Encyclopedia of Language and Linguistics*', Vol. 8, Pergamon Press, pp. 4071-4073.

Tan, Ha Van, (1965), 'Tu mot cot kinh Phat nam 973 vua phat hien o Hoa Lu-Some problems rising from the stone column with Buddhist prayer-text in Hoa Lu', *Historical Studies Magazine*, Issue 76.

Thai Van Chai (1997), '*Tieng Khmer-The Khmer Language*', Hanoi.

Thien uyen tap anh (1980), '*An Anthology of the Most Talented Figures in Ch'an Park*', Publishing House for Literature, Hanoi, Vietnam.

Tran Dinh Huou, '*Nho giao va anh huong cua no trong van hoa*', '*Vietnam-Confucianism and its influence in Vietnamese culture: Almanac of Vietnamese culture*', Van Hoa Viet Nam–Tong hop.

18 Vietnam Tourism: Potential and Perspective

Tran Phong Binh

Vietnam has a beautiful geography dotted with beaches, mountainous regions and places of historical importance making it attractive for tourism. Vietnam wants to develop tourism as a spearhead economic industry and gradually develop itself as a major tourism centre in the region. It wants to develop tourism in sustainable way together with conservation of natural resources, and showcasing and promoting national cultural value.

Tourism Potential in Vietnam

Vietnam provides world class infrastructure and tourism facilities. Vietnamese hospitality is one of the most well-known in the world. Vietnam also has one of the world's finest cuisines. 'Pho' is a favourite dish for local people and foreign visitors. Vietnamese Spring rolls are one of the most well-known dishes in the world. Besides, there is enough 'night life' and entertainment in Vietnam.

About 6.5 million international tourists arrived in Vietnam in 2012. International tourists market share in Vietnam was about 26 per cent from Northeast Asia, 19 per cent from China, 16 per cent from ASEAN, 15 per cent from Europe, 9 per cent from North America, 6 per cent from Oceania and 9 per cent from other regions of the world. There were about 30 million domestic tourists in Vietnam in 2011. Vietnam received about US$ 5.7 billion (US$ 1 = 20,851.64 VND) in tourist revenue in 2011.

Vietnam has about 13,000 classified units of accommodation comprising of about 2,50,000 rooms. Out of this 52 are 5 star accommodations, 137 are four star hotels, and about 300 three star hotels. There are about 1040 tour operators and travel agents catering to international tourists, and about 5000 tour operators and travel agents catering to domestic tourists. Vietnam has about 6,000 tourist guides, out of which 43 per cent are English language guides, 23 per cent Chinese language, 10 per cent deal with French, 8 per cent deal with Japanese, 3.9 per cent speak German, 1.3 per cent speak Spanish and 10.8 per cent speak other languages.

There are five airlines in Vietnam: Vietnam Airlines, Pacific Airlines, Vasco, Viet Jet Airlines and Air Mekong, and 49 operational international routes to Vietnam. Forty three foreign airlines have their representative offices in Vietnam. Vietnam is connected by road to China, Laos, Cambodia, Thailand and other ASEAN countries. There are 11 international seaports in Vietnam.

Vietnam has bilateral visa exemption for ASEAN countries except Myanmar. It also has unilateral visa exemption for people from Japan, Republic of Korea, Sweden, Norway, Finland, Denmark and Russia. Vietnam grants visa on arrival at international airports. There is visa exemption for tourists who visit Phu Quoc Island. Visa is also exempted for Vietnamese staying overseas, who want to visit Vietnam.

Vietnam's top ten tourists markets in 2011 were China, Korea, Japan, US, Cambodia, Taiwan, Australia, Malaysia, France and Thailand. Short-haul source markets for Vietnamese tourism comes from Northeast Asia (Japan, Republic of Korea, Taiwan), China (Hong Kong, Macau), ASEAN, Western Europe (France, UK, Germany, Spain, The Netherlands), Northeast Europe, Scandinavian nations, Russia and Eastern European nations, North America (USA, Canada) and Oceania (Australia, New Zealand) region. Vietnam is looking for potential tourist markets from India, Middle East and Latin America.

Scope for Cooperation with Vietnam

According to Indian Tour Operators Promotion Council there were about 11.07 million Indians going abroad in 2011, out of this only 0.14 per cent of Indian tourists visited Vietnam and rest 99.86 per cent people visited other countries. There is great potential for Vietnam to attract these tourists. Vietnam can attract from key tourist markets in India like Mumbai, Delhi and other major cities like Kolkata, Chennai, Bangalore, Hyderabad, Ahmadabad, etc. Only two Indian cities, Mumbai and Delhi, account for about 59 per cent of the total tourists going abroad from India in a year.

Some of the main cities attracting tourists in Vietnam are Hanoi, Sapa, Hue and Ho Chi Minh City. Mekong River with its dense system of canals, floating markets and islands with lush orchards, is also an attractive tourist destination. Besides, Ha long Bay, Phong Nha Cave, Hoi An ancient town, My son holy land, Ca Na Beach, Nha Trang beach, Vinpearl resort, Chenh Da Dia Phu Yen, etc., are some specific places of major tourist attraction.

Index